de Gruyter Studies in Organization 14

Oshagbemi: Leadership and Management in Universities Britain and Nigeria

de Gruyter Studies in Organization

An international series by internationally known authors presenting current fields of research in organization.

Organizing and organizations are substantial pre-requisites for the viability and future developments of society. Their study and comprehension are indispensable to the quality of human life. Therefore, the series aims to:

- offer to the specialist work material in form of the most important and current problems, methods and results;
- give interested readers access to different subject areas;
- provide aids for decisions on contemporary problems and stimulate ideas.

The series will include monographs, collections of contributed papers, and handbooks.

Titus Oshagbemi

Leadership and Management in Universities
Britain and Nigeria

Walter de Gruyter · Berlin · New York 1988

Dr. Titus A. Oshagbemi
Senior Lecturer and Acting Head
Department of Management Studies
University of Jos, Nigeria

Library of Congress Cataloging in Publication Data

Oshagbemi, T. A. (Titus A.)
Leadership and management in universities : Britain and Nigeria / Titus A. Oshagbemi.
p. cm. — (De Gruyter studies in organization : 14)
Originally presented as the author's thesis (doctoral).
Bibliography: p.
Includes index.
ISBN 0-89925-426-8 (U.S.)
1. Universities and colleges--Great Britain--Administration--Case studies. 2. Universities and colleges--Nigeria--Administration--Case stuides. 3. College administrators--Great Britain--Case studies. 4. College administrators--Nigeria--Case studies.
I. Title. II. Series.
LB2341.8.G7084 1988 88-29749
378.41--dc 19 CIP

Deutsche Bibliothek Cataloging in Publication Data

Oshagbemi, Titus:
Leadership and management in universities: Britain and Nigeria / Titus Oshagbemi. - Berlin ; New York : de Gruyter, 1989
(De Gruyter studies in organization ; 14)
Zugl.: Bradford, Univ., Diss.
ISBN 3-11-011514-X
NE: GT

♾ Printed on acid free paper.

Typesetting: Asco Trade Typsetting, Hongkong. - Printing: Gerike GmbH, Berlin. - Binding: D. Mikolai, Berlin. - Cover Design: Hansbernd Lindemann, Berlin. - Printed in Germany.

Preface

This is an exploratory study designed to identify ways in which universities could improve their management policies and practices through an examination of the job characteristics and perceptions of their academic leaders. The impetus for the research arose from the concern to provide ways of enhancing university performance, a need arising from the increasing environmental turbulence which universities experience and which manifests itself in the shortage of funds, increased governmental intervention in their internal activities, public criticisms, and the alleged mediocre performance by the universities. Universities in most countries seem to be experiencing zero-growth or decline conditions with the resultant need for new and better management capabilities. This is especially so as the experiences of many academic leaders seem to be limited to the expansion era which is a sharp contrast to the current situation of stagnation and recession.

The central hypothesis is that academic leaders spend most of their time on administration and management and not on research or teaching as the public impression seems to be. Given that the hypothesis is true, and considering the important administrative and management positions which academic leaders occupy in the university organizational structure and decision processes, especially their policy formulation function, it becomes expedient that academic leaders be adequately equipped to perform their administrative and management duties better. There were a number of research questions which the project concerned itself with. For example, there was the desire to find out the extent to which academic leaders know the nature of their jobs and whether cultural differences affect the nature of these jobs significantly. Answers to these and other related questions are relevant to exploring measures designed to make the universities more effective.

Employing multiple research methodologies, and collecting data from both Nigerian and the British Universities, the study proceeded to test the central hypothesis and to answer its many research questions. This involved using, in part, appropriate computer-based statistical techniques such as cluster analytical procedures. The findings of the research confirm the central hypothesis and reveal that academic leaders spend about half of their working time on administration and management, spending on the average more time on this activity than on the combined research, teaching, and consulting functions. It is also revealed, that academic leaders are poor estimators of how they spend their time and that British and Nigerian academic leaders' jobs are roughly similar. Before the summary and conclusions, the book examine important issues, such as the selection and training of academic leaders, which directly affect academic leadership and management practices, and ends by highlighting the theoretical as well as the practical implications and applications of the study.

This book is addressed to all academics and to all those people, including government officials, who are connected with or interested in improving the performance of higher education. The book is also aimed at students of management and organizational behaviour who are interested in the problems and challenges of improving managerial performance in organizations. As the focus of the book is on managerial work, it is directed at practising managers in both the public and private industries. Finally, the book is recommended to researchers in the social and behavioural sciences who may find the methodological approach particularly useful.

The research which led to the writing of this book was initially reported in the authors doctoral thesis. From the pilot and data gathering stages, several individuals contacted me and indicated their interest in obtaining a copy of the finished work. This, in addition to the important issues raised, has encouraged me to make the report of the thesis available in a book form to a wider audience.

I received various forms of assistance and encouragement from many people when writing the original thesis. These people include Dr. John Sharp, Dr. Nasir Hussain, Dr. Geoff Mallory, Prof. J.C. Higgins, Dr. Graham Hooley, Dr. Barnabas Agbonifoh, Mr. Bamidele Adepoju, Prof. Peter Buckley, Dr. Jim Lynch, Mr. Yakubu Isa, Mr. Joshua Omuya, Prof. David Hickson, and the members of the Human Resources Research Group, University of Bradford Management Centre. I continue to be grateful to them all. However, I would like to distinguish Dr. Peter Wright who supervised the doctoral work and offered invaluable suggestions.

I would also like to mention my appreciation to the academic leaders who responded to the survey including the pilot work, and especially those who completed the diaries over a duration of one week. Similarly, I thank the University of Jos for granting me leave of absence from work during the period when I worked on the initial project. Finally, I am indebted to my wife for her moral and practical support which facilitated the preparation and the completion of this book.

Jos, August 1988 *T.A. Oshagbemi*

Contents

List of Tables and Figures

Chapter 1
Introduction

1.1 Introduction

There has been a general upsurge in management researches in the last three decades or so. [1] Despite this fact, empirical studies on managerial work activities have been limited in number and in scope. [2] Researchers seem to have focused more attention on the functional areas of management which are less ambiguous and which lend themselves to greater quantification. Mintzberg echoed the paucity of work in the managerial role area, and he emphasised the need to investigate more into what the manager actually does in the following words:

> We still know very little about managerial work and we are in greatest need of more studies in which the researcher seeks to develop basic understanding[. . .]. We must devote considerable attention to the study of job differences[. . .]. We know almost nothing about work variations by culture[. . .]. [3]

In the same vein, Stewart referred to the dearth of materials in this area thus:

> We need a better understanding of managerial work for many reasons, most of all in the selection and training of managers[. . .]. The first and most important, is our ignorance of the differences between managers' jobs. The second is that we still know little about what the manager has to do, apart from the specialist aspects of his job. [4]

This research was undertaken partially in response to some of the above comments. It is an investigation into the nature of the academic leaders' jobs, their perceptions about these jobs, and their attitudes towards aspects of their jobs. Employing both survey and diary methodologies, the research attempts to examine academic leaders' job characteristics and perceptions with a view to seeing what can be done towards attaining a more effective academic management.

1.2 Background to the Study

In both Nigeria and the United Kingdom, universities have come under severe criticisms for poor performance. Central to these criticisms is perhaps the issue of funding and how universities spend available money. Traditionally, and up to the present time, British and Nigerian Universities have been funded in the main by their respective federal, state, or local governments. In both countries, there are few examples, if any, of very successful private universities as yet, although a move towards establishing a number of private universities was mooted sometime in Nigeria.

In U.S.A. however, there are several examples of private universities some of which in addition to possessing financial independence have distinguished themselves as centres of academic excellence all over the world. Generally, in fact, American universities whether public or private tend to have good relationships with industry and commerce and they have strong connections with their communities. They tend to possess the entrepreneurial spirit and are concerned with attitudes to the world outside higher education. Consequently, they generate money in a fashion and at a degree yet to be emulated by universities in Britain and Nigeria.

Unlike some of the American universities that generate much of their funding, British and Nigerian universities are, as we mentioned before, financed by their governments. These governments sometime contribute up to 95 per cent of some of their universities' annual budget in direct subvention and normally do not contribute less than 70 per cent to any of the university's annual expenditure. The amount of money involved normally runs into hundreds millions of pounds. Over time, governments continue to shoulder more and more heavy financial responsibilities. As universities consume a sizable portion of various State or local budgets, it dawned on governments that universities are very expensive ventures which they will have to watch and control.

As the saying goes, "he who pays the piper dictates the tune". Consequently, governments started prying into hitherto reserved areas and functions of the university—freedom to mount desired programmes, liberty to research into areas or issues of interest to the academics, freedom to admit whosoever is academically qualified and can benefit from higher education, and so on.

In the British situation, there are debates on selective funding between teaching and research in the same university or selective funding of research projects among several universities. Both the University Grants Committee and the National Advisory Body for Public Sector Higher Education are suggesting ways of adopting funding mechanisms that will minimize cost and reduce overall government funding of universities. [5] There are complaints that the British university system harbours a lot of inefficiency and that it is wasteful. For example, it is argued that the figures for Ph.D. completion rates and completion times are very low and unnecessarily so. Indeed, the University Grants Committee now blacklists some universities for lack of performance in this area and would not allow University Grants Committee sponsored Ph.D. candidates to go into such blacklisted institutions. Consequently, the desirability of the continuation of the apprenticeship model of doctoral training has been called into question. There are suggestions that there should be a shift in emphasis towards taught and assessed research skills and away from lone original research. This issue is of course important enough to be a subject of national conferences. In one of such national conferences, the concern of the participants were to examine four related issues. Specifically, they considered whether:

a) the nature of a British doctorate has changed, and if so how has it changed?
b) the shift in emphasis towards taught and assessed research skills and away from lone original research is a desirable one?
c) the apprenticeship or a programme model doctorate is an appropriate qualification for an academic career?
d) the doctorate is an appropriate qualification for other careers? [6]

Thus, while British universities have, no doubt, contributed immensely to the development and progress of the country, the government is of the opinion that the economic performance of the U.K. since 1945 has been disappointing compared to the achievement of others. The British government believes that it is vital for their higher education to contribute more effectively to the improvement of the performance of the economy and that there should be changes to make higher education more flexible to respond quickly to new needs. [7] Towards this objective, management systems, academic leaders' activities, university structures, and other areas are criticized and changes are recommended in them.

In the Nigerian situation, the picture of the universities is not much different from what it is in the U.K. If anything, it is perhaps worse. Unlike in the U.K. where there were universities as early as in the 12th Century, the first university to be established in Nigeria is the University of Ibadan which started as a University College in 1948. Since then, as many as twenty-four Nigerian universities have been established. [8]

Since pre-independence days, universities in Nigeria have assumed positions of eminence in contributing to and in shaping the socio-economic progress of the country. Considering the resources at their disposal, they have performed rather creditably insofar as the production of high-level manpower is concerned.

While recognising their modest achievements and limitations, commentators have argued that the Nigerian universities are not doing enough. It is said, for instance, that while concerned with the manpower statistics, Nigerian universities have neglected the development of and the inculcation of national consciousness, unity, understanding, and peace. It is argued that unless the development of the total human being through the development of his or her mind is pursued, Nigeria may continue to be a directionless society. The universities would then have failed in their central mission of helping to shape the society for good. [9]

Other critics say that the Nigerian universities have not been effective and that they hardly justify the public expense on them. Some claim that university management practices are not effective because academic leaders are not professional managers. [10] That in terms of relevance, Nigerian university researches and some of their programmes hardly justify their funding. It is said that the medical sciences, for example, despite the colossal amounts spent on developing teaching hospitals, have not being able to come up with the cure or the solution to essentially tropical diseases like sickle cell. It is further contended by critics that the culture of the Nigerian universities is not significantly different from that outside the university. Inefficiency obtains in both systems. The attitude to time, the disposition to work, and the consumption habit are not distinguishable in the sectors.

In both Nigeria and the U.K., academic programmes are now therefore being rationalised as there are reduced levels of funding. There are no longer threats, there are now real academic redundancies in universities in both countries, and academic leadership is a current and topical issue in Britain and Nigeria. The picture seems to be a call by governments and people of both countries to evolve universities that will be managed as efficiently and as professionally as possible. [11] Towards this end, various suggestions have been made and are being made even by the universities themselves [12].

This research is not concerned as such with the pros and cons of the topic of university effectiveness in Britain and Nigeria. Rather, we take the position that while recognising and applauding the laudable efforts of universities in these countries, they can still be made more effective through improved management practices on the part of their leaders. However, management practices cannot be improved meaningfully, unless the job characteristics and the managerial work activities of academic leaders are ascertained. The present effort attempts to do this as a prerequisite to effective management policies and practices.

In essence, therefore, the background to this study arose from the concern of the researcher, himself a lecturer in one of the universities, in investigating what academic leaders actually do as a step towards assisting them to perform their functions better.

It should be mentioned, however, that although the initial background to this study was the concern for the Nigerian and British Universities, it is to be noted that universities in other countries were also experiencing organizational difficulties and management problems similar to what we have discussed earlier. In particular, universities in Africa, other Third World, and European countries face similar public criticisms on their activities and performance. Thus, it is hoped that recommendations emanating from the research data gathered from these two countries would be applicable to other African and European countries. Because the choice of sample was carefully chosen to include a developing and a 'developed' country, there was the interest to examine the extent to which cultural differences affect the nature of academic jobs and perceptions.

1.3 Aims and Objectives of Research

This study aims to contribute to a greater awareness and a better understanding of the activities of academic leaders—a group that seems to have been hitherto neglected, though whose potential for significant contribution to societal development is not in doubt.

One of the major objectives of the study is the determination of the nature of the academic leaders' jobs. The approach we adopt is to identify the major activities of the academic leaders and find out their time allocation amongst these. The intention is to test the central hypothesis that academic leaders spend most of their time on administration and management, and not on research or teaching as the popular belief seems to be. If this hypothesis is true, there would be important implications for the selection and training of academic leaders especially as academic leaders occupy important organizational positions where policies of strategic consequences are being formulated.

It is also the objective of this study to compare the job characteristics of British and Nigerian academic leaders to see if there are significant differences between them. In this, the intention is to identify the extent to which cultural differences affect the nature of academic leaders' jobs. Furthermore, it is hoped to compare academic leaders' jobs with those of the industrial managers to test the applicability of the concept of the universality of managerial functions. Another objective of the study is to examine the academic leaders' preceptions, beliefs, and attitudes on aspects of their jobs. The latter consideration is important in the recommendation of acceptable policies.

It is felt that the results of the research will lead to useful and interesting implications, apart from providing a better understanding of the activities and the job characteristics of academic leaders. The findings of the study may also lead to a greater appreciation of academic leaders' jobs and roles.

In essence, this research seeks to examine the work characteristics of academic leaders, particularly how academic leaders spend their time. The ultimate objective of the research is to contribute towards a more effective academic management. In particular, it would be helpful to know whether the selection processes of academic leaders can be improved and the training programmes that can usefully be introduced or the managerial skills that can benefically be developed among the academic leaders. For instance, McCall, Morrison, and Hannan suggest that in order to benefit practising managers, researches so far indicate that management trainers should focus on such things as:

- How to handle a two-minute interaction;
- How to use staff assistants and consultants;
- How to handle ceremonial events;
- How to decide when a meeting is necessary and who should attend (as opposed to how to run a meeting),
- How to delegate in an oral environment;
- How to plan in the midst of chaos. [13]

The question is, to what extent, if at all, would academic leaders benefit from such a training programme as detailed above?

1.4 Summary of the Chapters

Chapter One introduces the book, stating the aims and the objectives of the research as well as the background to the study. Chapter Two presents an overview of the Nigerian and British University Systems, highlighting both the structure and management as well as the problems and challenges facing the institutions. In Chapter Three, the theoretical basis of the thesis is laid with a review of the nature of the jobs of managers in general and the jobs of the academic leaders in particular. Chapter Four documents the research design and the methodology, detailing definitions, sample selection, distribution, and responses. It also provides data analyses methodology.

Chapters Five and Six detail the findings on the nature of the academic leaders' jobs. The chapters discuss not only the activities which the academic leaders performed and with whom, but also the subject of the activities, their location and duration, and the contacts which the academic leaders made. Chapter Seven classifies the academic leaders into five job profiles on the basis of 24 criteria of their job characteristics. Chapter Eight discusses the research findings on the academic leaders' perceptions of how they spent their time as well as their perceptions of aspects of their jobs. Chapter Nine focuses on issues such as selection and training which affect academic leadership and management practices more directly. Chapter Ten provides a summary of the research and its findings, while Chapter Eleven presents conclusions, implications, and the applications of the study.

1.5 Notes and References

[1] Koontz, H.J., The Management Theory Jungle, *Journal of The Academy of Management*, Vol. 4, No. 3, December 1961, pp. 174–188.

[2] Mintzberg, H., The Manager's Job: Folklore and Fact, *Harvard Business Review*, July–August 1975, pp. 49–61.

[3] Mintzberg, H., *The Nature of Managerial Work*, Harper and Row Publishers, New York, 1973, p. 197.

[4] Stewart, R., *Contrasts in Management: A Study of Different Types of Managers' Jobs; Their Demand and Choices*, McGraw-Hill, London, 1976, p. 1. See also, Stewart, R., The Nature of Management? A Problem for Management Education, *Journal of Management Studies*, Vol. 21, No. 3, July 1984, p. 325, where the author reiterated: "An understanding of the nature of management requires a conceptualization of what it is that managers do [. . .] we need to understand what it is that managers do before we can decide what managers should know and how they can best acquire this knowledge".

[5] *The Times Higher Education Supplement*, April 5, 1985.

[6] Workshop Briefing on 9th Annual Workshop on Doctoral Research in Industry and Employment, Scottish Business School, 6–7 Sept., 1985.

[7] *The Development of Higher Education into the 1990s*, Cmnd. 9524, Her Majesty's Stationery Office, London, May 1985.

[8] Chizea, C.A., (ed.), *Bulletin of the National Universities Commission*, Lagos, Nigeria, Dec., 1984, p. 4. Actually, the number of universities in Nigeria was only reduced to 24 in 1984 when the Federal Military Government merged the 7 former Federal Universities of Technology into 3. In the same year, i.e. 1984, the Open University was suspended indefinitely from operating on the grounds of scarcity of funds and inadequacy of necessary facilities.

[9] Ike, M.C., Manpower or Manhood? *Management in Nigeria*, Jan. 1977, pp. 6–17.

[10] Odeleye, A.O., Professionalism in Management and Administration, *Management in Nigeria*, Jan. 1979, pp. 19–21.

[11] Sir Alex Jarrat (Chairman), *Report of the Steering Committee for Efficiency Studies in Universities*, 29 March, 1985.

[12] *Committee of Vice-Chancellors and Principals' Press Briefings* on Jarrat Committee Reports on Efficiency in Universities, 29 Tavistock Square, London, April 1985.

[13] McCall, M.W., Morrison, M.A., and Hannan, R.L., Studies of Managerial Work: Results and Methods, *Centre for Creative Leadership*, Technical Report No. 9, North Carolina, 27402, May 1978, p. 42.

Chapter 2
Nigerian and British Universities—An Overview

2.1 Introduction

Universities all over the world are organizations established for the propagation, dissemination, and the application of knowledge. The stock-in-trade in universities, as in all institutions of higher learning, is knowledge. Details of university structure or management systems may differ from one country to another. We pointed out in Chapter One, for example, that the issue of funding and hence control is one distinguishing factor between American universities on the one hand and British and Nigerian universities on the other. However, even within the same country, differences in organizational structure and management practices may be experienced by universities. Generally, however, it is hoped that the programmes established by universities, the courses taught, and the emphasis laid on scholarship will tend to be, in part, a function of national aspirations and objectives.

British and Nigerian universities are similar in many respects—in structure, governance, and management, although the problems and challenges that they face are different. There is a long-standing relationship between British and Nigerian universities which dates back to the colonial era when Nigeria was under the British rule. Indeed, the first university to be established in Nigeria—the University of Ibadan—was an affiliate of the University of London. After political independence in 1960, Nigeria adopted the political and educational systems of the British. Hence, a detailed examination of the Nigerian university system will, to a large extent, reflect many practices in British universities.

In the first part of this chapter, we shall undertake an examination of the Nigerian university system. This will be followed by a relatively brief analysis of British universities where the emphasis will be on a general comparison between universities in the U.K. and Nigeria. In this short section, attempts will be made to identify similarities and differences in the two sets of universities, statistics on the Nigerian universities having already been detailed.

2.2 Nigerian Universities—Structure and Management

The history of the Nigerian University System began in 1948 when the then University College, Ibadan (now University of Ibadan) was established as an affiliate of the University of London. [1] Following the Ashby Committee Report of October 1960, four new universities were established in 1962. [2] The University of Lagos was established by the Federal Government while the three Regional Governments each established a university. These were the Universities of Ife, Nigeria, and Ahmadu Bello.

In 1972, the then Mid-Western State (now Bendel State) established the University of Benin. This brought the number of universities in Nigeria to six. In 1975, the Federal Military Government took over the responsibility of the Regional Universities and established seven new universities. [3] In 1979, the Military Government created another seven new universities of technology on its way out of office. This brought the number of universities in Nigeria to twenty. However, in 1984, the number of the Federal Universities of Technology was reduced by the new Military Government from seven to three. [4]

Between 1979 and 1983, when there was a Civilian Administration in the country, some States passed laws establishing State Universities. This was in conformity with the 1979 Nigerian Federal Constitution which classified university establishment within the jurisdiction of States. The period 1979 to 1983 thus witnessed a boom in university establishment, and eight State Universities were created. [5] Since 1984, however, when the military regained control of the government, and as a result of the downturn in her economic position, a temporary stop has been placed on university establishment. In fact, the Open University, one of the universities started by the preceding government, was halted because of lack of or inadequate facilities.

Nonetheless, it can be seen that from independence in 1960 to 1984, the number of universities in Nigeria grew from only one to twenty-four, the correct figure as at the beginning of the 1984–1985 academic session. [6] In the 1980–81 academic session, the 13 Federal Universities (excluding the then 7 new Federal Universities of Technology) recorded an enrolment of over 77,000 students and employed more than 52,000 persons. [7] In the 1982–1983 academic year, the total enrolment in the Nigerian Federal Universities stood at exactly 92,116. [8] This figure excluded the enrolment figure in the State Universities. During the 1981 fiscal year, the Nigerian Universities attracted government subvention of about three hundred and fifty million Naira for their recurrent operating needs alone. This was in addition to about thirty million Naira which was estimated that the universities generated internally. [9] These statistics easily point to the importance accorded to university education in Nigeria.

The remaining part of this section is broadly divided into two. The first portion deals with the structure of and the management in Nigerian universities, while the second part attempts a diagnosis of the problems and challenges facing the institutions. In the second and conluding section to this chapter, we discuss the British universities briefly and compare them with their Nigerian counterparts.

2.2.1 Structure

The structure and the organization of Nigerian universities are very similar to one another and are patterned along the British lines. As corporate entities, universities in Nigeria were brought into existence either by means of military decrees or by acts of parliament. The statute of incorporation defines the constitution of each university. It normally provides for a governing body or a Council who controls the university's property and finances. The Council interferes very little on academic matters, a function left to the Senate. The Chairman of the Council is the Pro-Chancellor, while the Chancellor, an elder statesman or an eminent public figure, is the titular or the ceremonial head of the university. The constitutions of Nigerian universities also provide for the role of the Visitor (who is the Head of State or the President of the Country) who has the visitorial powers of State as proprietor and provider of funds to order visitation. However, these powers are normally exercised only as a last resort either when there is a fundamental problem or to adjudicate in the event of dispute between the Council and the Senate. In addition, there is a body known as the Congregation, consisting of all graduates of the University which may make recommendations to Council or to Senate on any issues of general interest.

Thus, the traditional hierarchy of the university structure is the Chancellor, Pro-Chancellor, Vice-Chancellor (who is the chief executive of the institution), Directors (if any), Deans (heads of faculties, schools, or colleges), and Heads of Departments. Structurally, the constituent bodies are, in order of superior authority, Council, Senate, Faculties, and Departments.

2.2.2 Management System

The primary vehicle of administration in the universities is the Committee System. This management system is used for administering the university on democratic principles. It is the technique used for achieving joint participation, and for ensuring proper delegation. The numbers of the committees varies from one university to the other; depending generally on size and complexity of purpose. Committee numbers of about 30 to 50 are common in the older universities.

As stated under the immediate section above, all matters of internal management are ultimately referred to the Council whose powers are subordinate only to the Visitor's. The registrar and his department are responsible for the day-to-day administration of the university. A recent development is the suggestion for the abolition of the present forms of the posts of the registrar, bursar, etc. [10] and to substitute this with a cabinet of deputy vice-chancellors, each to be in charge of broad divisions of management. Presently, some universities, e.g., University of Jos, have two deputy vice-chancellors, one for academic and the other for administrative matters. It is suggested that if the number of deputy vice-chancellors is increased, some could be in charge of finance and accounting, student welfare, etc. The central idea is to reduce the red-tapism resulting from the centralised activities of large and complex multi-campus universities, and make universities more responsive. The existence of the use of modern management techniques, such as Management By Objectives, Project Management, etc., do not appear to be many in Nigerian universities. This is partly because such techniques may have little relevance in the university setting, or more likely because, as Adamolekun suggested, universities have conservative tradition on matters of the practice of administration. [11]

2.2.3 Selection and Development of Academic Leaders

"Academic Leaders" are formally defined in Chapter Four. It is sufficient, for our discussion here, to regard them as academics occupying formal administrative positions within the university organizational setting. This group includes the vice-chancellor, the director, dean, head of department and their deputies, or incumbents of equivalent positions.

The process of the selection of vice-chancellors requires the Senate to recommend three names to the Council from the existing full professors of the university. Recommendations are to be made in order of merit. The Council, in turn, recommends three names in order of merit to the Visitor whose prerogative it is to select the Vice-Chancellor from his list. In selecting the Vice-Chancellor, the Visitor is free to appoint the third candidate in the list of names submitted to him, just as the Council may forward Senate's recommendation in the re-arranged order of its own. A vice-chancellor is appointed for a term of four years. This can be renewed for another period of three years only.

Deputy vice-chancellors and directors are nominated by the vice-chancellors and these are normally ratified by the Senate and the Council. If rejected, the vice-chancellor has to suggest alternative names. Deans are elected by the academic members of a faculty. They run a term of two years which is renewable for a further two years. Although details vary, to qualify as a dean, a candidate must usually be a full professor or be the head of a department and not below the rank of a Senior Lecturer.

A head of department is chosen by the vice-chancellor who has the prerogative to choose anybody. However, the most senior academic member usually not below the rank of a senior lecturer is commonly appointed. In some universities, e.g., University of Jos, the most senior academic member is normally chosen irrespective of nationality. In some other universities, such as Ahmadu Bello, consideration is often given to Nigerian academic staff members in addition to seniority. Therefore, a Nigerian senior lecturer may for instance be the head of a department where there is, say, an Asian professor. The latter may not want or he would not be given administrative roles.

There are no conscious training programmes or development courses offered to assist academic leaders in the performance of their duties. This observation is true for both newly appointed academic leaders as well as for the older ones. It is hoped that a director, for instance, would have been previously a head of department and a dean before being appointed. Since this assumption may not always be true, perhaps some form of assistance should be given to academic leaders. This may help them to perceive their roles properly and to perform their managerial duties more effectively.

2.2.4 What Academic Leaders Do

The writer is unaware of any documentation of the activities and the job characteristics of Nigerian academic leaders. Yet, in order to know the type of assistance they need and provide just that, an understanding of what they do and how they perceive their role, is desirable. The present effort attempts to do this. As would be seen from the literature review in the next chapter, very little is in fact known about the nature of the academic leaders' jobs in other countries as well.

2.3 Problems and Challenges

There are big challenges currently facing Nigerian universities. These problems are dynamic, complex, and interrelated. The emphasis in this section is on the diagnosis or the identification of these challenges as opposed to prescribing remedies or solutions for them. We shall discuss the problems of the relevance of activities, the proliferation of institutions, government interference, and the challenges of effective management and academic leadership.

2.3.1 Relevance

One of the major difficulties confronting these institutions of higher learning is that of relevance, i.e. the problem of identifying more closely with their environment. Historically, the people of Nigeria, the various governments as well as the university people themselves seem to have believed that carbon copies of Oxford, Harvard, Cambridge, and Moscow universities in Nigeria would effectively serve their needs of transforming the economy and that of improving the lot of their people. [12] Thus, some buildings of foreign architectural designs were put up and foreign courses such as English legal system, American geography, British history, and industrial relations were included into their curricula. The universities, in their bid to be "international" in outlook, also encouraged foreign values, taste, and culture. It borrowed personnel, equipment, ideas, and practices generously from the East and the West, believing that a university is an international organization and therefore knows no national boundary. Nigerian academics, indeed African academics, therefore have tended to conform to Lord Macaulay's ideal of a well-educated Indian of the 19th Century: "A person, indian in blood but English in thought, language, religion, and culture." [13]

In the perception of its role, Nigerian universities face the challenge of relevance. As Fafunwa explained, a university in an affluent and technologically advanced society has a different role to play vis-à-vis a similar institution in a developing country. What is universal in universities is the quest for knowledge and truth, not necessarily curricula and organization and certainly not structures. [14] Given the current modus operandi in Nigerian universities, it is doubtful whether such developing countries will ever develop. Relevance means that in its twin functions of teaching and research, Nigerian universities must emphasize indigenousness. Peculiar economic, socio-cultural, and political problems facing the country should be the prime concern of Nigerian academics and this should be reflected in the type of researches they pursue and the publications they make.

Societies often make demands on higher education and on the intelligentsia. When the United States (U.S.) was facing the oil crises of 1974–1975, the U.S. Government turned to their academics for advice and for strategies that reversed the oil situation and subsequently forced serious concessions on otherwise unwilling O.P.E.C. members. Similarly, after the Second World War, there was pressure on the American Universities to expand enrolment, increase faculty staff, and so on. These challenges were, by and large, met successfully.

The challenge facing Nigerian universities is to identify with needs and aspirations of its people. This challenge of identification should be pursued in the universities' major functions: the propagation, the dissemination, and the application of knowledge. This is to justify their existence and their funding. They should develop the right mix needed for a relatively poor nation. Some of the graduates being produced by the Nigerian universities have no special skills to contribute to the development of the nation, having being trained in subjects which could not be of much use to the graduate or to his country. [15]

2.3.2 Government Interference

Another major problem confronting Nigerian universities at the moment is that of excessive government interference. It is unfortunate that Nigerian universities are far from being autonomous. In August 1972, the then federal government (military) announced that all the universities would be federalized and that higher education would be the sole responsibility of the federal government. In a decree promulgated in 1974, the responsibility for university education was removed from the federal cabinet and placed under the Minister for Education. Consequently, the National Universities Commission (N.U.C.) was to be responsible to the Minister for Education in all matters relating to university governance.

What currently happens in Nigerian universities is excessive control and regulation. If a department is to be established, for example, or another cancelled, or if a new academic programme is to be started or a member of staff is to be sent on a foreign training, the N.U.C. and consequently the Minister for Education and the federal government must be in the know, and their approval sought. What happens also is that in the appointment, renewal, or removal of the Vice-Chancellors of all federal universities (these are in the majority and they include all the older universities), the various Councils of respective universities only make recommendations to the Visitor. The President of the country is the Visitor to all federal universities, and he has the exclusive prerogative to choose who would be the Vice-Chancellor of a university.

On the one hand, this situation could have arisen because the universities were no longer conducting their affairs in a respectable manner. Petty jealousies and rivalries tend to erode the confidence that people place on them. The government justifies her position on the grounds that the occasions for the appointment of Vice-Chancellors in Nigerian universities had been periods of great tensions, that in at least one particular instance, "the issue degenerated into the most acrimonious debate between two rival ethnic groups". [16]

On the other hand, the bureaucrats in government could have been too anxious to wield enormous power. It is perhaps illuminating to note that since October 1977, when the federal government abolished tuition fees in all universities in Nigeria, and considering the fact that these institutions were totally funded by the same government, it can be assumed that the new government policy is in keeping with the dictum that "he who pays the piper dictates the tune". Otherwise, as Adamolekun remarked,

> calling for a list of candidates 'in order of preference' of the University Council and then approving the list, for example, in the reverse order is hardly a method likely to reduce 'ethnic antagonism' from 'flames' to 'smouldering embers'. [17]

Additionally, the theme of ethnic balancing which is understood in the peculiar situations of Nigeria is in fact incompatible with the goal of merit which universities pursue. [18]

Unfortunately therefore, in a number of cases, universities felt that unwanted personnel were imposed on them. Of course, the government does not have to justify his selection to anybody. At any rate, government can always plead "political expediency" and not merit. The implication of this is that some Vice-Chancellors find it difficult to secure the cooperation and the dedication especially of some professors. The government has therefore, perhaps unwittingly, introduced or heightened campus politics and politicking. It is an unfortunate situation to now see senior academics jostling for power from bureaucrats in government. What some Vice-Chancellors or aspirants allegedly do to gain or to remain in power is not fit for printing. Another serious implication of this process of selecting Vice-Chancellors is that once made a V.C., an incumbent does not owe allegiance or loyalty to his colleagues—but to the President. And it is the President alone who on the recommendation of the University Council can remove a V.C. Some V.C.s therefore tend to be too arrogant and powerful, without any appropriate university organs or processes to curb an individual's excesses or to remove him.

Lamenting the sorry situation, professor Fafunwa has said:

> The government interference in university administration and policy has now reached an alarming proportion and both the N.U.C. and the University Councils and Senates are fast becoming mere appendages. The permanent secretaries in the federal ministries of education, establishment, finance and in the federal cabinet office have tremendous influence over university governance. They wield enormous power and when they sneeze, the universities jump. [19]

It is a great challenge to Nigerian universities to reverse this situation and regain some reasonable autonomy. The university community must show that over-regulation and excessive interference lessens institutional flexibility essential to improve efficiency and productivity. Concomitantly, it must demonstrate that it has or it can develop satisfactory techniques for achieving self-imposed institutional accountability as well as acceptable self-administering procedures.

2.3.3 Proliferation

One feature of higher education in Nigeria at the very recent past was the proliferating universities and the unprecedented growth in enrolment figures.

2.3.3.1 Universities

The introduction to this chapter detailed how the number of Federal Universities grew from only one at independence in 1960 to 6 in 1972, 13 in 1975, and 20 in 1979. Including the State Universities, there are now twenty-four Nigerian Universities. This number would have been higher had the Federal Military Government not merged some Federal Universities of Technology with some older conventional ones in the country.

2.3.3.2 Enrolment

As with the growth in universities, the enrolment figures in Nigerian universities continue to sky-rocket: in 1948, the enrolment figure was about 210, and in 1953, it rose to about 400. In 1966, it went to about 8,700 while in the 1971–1972 session, the figure jumped to over 17,000. In the 1977–1978 academic year, the estimate was 47,000 while in 1982, enrolment figures totaled more than 80,000. [20] Thus, the pressure on expansion poses another challenge to Nigerian universities. This is especially serious, as we shall discuss later, in the current period of diminishing university funding and the general scarcity of financial resources.

Of interest is the rate of growth and the structure of that growth. Structurally, it appears that universities are merely duplicating each other and only providing avenues for graduating students. A recent innovation here is the federal government policy of making the bulk of the newer institutions universities of technology. But these are very much at their infancy or inception stages. Besides, as we noted earlier, their number has now been reduced from seven to three. Therefore, one cannot for now evaluate their contribution properly. The experience from similar British institutions in this regard was not encouraging. The institutions suffered from a status of inferiority as compared to the conventional universities. But perhaps this was largely because they did not label their own institutions as universities.

On the structure of growth, it is not certain whether the Nigerian society needs as many as twenty universities to cater for only 80,000–100,000 students. Although the number of students in British Universities tends to be relatively small, [21] in America, for instance, four or five big universities can have a student population of about 80,000. Considering the phenomenal cost of establishing universities, existing universities should, perhaps, merely expand their admission by opening more campuses or by expanding their present facilities accordingly. In this way, overhead cost is minimized. The savings from this could be substantial.

However, on the rate of growth of the universities themselves and of their enrolment figures, "political expediency" should not be allowed to override economic and educational rationality. The mushrooming and the high growth rate of universities poses problems, as there are no simultaneous growth in resources—human, material, and financial—to cope with this growth.

In conclusion, it is important to observe, however, that as from 1984, the previous phenomenal growth and expansion of Nigerian Universities seem to have stopped. Indeed, as we noted earlier, some universities have now been merged and others totally scrapped. This situation conforms to the international scene of stagnation and recession which universities currently seem to be experiencing.

2.3.3.3 Implications

Nonetheless, one of the implications of the previous high growth rate in the Nigerian Universities is that there are congestions in lecture halls, laboratories, libraries, residential halls, et cetera. Murtala Opoola in an investigative report of the situation at the University of Ibadan, the premier university in Nigeria, said, "lecture halls are usually jam-packed with students so much so that some peep through spaces between lourves and use walls for tables". [22] The residential halls too, according to Mr. Opoola, are so full that in some of them, like Zik and Idia, the common rooms have been turned into "sleeping places". At the University of Ibadan, utilities in every hall is said to be broken down.

> In Mellamby—the oldest hall, toilets without seats and covers overflow with human faeces, burst pipes ooze out human defalcation and bathrooms have become slippery because of the growth of moors on the walls and on the floors. [23]

Because there is shortage of finance to maintain and expand resources, there is the challenge of maintaining and protecting institutional quality—equipping laboratories, accumulating library collections, constructing new buildings and maintaining old ones, hiring academic members, and so on. Presently, some new universities are described by critics as "glorified secondary schools". Buildings are dilapidated and practicals are held less frequently because there are no laboratory materials to conduct experiments. Commenting on the deplorable situation at Ibadan, a third year student of history was reported to have said: "U.I. is in an advanced stage of decay . . .". [24] Unfortunately, what happens at Ibadan is not an isolated case.

The staffing problems in Nigerian universities deserves particular attention. In one of the universities, it is alleged that as many as 80 percent of the senior academics are Asians. Some of this group of lecturers in Nigeria have difficulties in the medium of instruction—the English language. One expects that as a result of this, the standard of teaching and that of learning would both fall. There is an important challenge on the part of Nigerian universities to train and indigenize its teaching staff. A situation where the number of the non-Nigerian academic staff is actually higher than the number of the Nigerian lecturers should simply be unacceptable. Yet, unfortunately, as of the 1981–1982 academic session, that was the reality in at least one Nigerian University. [25] This is not to say that universities should not harbour international figures who are eminent scholars. However, no nation develops meaningfully by relying largely on foreign personnel. True development must be indigenous.

One consequence of the hitherto growing number of universities is that some academic members were hired and promoted to ranks in numbers and proportions previously unknown. In all this, there is the challenge to ensure that quality is not compromised.

Another consequence of the proliferating universities is that available faculty members are often stretched to the full with teaching, the quality of which invariably falls. Lecturers are also not afforded opportunities or allowed time for research. The result is that the great majority of the books, journals, and teaching materials in use were produced by foreign academics writing for their own students. Especially in the behavioural sciences, the use of case studies and in the teaching of courses such as industrial relations, personnel management, and interpersonal behavior, there must be some cultural relevance. Besides, there is a symbiotic relationship between teaching and research. There is a challenge on the part of Nigerian universities to produce indigenous teaching materials and references. As argued elsewhere,

> . . . as long as the textbooks and teaching materials used in a country are foreign, the educational system is also foreign even if the teachers are indigenous. [26]

2.3.4 Management

One major challenge confronting the Nigerian universities is that of poor management. As noted in Chapter One under the background to the study, critics of the Nigerian Universities allege that the culture and the operation of the institutions are not different from that which obtains in the larger society. It is stated that inefficiency, red-tapism, and corruption exist in the universities as it does outside the system. Furthermore, the disposition to work, the attitude to time, and the consumption habits are characteristics that do not distinguish the universities from the larger society.

In as much as the university is a microcosm of the society of which it is a part, wonders can hardly justifiably be expected from the universities. Moreover, the object of the university is intellectual, not moral. The university is an integral part of the society; in fact, it can be regarded as a mere mirror of the society. Nonetheless, either rightly or wrongly, the society places a high premium on the ability of universities to tackle the problems affecting the society and deal with these effectively. We observed earlier that societies do make demands on higher education. Nigeria should not be an exception. The point is that if the universities themselves are no better than the larger society, it cannot morally justify assisting the latter. There are three areas in the management consideration that pose serious challenges to Nigerian universities—finance, general administration, and human problems.

2.3.4.1 Finance

Education generally, and university education in particular, are very expensive ventures. In Nigeria, education has enjoyed a high priority in national development planning and in the annual budgets. In the 1962–1968 National Development Plan, education ranked fifth judged by the magnitude of financial resources allocation. [27] In the second National Development Plan (1970–1974) the priority rating of this sector was second only to transport. Out of the gross public sector investment of about 2,000 billion Naira, education took a share of 77.8 million Naira. The actual capital expenditure for all the universities in the 1979–1980 session was more than 30 million Naira. This represents about one-third of the total education capital expenditure for that year. In the two years 1979 and 1980, when total appropriations for education were 531 million Naira and 690 million Naira respectively, N.U.C.'s share amounted to about 30 percent in each year. [28] Abdul Salami reveals that federal government's direct subvention to the universities is as high as 95 percent in respect of new universities and never less than 70 percent in respect of older ones. University education has therefore remained high in the national priority. In Britain, Mr. Salami states that government direct and indirect grants to universities range annually between 80 percent and 90 percent of total university revenue. [29] From the figures above, two points stand out: (a) Universities are expensive ventures, and (b) Various governments invariably shoulder the bulk of the funding.

Unfortunately in the recent years, following the downturn of its economy, the finances of the Nigerian Universities have been in a crisis of scarcity. Subventions now decrease in real money terms from one year to the other. The financial crisis has perhaps become directly or indirectly the most important single cause of uncertainty, stresses, and anxiety. However, the experience of Nigerian Universities is not an isolated one in this regard. British Universities, for example, experience similar financial stringences, and some British academics now face the threat of redundancies.

It is a challenge for academics to demonstrate the short-sightedness of cutting public funding for the universities. The point made by Bowen should be reiterated: that in terms of slow economic growth, the best investment that society can make is in educating its most important resource—(human beings)—and in encouraging research that will enhance growth, increase productivity, and improve the quality of life. [30] After all, "human resources, not capital, nor material resources, is the ultimate basis of the wealth of nations". [31]

It is also a challenge to universities to manage their available financial resources judiciously. In the past, emphasis seem to have been focused on the accountability function. In the future, greater attention should be placed on the generation of funds and on the utilization of available funds. Finance and investment managers, and not just accountants (as the traditional emphasis has been) would be needed, as emphasis should not just be on allocating and recording the flow of money. Needless to say, in other to generate confidence in the system, Nigerian universities must design accounting and financial regulations that would minimize embezzlements and other financial misdemeanors obtaining in some of the present systems.

In addition to financial resources, physical resources must also be managed efficiently; buildings, machinery of all sorts, vehicles, and laboratory hardware and software.

2.3.4.2 General Administration

The second problem in the management area concerns general administration and the effectiveness of the supportive services necessary to carry out the universities' main functions. The bursary, registry, health, maintenance, and other units are administrative organs existing to work in collaboration with the academic departments for greater and better organizational output. In Nigeria, unfortunately, the supportive offices frequently act as drawbacks in effectively implementing policy decisions. For example, because of slow administrative machinery, it takes a long time to appoint new faculty members, pay for external consultants or to appoint an external examiner. Besides, the elements of public relations, the attitude to work or to time seem to be hopelessly beyond reach of effectiveness. Obviously, the effectiveness of faculty members are adversely affected by their time consuming involvement in university administration such as personnel administration—leave arrangements, sick-offs, student record keeping, admissions, discipline, research grant administration, answering telephones, filing, photocopying, and so on. We note that effectiveness in teaching and in research can be improved if administrative effectiveness is higher.

2.3.4.3 Human Problems

The other general management concern is related to the problem of student unrest, interpersonal behaviour, and industrial relations. As a result of complex factors, the incidence of student unrests is high. There is also the difficulty of creating a good social image for the university as well as motivating members of the academic staff beyond pecuniary considerations. The turnover rates in Nigerian universities, especially in marketable disciplines such as accounting and business administration is high. It remains a challenge to attract and retain eminent scholars. Many people tend to use the universities as spring boards to other professions. Also because of the higher salary levels in the business world, professions which are related to business pursuits experience the problem of keeping staff. The universities must not be allowed to be institutions where people stay who do not have any other choice of work or profession.

2.3.5 Leadership

The greatest challenge facing Nigerian universities, however, is that of effective leadership. This is because the right leadership is crucial to the solution of the hitherto enumerated problems. Leadership is the element that makes the difference between an organization "muddling through" or merely surviving and another that is really making enviable progress. There are immense stock of latent energies in any organization. Effective leadership makes use of these latent energies for increased output. The importance of leadership in Nigerian universities cannot be over emphasized. To a large extent, it affects motivation and job satisfaction, productivity, and organization success however defined.

Leadership can be looked upon as a subset of the management function. However, it seems to occupy a central and an important position in the diagnosis of the problems of Nigerian universities to justify a separate treatment.

Rather ironically, universities seem to have shun the idea of the need for organized management training, especially for the academic leaders. Instead of encouraging the cultivation of administrative and leadership skills for its managers, universities traditionally emphasize technical and academic proficiencies. The result is that some academics assuming important administrative positions rarely have leadership training or administrative work experience. The assumption is that a professor would make a good dean, director, or a good vice-chancellor. Little accepted is the notion that academic competence may not necessarily confer leadership and administrative capability. The culture of universities the world over seem to exaggerate the importance of the accumulation of knowledge and research skills per se over leadership or management abilities. Specialism is often pursued at the expense of broad-mindedness and realism. Surely, if there were any relationship between theory and practice (and the universities exist to show that there is) then some measure of management and leadership training seem advantageous for potential and practicing academic leaders in assisting them to perform their duties more effectively. This is especially true as universities now seem to face an unprecedented environmental hostility and economic-financial recession.

The leadership challenge facing Nigerian academics is that of effectiveness. Nigeria is in need of men who will spearhead researches and moves to liberate the African from all that hampers his well-being physically, mentally, and materially.

It is believed that with better leadership skills and behaviour on the part of its academics, Nigerian universities can be the principal sites at which substantial social, political, economic, and cultural issues could be examined for appropriate remedies. This is because universities harbour a concentration (not a monopoly) of the best brains in a country. However, the academics must develop their leadership skills and behaviour if they are to bring about the much needed university effectiveness which is a catalyst in societal advancement. To know which skills to develop or what management courses to run, it is desirable to know the job characteristics and perceptions of academic leaders.

2.4 British Universities

The first part of this chapter has attempted a thorough examination of the Nigerian University system—structure, management, and challenges. In terms of structure, British and Nigerian university systems are roughly identical. In the administrative structure, you have the Vice-Chancellor as the chief executive with directors of schools, deans of faculties, and heads of departments in the academic setting. Heads of Departments in the services and supporting units include the registrar, bursar, librarian, directors of health, and so on. This arrangement is not significantly different from the Nigerian practice.

The administration of universities in the U.K. is generally along the lines of the Committee System as the practice in Nigeria. However, unlike in Nigeria, the University Council is the supreme authority in a British university (except on academic matters where the University Senate has the final say), its decisions subordinate only to that of the courts. There are both standing as well as ad-hoc committees of Councils and Senates. Universities in both countries are managed essentially by these committees and their subcommittees.

In the current debates in United Kingdom, however, there are suggestions that universities in that country should have diminishing democracy in non-academic matters. If this suggestion is implemented, the argument goes, it will make universities more business-like and more responsive to changes and current needs. As opposed to scholars carrying out Senates will, Vice-Chancellors in both countries are becoming more of chief executives actually directing the affairs of their universities, influencing goals, and dictating courses of action. This situation is particularly true in the Nigerian case although ironically, or perhaps expectedly, it is in Nigeria that there seems to be more clamour for entrenching more committee management in all aspects of university administration.

As a result of different levels of development and different cultures, the practice of management in universities in U.K. is perhaps marginally better than it is in Nigeria. For example, U.K. has superior telephone and communication facilities than Nigeria and this factor can have significant effects in the management of meetings and committees. Nonetheless, like the practice in Nigeria, there is no systematic training and development of academic leaders in Britain.

Universities in the U.K. and Nigeria developed over distinct time periods. Whereas almost all the universities in Nigeria were established during the second half of this Century, some universities in Britain have long historical development, sometimes dating back to the 12th Century. Consequently, perhaps, there are more universities in the U.K. than in Nigeria. The 1982 Commonwealth Universities

Yearbook listed 47 universities in the U.K. This number is about double the official figure of 24 universities in Nigeria. Thus, while Nigeria with a land area almost four times that of the U.K. and possessing an estimated population of at least 150 per cent that of the U.K., it has only about 50 per cent of the number of U.K. universities. Yet, because of different levels of development, Nigeria is already complaining of having too many universities. These comparisons are intended to explain that the problems and challenges facing universities in the U.K. and Nigeria cannot reasonably be expected to be the same. Whereas universities in Nigeria are generally trying to get off the ground and establish some tradition, those in the U.K. are debating new emphasis and new directions in a changing and competitive world.

Some of the issues of the debates on higher education in U.K. today include (a) what the nature of postgraduate training should be—the more structured versus the less programmed training in research skills; (b) whether courses of higher education should be available to all those who, following the Robbin's Committee axiom, are "qualified by ability" and attainment to pursue them and who wish to do so, or should access to higher education be limited to those who possessing the wherewithal, are "able to benefit" from them and wish to do so; (c) how universities should be structured and managed—whether the industry model which is less democratic, more responsive, and more goal focused should be practised or whether the Committee Model which is the opposite in characteristic should continue to be operated; (d) how universities should be funded—whether totally by the government or in large measure by the money internally generated by the universities themselves to be supported only by government subventions; (e) whether academics should be free to continue to select their areas of research interest or whether funding bodies should stipulate on what they want research money to be spent? This is a healthy debate, and both parties are likely to be better off after it.

2.5 Notes and References

[1] Chizea, C.A. (ed.), *Bulletin of the National Universities Commission*, Lagos, Nigeria, Various Dates.

[2] In May, 1959, a commission headed by Sir Eric Ashby of Cambridge University was appointed to "conduct an investigation into the Nigerian needs in the field of post-secondary school certificate and higher education over the next 20 years, 1960–1980." The team included Professor Frederick Harbison, a noted American Economist who was asked to estimate Nigeria's need for higher-level manpower between 1960 and 1970, and their educational implication for the future in terms of training.

[3] These are the Universities of Calabar, Jos, Maiduguri, Sokoto, Kano, Ilorin, and Port-Harcourt.

[4] Chizea, C.A., (ed.), *Bulletin of the National Universities Commission*, Lagos, Nigeria, Dec. 1984, pp. 2–3. The four former Federal Universities of Technology now run as campuses of some older universities in the country as follows: The Federal Universities of Technology Abeokuta, Bauchi, Markurdi, and Yola were merged with the Universities of Lagos, Ahmadu Bello, Jos, and Maiduguri respectively. The remaining three Federal Universities of Technology, i.e. those located at Owerri, Akure, and Minna continue to function as autonomous full fledged institutions.

[5] Ibid., pp. 4–5. These are Imo, Lagos, Bendel, Anambra, Rivers, Cross Rivers, Ondo (Obafemi Awolowo), and Ogun State Universities.

[6] Ibid., p. 4. Sixteen of these are federally owned and eight state owned. The Bulletin referenced revealed that: "Five of the Federal Universities have campuses in towns other than where the main campuses are located. Three of the federally owned Universities are Universities of Technology while the other thirteen are conventional ones. Only two of the State Universities are not conventional Universities. These are the Rivers State University of Science and Technology at Port Harcourt and Anambra State University of Technology, Enugu."

[7] Report of the Presidential Commission on salary and conditions of service of university staff, Nigeria, 1981.

[8] Chizea, C.A. (ed.), *20 Years of University Education in Nigeria*, National Universities Commission's Publication, Lagos, Nigeria, 1984, pp. 86–87.

[9] Report of the Presidential Commission on salary and conditions of service of university staff, 1981.

[10] Public Service Review Commission, (Lagos, Federal Ministry of Information, 1974) Main Report Paragraph 637.

[11] Adamolekun, N.K., Universities and Polytechnics, in: Adamolekun and Gboyega, (eds.), *Leading Issues in Nigerian Public Service*, Proceedings of a National Symposium, April 1975, University of Ife Press, Ile-Ife, Nigeria, 1979, p. 114.

[12] Fafunwa, B., Nigerian Varsities: Problems and Challenges, *National Concord*, 12 January, 1983.

[13] Ibid.

[14] Ibid.

[15] Ibid.

[16] Government views on The Report of the *Public Service Review Commission*, Dec., 1974. Paragraph 69 of the White Paper.

[17] Adamolekun, op. cit., p. 99.

[18] Ibid., p. 98.

[19] Fafunwa, B., loc. cit.

[20] Chizea, C.A. (ed.), *Bulletin of the National Universities Commission*, Lagos, Nigeria, Various Dates. In the 1982–1983 academic session, the total en-

rolment in the Nigerian Federal Universities stood at exactly 92, 116. See reference [8] above.

[21] The Association of Commonwealth Universities, *Commonwealth Universities Yearbook*, 1982, Vol., I A–B, pp. 206–833. Excluding the Open University, only 6 of U.K.'s 47 universities have total student enrolment figure greater than 10,000 as of the 1978–1979 session. The six universities in order of size of enrolment are London, Wales, Manchester, Oxford, Cambridge, and Leeds.

[22] Opoola, M., Ageing U.I.: Coping with the problems of university education, *New Nigerian*, May 24, 1983.

[23] Ibid.

[24] Ibid.

[25] Chizea, C.A. (ed.), *20 Years of University Education in Nigeria*, op. cit. The Table on "Academic Staff By Nationality, Institution and Academic Year, 1973–74—1981–82", no page, reveals that as of the 1981–82 session, there were 99 non-Nigerian lecturers as against 94 Nigerian academic staff members at Sokoto University. See also, Aliens and Our Universities, *Daily Times*, Editorial, February 28, 1985, p. 3.

[26] Oshagbemi, T.A., *Nigerian Business Policy and Strategy*, Hutchinson, London, in press.

[27] Salami, A., Universities: Alternative Sources of Finance to Government Funding, *Sunday Standard*, October 31, 1982.

[28] Ibid.

[29] Ibid.

[30] McCorkle, C.O. and Archibald, S.O., *Management and Leadership in Higher Education*, Jossey-Bass Publishers, San Francisco, 1982, p. 8.

[31] Harbison, F.H., *Human Resources as the Wealth of Nations*, Oxford University Press, New York, 1973, p. 3.

Chapter 3
Managerial Jobs

3.1 Introduction

A manager is generally described as someone who gets activities performed through other people. The question of what exactly he or she does has been a subject of inquiry for many management writers since the beginning of the century. In seeking to understand managers' activities, various questions have been asked: What amount of time do managers spend on the various aspects of their work? What kinds of decisions do they make? What is the content or the subject matter of these decisions? Has the manager's work any pattern? With whom does the manager interact and how frequently? What information processes do managers utilize? And so on.

Answers to these questions are valuable as they help the manager in self management for greater effectiveness. They also make the processes of selecting managers and staffing organizations more manageable. Additionally, awareness of the nature of the job characteristics, contacts, perceptions, and activities of managers help in the design of appropriate courses for training particular managers, or for general management development programmes.

A brief review of the past studies of the manager's job shall be attempted in this chapter. First, the classical views of the functions of the manager shall be presented. This is to be followed by a literature survey of the work-activity studies. Next, other studies that do not readily fall into any of the above two categories shall be examined, after which researches specifically centered on the academic leaders' job are looked at in detail. Finally, the methods used to study what managers do are briefly outlined and appraised. The summary and conclusions to this chapter noted, with surprise, the relative neglect of studies of the academic leaders' jobs and expresses the opinion that such studies are not only justified, but long overdue.

3.2 Classical Views

The earliest view on managerial work activity was documented in the early part of this century by the management practitioner Henri Fayol: Reflecting on his distilled personal experiences, Fayol posited that managers plan, organize, coordinate, command, and control. [1] Although published in 1916 in the French language, Fayol's work was "eclipsed by the bright lights of his contemporary, Frederick Taylor, and clouded by the lack of a widely available English translation until 1949". [2] However, his five basic managerial functions were the first, and for a very long time, the most prevalent explanation on what managers actually do. Fayol believed that management was a universal process, [3] and this belief was consistent with his theoretical exposition which explained managerial duties in terms of a set of discrete and discernible roles and functions.

The classical view of managerial functions (fathered by Fayol), was very popular, generally accepted, and as such, was frequently referred to by later writers. [4] As Mintzberg observed, it permeated the writings of popular theorists such as Peter Drucker and industrial leaders such as Ralph Cordiner. [5] Sune Carlson also noted that the classical thinking was evident in the mind of Chester Barnard in the latter's analysis of the functions of the executive. [6]

However, Fayol's basic ideas were to be revised and modified by subsequent writers who were not satisfied with its original form. In 1937, for example, Luther Gulick extended Fayol's ideas and coined POSDCORB, a mnemonic for the classical managerial functions: Planning, Organizing, Staffing, Directing, Coordinating, Reporting, and Budgeting. [7] Similarly, Newman introduced "assembling resources", [8] and Terry, "leading human efforts" [9] while Richman and Farmer contended that:

> A useful division of managerial function is: planning and innovation, controlling, organising, staffing and direction, communication, leadership and motivation. [10]

However, Fayol's basic contention was not disputed by these authors. Indeed, Fayol's importance was never questioned even by Mintzberg and Stewart. While the former refers to him as the "founding father" of the "classical school" of management theory, [11] the latter accepted that Fayol's ideas "promoted an analytical approach to managerial work and the recognition that it has distinctive characteristics". [12]

Dissatisfaction with Fayol's theory nonetheless started in earnest when an empirical approach to studying the manager's work begun. Originated in 1951 by Carlson, there was a recognition of the poor conceptual foundations inherent in Fayol's Principles. It was found difficult to relate Fayol's elements to actual managerial activities or to distinguish among the five elements he propagated. In the report of his own studies, for example, Carlson noted,

> If we ask a managing director when he is co-ordinating, or how much co-ordination he has been doing during a day he would not know, and even the most highly skilled observer would not know either. The same holds true of the concepts of planning, command, organization, and control. [13]

Mintzberg suggested that Fayol should be blamed for initiating the use of ambiguous terms in management theory. He gave an example of Goodman, an academic, who in 1968 proclaimed that:

> It must be admitted that most managers both manage and do, but at the time they are doing, they are not managing. [14]

Such imprecise and confusing terms as "manage and do" unfortunately flooded the management literature. Mintzberg noted that the problem of imprecision was compounded whenever other writers utilized Fayol's terms, as there was no objective comparability.

The conclusions reached by the critics of the "traditional" or the "universalist" school, and critics of its intellectual progenitor, Henri Fayol, led researchers to direct their investigations into what managers actually do as opposed to what they are supposed to do. This new orientation had profound consequences on both the methodology adopted in subsequent studies as well as on the assumptions. For instance, later studies dropped the assumptions that the manager's role was already known in favour of exploratory enquiries. Additionally, investigations turned from indirect qualitative studies to more direct empirical researches, a move away from Fayolism towards more empiricism.

In summary, the classical writers, in the main, sought to describe managerial practices in terms of general principles and in terms of composite functions. Basing their writings on unstructured observation and experiences, they provided analytical insight into the nature of managerial work. That is why Fayol is still regarded as the father of pioneer writers in this area even by empirically inclined researchers such as Mintzberg and Stewart. As Koontz remarked,

> Certainly not even the most academic worshiper of empirical research can overlook the empiricism involved in distiling fundamental from decades of experience by such discerning practitioners as these. Admittedly done without questionnaires, controlled interviews, or mathematics, observations by such men can hardly be accurately regarded as a priori or "armchair". [15]

However, the classical writers tended to provide an over simplified picture of the manager's functions. Some of their principles are too general and broad to be operationally useful. Some of them are also contradictory, vague, and confusing.

3.3 Work-Activity Studies

As a result of the great dissatisfaction with the classical views of the functions of the manager, attention focused on what has become known as the "work-activity school". [16] This unique approach to management theory has three characteristics: (1) It utilized direct methods of gathering data on managers' activities; (2) It led to the generation and the production of quantitative data as the basis of the opinions held; (3) It focused on recordable, testable, quantifiable, or observable behaviour of managers when they perform their functions. [17]

3.3.1 Origins

The origins of managerial work-activity studies predates Carlson's study and can conceptually be traced to the work study method as developed by Frederick Winslow Taylor and the Scientific Management School. [18] The commonality in methodology between the work-activity studies and Taylor's Scientific Management was indirectly alluded to by Mintzberg, [19] but more clearly stated by Gibbs. [20] The similarities include the following:

> "First", Taylor said, "find 10 or 15 different men preferably in as many separate establishments and parts of the country".

Carlson found 9 chief executives from 9 different organizations in Sweden. [21] Stewart found 160 senior and middle managers in Britain. [22] Mintzberg got 5 willing executives in America. [23]

"Second, study the exact series of elementary operation which each of these men uses in doing the work".

Researchers of the work-activity school recorded details of the work characteristics of the managers they studied. These details included where the managers worked, with whom, what their work entailed, and so on.

"Third, proceed to considering and establishing the best way of doing the job."

The ultimate outcome of the work-activity researches, it is hoped, would be the improvement in the selection, training, and management development of managers eventually leading to more effective management practices.

Notwithstanding the above observations, the origins of empirical studies of the manager's work is dated to Carlson's pioneering work of 1951. In the above illustrations, Taylor was concerned only with the analysis of manual work at the factory level. However, as the above illustration depicts, and contrary to Gibbs' conclusions, [24] the work-activity methodology is indeed an extension of Taylorism from manual to managerial jobs.

Carlson, a professor of Business Administration at Stockholm University, met with some dissatisfaction when he and a group of managing directors were investigating into the tasks that only top executives perform in an organization. Their difficulties were further compounded by the absence of relevant literature in the subject area, a factor which led Carlson to undertake his studies. The aim was to find common managerial "behaviour patterns and some general relationships which characterize these patterns". [25]

Carlson developed and used a diary, (see figure 3-1 for a sample) a method which was to gain wide popularity. For each activity, they noted the place of work, the person or persons involved, the nature of the questions being handled, the kind of action taken, the technique of communication, and so on. Carlson's conclusions were of three types. These were related to working time, communication, and to work content.

Carlson found out that executives were extremely busy people, their working loads averaging between 8.5 and 11.5 hours a day. However, executives experienced a number of interruptions during their working sessions, the typical "alone" interval of only 10–15 minutes duration and averaging only about an hour each day.

Date: 3/11 49 Telephone: In [ ] Out [ ]

Time: 10.45-11.05

Place (other than own office): ______________

Person: ______________

____

Manuf. dir.	[ ]	Comptr.	[ ]	Adv. dir.	[ ]
Works man. A	[ ]	Account.	[ ]	Pers. dir.	[ ]
Works man. B	[X]	Sales dir. Swed.	[ ]	Assistant	[ ]
Organ. dir.	[ ]	Sales dir. exp.	[ ]	Secr.	[ ]

A. Question handled		Kind of action	
Finance, legal	[ ]	Getting information	[X]
Accounting	[ ]	Systematizing information	[ ]
Buying	[ ]	Taking decisions	[ ]
Production	[X]	Confirming or correcting decisions of others	[ ]
Product research	[X]		
Sales	[ ]	Giving orders	[ ]
Personnel	[ ]	Advising, explaining	[ ]
Public relations	[ ]	Inspecting, reviewing	[ ]
Organiz. planning	[ ]	Executing	[ ]
______	[ ]	______	[ ]
______	[ ]	______	[ ]
______	[ ]	______	[ ]
Private	[ ]	Personal development	[ ]

B. Question handled		C. Question handled	
Development	[X]	Policy	[ ]
Current operations	[ ]	Application	[X]

Figure 3-1: A Sample of Carlson's Diary
Source: Carlson 1951, p. 46.

The findings include the fact that the managing directors spent a large amount of time outside their organizations. They also had a false perception of how they allocate their time on many activities such as reading and tours. Carlson discovered that the communication network of the chief executives were very complex, and that written communications were infrequently used as compared to oral ones. He also found that the managers received, on the average, a greater number of letters than they initiate every day. Unfortunately, Carlson could not be categorical about his findings on the actual content of the executives' activities. He found out that the executives gave different interpretations to his categorizations on the subject matter of the contents of their jobs.

3.3.2 Subsequent Diary Studies

In 1951, Carlson could only find two, if somewhat irrelevant studies of the work activities of managers. Some thirty years later, in 1981, McCall, Morrison, and Hannan needed to utilize the services of the computer to help them identify and locate the many references where work had been done in this area. Their search produced over a hundred relevant articles and books, forty of which presented data in sufficient detail to justify their inclusion in their substantive review. [26] The vast majority of the studies on the work-activity of managers were conducted in Western Europe and the United States of America, and these were conducted mostly in the private industry. It included managers at all levels from the chief executive to the supervisor, and in a variety of organizational settings. A list of the sample of the major diary studies consulted in our review is presented in table 3-1.

The first follow-up study was undertaken by Tom Burns and published in 1954. [27] Here, Burns studied the relationships among four middle managers in a manufacturing plant for five weeks. This was after the managers had estimated their allocation of time among various activities. His conclusion was that managers are poor estimators of how they spend their time, especially the time spent with people, or on human affairs. The second study, also by Burns, utilized a larger sample of managers (76) and, unlike his first study, extended to eight different firms. This latter study led to some of his more important findings. One of these was the finding that managers spent a high proportion of their time in oral conversation with the tendency to spend considerable time with some selected individuals. [28] Burns also found that managers spent much time on horizontal and lateral communication, findings that were later replicated by other researches.

Table 3-1: A Sample of the Major Diary Studies Reviewed

Researcher(s)	Date	Sample Size	Level of Managers*	Number of Organizations
Carlson	1951	9	Top	9
Burns	1954	4	Middle	1
Burns	1954	76	Senior	8
Copeman	1963	58	Top, senior, middle	Not reported
Dublin & Spray	1964	8	Senior, middle	3
Brewer, Tomlinson	1964	6	Senior, middle	6
Hinrichs	1964	232	Middle, low	1
Horne, Lupton	1965	66	Middle	10
Thomason	1966	30	Middle, low	7
Thomason	1967	26	Senior, middle, low	4
Stewart	1967	160	Senior, middle	Not reported+
Marples	1968	8	Middle, low	1
Lawler, Porter, And Tennenbaum	1968	105	Middle, low	5
Dahl & Lewis	1975	12	Senior, middle	1
Hinrichs	1976	142	Middle, low	1
Stewart	1976	16	Senior, middle, low	9

+ However, it covers over 17 industries
* 'Top' refers to the chief executive

Copeman was concerned generally with the contrasts in the work of the chief executives with that of departmental managers. Specifically, he compared in detail the time allocations between chief executives and departmental heads. [29] One of his more interesting findings was that chief executives had longer working hours than do departmental heads (53 versus 43 hours per week). The finding is interesting because it implies that the higher the managerial level, perhaps, the longer the manager tends to work. If this finding is supported by subsequent researches, it means that one would be able to rank how hard managers work in order of their seniority.

Dublin and Spray studied the work behavior of eight American managers for two weeks, and found little uniformity in the executives' functions. Dublin and Spray also found that top executives tend to engage in more contacts with people outside the organization and they have a wider scope of activities than junior managers in the same organization. [30]

Horne and Lupton [31] on their part attempted to study the content of managerial jobs using FOUR, representing Formulating, Organizing, Unifying, and Regulating, a mnemonic which Mintzberg calls a "surrogate" for POSDCORB. They also measured what the manager thinks he does against what he actually does, and concluded that managers are poor predictors of their own activities. They did this by first asking the managers' estimation on the allocation of their time. This was later compared with the diary recordings filled by the managers. Contrary to some earlier notions, Horne and Lupton found that their managers, though very busy, were not over-worked. However, like many studies suggest, they also discovered that managers spent a lot of time on routine, non-policy issues.

Two reports were published from Thomason's studies, a series of investigations conducted with the assistance of management students. The first report concentrated on executives' communication structure [32] while the second one focused on the variations in executive jobs due to functional specialties. [33] Thomason found interesting variations in jobs by functional areas. For example, he found that top managers spent less time on production, and more on policy matters as compared to lower-level managers.

Other relevant diary studies were conducted by Marples, [34] Brewer and Tomlinson, [35] Lawler, Porter, and Tennenbaum, [36] and Hinrichs, [37, 38]. Brewer and Tomlinson were "concerned with the elements of managerial behaviour that are common to all situations" [39] while Hinrichs undertook a work sampling study of on-the-job time allocation of technical men in a large Research and Development Organization. On their part, Lawler, Porter, and Tennenbaum studied the psychological dimensions of managerial behaviour and attempted to ascertain why or how managers react to different behaviour episodes. Marples concentrated on attempting to distinguish the origins and the character of the problems that different managers face. A further review of the latter set of work, and indeed of other reported small-scale studies, would not appear either to add significant dimensions to the methodological approach or to our understanding of what managers do.

However, Stewart's study was comprehensive and her sample size of 160 managers was quite extensive. Her research therefore provided a major contribution to our understanding of variations in managerial jobs. Stewart studied how mangers spent their time in detail discovering that managers averaged about 42 hours of work per week, and spending sixty percent of their time in discussion. She also stated the arithmetical averages of the percentage times spent in own establishment (75%), offices (51%), alone (34%), with immediate subordinates (25%), and so on, depicting the variety of and the fragmentation in work. [40] However, because of methodological problems resulting in inaccuracies in the data obtained, she abandoned collecting information on the work content of managers. She used cluster analysis to classify managers on the basis of how they spent their time. Her results showed five clusters which she labelled the Emissaries, the Writers, the Discussers, the Trouble shooters, and the Committeemen.

3.3.3 Observational Studies

Instead of the manager recording his own activities, as in the case of the diary studies, researchers using the observational method stay with, observe, record, and interpret the manager's activities. A list of the sample of the major observational studies consulted in our review is presented in table 3-2.

The series of observational studies started with Blau who observed the patterns of interactions among 16 middle-level agents in one government law-enforcement agency in 1954. He found out that it was not only agents who were highly competent, but also those who had extensive informal relations who received a disproportionately large number of contacts (signifying more power and prestige) in the course of social interaction. [41] Guest [42] and Jasinki [43] reported a detailed one day observation of the activities of 56 foremen in an automobile assembly plant, keeping records of location, contacts, and the nature of their interaction.

Guest studied in detail, how the managers spent their time, and found that the managers were involved in a large number of incidents (an average of 583 per day). Managers also exhibited a rich variety of job types, a high frequency of contacts and interruptions, but a low idle time.

Jasinki found that during the eight-hour day when he carried out his investigations, the average foreman was in contact with someone else for 58 percent of his time. In addition, Jasinki found out that 46 percent of the average foreman's "interacting" time was spent with his own workers, i.e. people in his formally designated work group. In one department, comprising of eleven foremen, Jasinki found that

Table 3-2: A Sample of the Major Observational Studies Reviewed

Researcher(s)	Date	Sample Size	Level of Managers*	Number of Organizations
Blau	1954	16	Middle	1
Guest	1956	56	Low	1
Jasinki	1956	56	Low	1
Ponder	1957	24	Low	1
Dale & Urwick	1960	10	Top	10
Landsberger	1961	3	Middle	2
Luijk	1963	25	Top	Not reported
Kelly	1964	4	Middle	1
Sayles	1964	75	Middle, low	1
Mintzberg	1973	5	Top	5
Cohen & March	1974	42	Top	42
McCall and Lombardo	1979	20	Top	1
Gibbs	1982	1	Top	1
Kurke and Aldrich	1983	4	Top	4

* Foremen are classified as low-level managers

about seventy five percent of all contacts for the average foreman were either with the foreman immediately preceding or immediately succeeding him on the assembly line. [44]

Ponder [45] carried out his observation at the General Electric Company. It was designed to differentiate between the work patterns of effective and ineffective foremen. He discovered that the effective foremen (as rated by superiors and subordinates) had less number of activities, concentrated more on personnel as opposed to production problems, and generally seemed to delegate more than ineffective foremen. Both effective and ineffective managers, however, spent about the same amount of time with their subordinates.

Dale and Urwick [46] were interested in the top executives of ten different organizations, while Landsberger was concerned with horizontal relationships and interactions in three comparable companies. [47] Dale and Urwick found that the chief executives spent more time than the other managers on external contacts and that the nature of this contact is very broad. Landsberger established that managers in equivalent positions, but in different companies tend to take the same stands on various controversial organizational issues. He also noted that the frequency of horizontal interactions was high.

Luijk [48] made a systematic study of the chief executive's job and how the executives handle administrative situations. He discovered a high-level of personal and telephone interruptions in the course of an executive's working day, a situation which, he observes, hinders their creative work. Luijk also observed that the executives were poor at organization, and that they handle administrative situations badly. Because of this and other factors, Luijk estimated that the chief executives in his study wasted about one third (32%) of their working time.

Joe Kelly [49, 50] used activity sampling to study the work of four section managers of the Glacier Metal Company, detailing in particular, how the managers spent their time with various other people: unit managers, colleagues, subordinates, and so on. His conclusions are very important:

> The important single conclusion to emerge from this study is the fact that the task is the principal determinant structuring the behaviour of section managers. What follows as a corollary is that personal factors are of limited significance in determining behaviour. [51]

Perhaps the most significant observational study to date is the one undertaken by Mintzberg. [52] Mintzberg carried out a comprehensive empirical study from which he exploded some myths about managerial behaviour. [53] One of these is the notion that the manager is a reflective, systematic planner. Another piece of "folklore" is that management is quickly becoming a science. While consenting to the idea that there is a common set of managerial roles, Mintzberg disagrees with the components of these duties as put forward by the classical writers. From his study, Mintzberg proposes ten managerial functions which are subsumed within three broad roles: interpersonal, decision-making, and informational. These, he hypothesizes, are common to all managers.

Kurke and Aldrich's study was a replication and an extension of Mintzberg's work, [54] while McCall and Lombardo's was a simulation study of a glass company to probe into how environmental uncertainty affects managerial behaviour and effectiveness. [55]

In summary, the work-activity studies sought to be more empirical and more scientific in methodology. As was pointed out earlier in this chapter, however, the technique of recording work activities empirically is not new. Taylor applied it to manual jobs at the turn of the century. [56] What we now have is an extension of activity recording from manual to managerial jobs. There is much in common between managerial work activity studies and work study methods as developed by the Scientific Management School. These similarities we have already pointed out.

3.4 Other Studies

This section incorporates the review of some other studies of manager's work that do not fall neatly into the previous two categories. One of the important studies in this section is Sayle's anthropological investigation. [57] An anthropological study is one in which a researcher lives with the people he is studying for an extended period of time in an attempt to understand their complex relationships and attitudes. Sayle's research has been criticized on the grounds that there is no systematic research methodology which can be replicated, and that little hard data are presented as such. His book nonetheless shows an appreciation of the complex activities, relationships, and roles inherent in managerial work. He sees the goal of the manager in maintaining the regular pattern of work and in doing this, the manager exhibits both the roles of a leader and a monitor. Seeing the dynamic nature of managerial work, he criticises the classical view of managerial work in favour of an open system of "moving equilibrium".

Other important studies in this section include the Ohio State Leadership Studies. This is a group of studies undertaken at the Ohio State University on managerial work. [58] Although it was originally intended to be a ten-year study, its many publications extended from the 1940s to the 1960s. One of their primary objectives is the accumulation of knowledge and the development of research methodology that will "aid in the education, selection, training, and assignment of persons to leadership positions in business and industry, government, and education". [59] Employing essentially a survey methodology and employing factor analysis in reducing and interpreting the resulting mass of data, various categorizations of managerial activity have been presented in the many studies under the same umbrella of the Ohio State Leadership Studies.

Fleischman's "initiating structure" and "consideration" are popular statements of the author's conclusion that all variations in managerial activity could be explained by two major dimensions. [60]

Items in the "consideration" dimension were concerned with the extent to which the leader was considerate of his workers' feelings. It reflected "human relations" aspects of group leadership. Items in the "initiating structure" dimension reflected the extent to which the leader defined or facilitated group interactions towards goal attainment. [61]

One of the studies was particularly focused on managerial work. [62] Hempill collected and analyzed responses from 93 people selected at various management levels from different large companies in America. He performed factor analysis on his data, and this isolated ten factors. The factors are:

Factor A: Providing a staff service in non-operational areas
Factor B: Supervision of work
Factor C: Internal Business Control
Factor D: Technical aspects of products and markets
Factor E: Human, community, and social affairs
Factor F: Long-range planning
Factor G: Exercise of broad power and authority
Factor H: Business reputation
Factor I: Personal demands
Factor J: Preservation of assets. [63]

Hempill tabulated his ten factors against the three management levels (upper, middle, and lower management levels), and the five functional areas (research & development, sales, manufacturing, general administration, and industrial relations). His findings were that top management tended to rank higher on business control and planning, (factors C and F) while the most junior management levels appeared to rate higher on technical products and markets, and staff services (factors A and D). Among the functional areas, research and development tended to be strong on factors A, F, and D, while manufacturing and sales were both apparently strong on business control (factor C). Industrial relations was outstandingly high on staff service (factor A) and high on business reputation (factor H).

A number of miscellaneous studies such as that by Neustadt, [64] Homans, [65] Stieglitz, [66] Wikstrom, [67] Walker, Guest, and Turner [68] have been reported. These do not appear to be particularly directed at uncovering what managers do, although they can hardly be dismissed as irrelevant. Wikstrom's investigation, for example, was to try and find out whether the foreman is a manager, while

Walter, Guest, and Turner wanted to know the work content of foremen. Additional reviews of these would appear to add little to the information to be obtained from the other studies already discussed.

3.5 Summary of Replicated Findings

Having carried out a general survey of individual contributions, it would now be useful to attempt a summary of what so far appears to be the consensus from the various authors and see where some questions still remain. McCall, Morrison, and Hannan set for themselves the task of such a summary. In their review, they suggested the following findings:

1. Managers work long hours
2. Managers are busy
3. A manager's work is fragmented, episodes are brief
4. The manager's job is varied
5. Managers are "homebodies"
6. The manager's work is primarily oral
7. Managers use a lot of contacts
8. Managers are not reflective planners
9. Information is the basic ingredient of the manager's work
10. Managers don't know how they spend their time. [69]

Similarly, the writers identified the following six question areas:

1. Do managers control their work?
2. Do effective managers do things differently?
3. What is the content of managerial work?
4. Do organizational variables matter?
5. Does managerial work cycle?
6. What causes stress? [70]

It is relatively easier to identify problem areas than it is to summarize consensus. For example, McCall, Morrison, and Hannan's review suggests that "the executive's work week typically consumes at least 50 hours and can go up to 90 hours for certain individuals". [71] The comment should be made, however, that although this conclusion is based on empirical data, some of the reports on managers' working hours, with the exception of Stewart's, were not detailed enough for easy generalization. It is useful to know, for example, if the computed working hours include lunch periods and periods taken off for social activities. It is also useful to know if every minute was accounted for, and whether or not the figures include work during the weekends. It should be mentioned that it is a little difficult to estimate, for example, the working hours of salesmen when they travel out or of academics when they are on conferences, say abroad. Working for as much as 90 hours a week must be regarded as very high indeed.

Similarly, it does not seem unreasonable to suggest that the activity levels of managers are high. However, to suggest that this may be as many as "at least 200 separate activities (incidents or episodes) during a typical 8-hour day", with averages of up to 583 incidents per day, [72] may, again, be an exaggeration. At any rate, "activities" are hardly rigorously defined by most of the studies. What passes for a "fleeting contact" in one study may be an "activity" in another, rendering comparability difficult. From our experience during the pilot study when an activity was not properly defined, the average activity level for our sample was about 25 per day. During the main study, when "activities are defined as incidents of 5 minutes or more in duration", the average activity level dropped to about half of the figure obtained during the pilot study. This is understandable because during the pilot work, a telephone conversation of four minutes duration would for instance be recorded as a separate activity, while during the main study, this would be treated merely as a fleeting contact. It is therefore important to be careful with generalizations.

3.6 Studies of the Academic Leaders' Jobs

The terms administration and administrator are still traditionally much more commonly used with regard to academic institutions than management or manager, which tends to find its extensive use in the private sector. That probably explains in part the relative neglect of the literature focusing attention on the public sector in general vis-à-vis the private sector. Yet, studies based upon the public sector would test whether generalizations could be made across the sectors. Higher educational institutions, especially the universities, provide an opportunity for a limited attempt to test the generalizability of the findings relating to the private industry.

Within the educational field, a number of previous studies had been documented. The more relevant research for our study was that made by Cohen and March. [73] This research was based on data collected from 42 college presidents (equivalents of vice-chancellors in Britain and in Nigeria) in the United States of America. The researchers had the secretaries of the presidents record the latters' activities and movements for two separate but non-consecutive days (a Tuesday and a Friday). The 24 hours in each day was divided into half hour periods. For each period, each president's time was coded in terms of (1) where he was, (2) with whom, (3) and in what size group. Their interest was in all the presidents' school related activities.

According to the secretarial logs, their estimates showed that the presidents worked for about 50 to 55 hours from Monday to Friday, while the authors assumed an additional 5 to 10 hours of work during the weekend. Their findings also showed that the college presidents spent 47% of their time on the campus, 14% in town, 16% at home, and 22% out of town. Of the time spent on the campus, the presidents spent about 75% of this in their own offices. Their figures for the times spent alone was 25%, 35% with one person, and 40% with two or more people. Similar figures obtained for the times spent with students and the faculty staff are 5% and 13% respectively. In conclusion, the authors claims that the "pattern of presidential activities is rather ordinary executive behavior heavily regulated by social expectations". [74]

Another study in the educational field was a diary investigation by Dahl and Lewis on 12 middle to high-level administrators in a single college. [75] The authors examined managerial work specifically with regard to stress and found that the problems of delegation were particularly stressful. Tom Lupton also reported the self-recording of the managerial activities of the director of a large teaching and research unit of a university. [76] The director used Mintzberg's ten roles to categorize his activities and claimed that this was fairly easy to do.

Additional somewhat distantly related writings have also been reported by Birley, [77] Hill, [78] Gibbs, [79] and Kogan and Van der Eyken. [80] Though connected with the educational field, the subject of the latter writings is outside the university framework and does not touch on the work of academic leaders. As such, they are of limited relevance to our study. So also are other published works such as McCorkle and Archibald's book on "Management and Leadership in Higher Education" [81] and Paul Jedamus' book on "Improving Academic Management". [82] The former book is addressed basically to administrators, although occasional references are made to faculty staff. The book addresses different organizational problems from the type being experienced in Nigeria, and the authors follow classical approaches, for example, in recommending role functions. The latter book is merely a compilation from 37 contributors on very diverse subject areas, none of which deals with the work activities of academic leaders. Apart from not being particularly focused, the approach of the latter book is also more philosophical than empirical.

3.7 Methods Used to Study Managerial Jobs

There are direct and indirect methods of studying what the manager does. Essentially, the indirect methods consist of asking the manager to estimate the duration, location, contacts, etc. of his or her activities. This is normally done through a survey or a questionnaire administration, which can then be followed up by an interview. Variations of this method include secondary sources useful for the study of the inaccessible manager, and critical incidence and sequence of episodes methods advantageous in probing deeply into important aspects of managerial work. [83]

The direct methods are of two main types. In one method, the diary, the manager keeps a record of the details of his or her activities over a period of time. Usually, such details are kept on pre-coded sheets designed by the researcher. The second major direct method of study is observational. In this method, the researcher observes the working manager and records the manager's activities himself. Again, variations of the direct methods include activity sampling while observation itself may be structured or unstructured.

The indirect method has some advantages over the direct methods. It is simpler, faster, and easier to get managers to cooperate. It can be used on a large sample of managers since it is relatively less time consuming and less expensive than the direct methods. In addition, the analyses of the resulting data are faster than those of the direct methods.

The problem with this method is that of reliability and validity. Managers' estimates may differ from the recorded facts, as managers may easily be biased or forgetful. This is more so since activities are varied, brief, fragmented, and primarily oral. McCall, Morrison, and Hannan have shown, for example, that many researches reveal that managers do not know how they spend their time. [84] Indeed, as Mintzberg suggests, this method may only show the perception of the manager and not the reality. [85] Self estimates also have the disadvantage that they cannot allow for variations in an individual's work characteristics.

When compared, the two direct methods have relative advantages and disadvantages. The advantages of the diary method over the observational method include the fact that it is not restricted in locality, and sample sizes can be larger. It also tends to be less expensive and it is recorded and classified by a person who knows what he or she is doing and why. All activities can usually be recorded unlike the researcher who may be barred from confidential meetings. One of the disadvantages of the diary is that there is a limit on the content and the scope of what can be studied. Only what will take minimum time from the manager and what can easily be pre-coded on the diary without ambiguity in meaning may usefully be investigated. Other disadvantages include the fact that the manager might either deliberately lie or simply forget to include some activities.

Conversely, the advantages of the observation over the diary include greater consistency in recording and an opportunity for greater details and more comprehensive recordings. [86] Furthermore, the record is likely to be more complete, as this is done by a full time researcher. [87] Unfortunately, only events capable of being observed can be handled by this method, which is incapable of assessing the non-observable activities such as planning and thinking. [88] Furthermore, as Hempill pointed out,

> We cannot understand a position simply by watching the man who holds it do things. The knowledge that he answered such and such a telephone call at 10:30, discussed such and such a project with Jones and Smith at 10:40, and so on through the day does not tell us nearly enough. There is more to a job than that. [89]

However, just as in the indirect methods, variations in the direct methods have their particular strengths and weaknesses.

3.7.1 Multiple Research Methodology

One general weakness with past studies is the reliance on one method of study to the exclusion of all others. And taken singly, each method tends to produce only a partial view of an essentially whole phenomenon. Another weakness is the excessively detailed concentration on a minute aspect of the manager's job as a way of obtaining a total picture. Some researchers have focused only on the manager's contacts, while others concentrate on executive roles, and so on. Like the blind men of Hindustan, each examines an aspect of the elephant and calls it the elephant. A full picture of the manager's job is a desideratum. For this purpose, almost all the writers have recommended the utilization of multiple research methods. McCall, Morrison, and Hannan stated that:

> The issue is how to conjoin purpose and activity so that they make sense together. Combined interview, diary and observational approaches seem to hold the most promise for accomplishing that goal. [90]

The authors argue that:

> The use of multiple methods should allow the researcher to capitalize on the combined strengths of a collectivity. If a description can be shown to agree with those provided by complementary methods, then it contains a degree of accuracy unattainable by a description that is consistent with only one method. [91]

3.8 Summary and Conclusions

We have, in this chapter, attempted a review of the literature on managerial jobs. The classical views, the work-activity studies, and other investigations were presented and discussed. Contributors as well as contributions were both highlighted. Finally, the research methods used to study managerial activities were described and evaluated. A conclusion arising from this is the desirability of multiple research designs in order to break with the "methodological parochialism" of the past and lead to more valid and reliable results.

In summary, it should be mentioned that studies by the diary and the observational methods are popular research types. However, one general weakness with them is their generally low sample sizes, often drawn from only a few organizations (see table 3-2, for example, where more than half of the studies reported were each conducted in only one organization). Generalizations have been made with samples of four, [92, 93] a sample of five, [94] and samples of less than ten are many [95, 96, 97, 98]. To be fair, access to data using these methods is very difficult. The observational method, in particular, could be very expensive and beyond the reach of otherwise qualified researchers. Despite these shortcomings, results from the diary and the observational studies are usually more accurate than with those whose methods are not based on direct methods of data collection, or those views that are not empirically based.

It was observed in this review that very little past studies had focused on the academic leaders and their jobs. This revelation of relative neglect is surprising in view of the fact that the managerial behaviour of other groups such as engineers, salesmen, and foremen have been studied, and well documented. Yet, in the majority of the cases, it is the academics themselves who conduct the investigations. Two reasons for the negligence can be proferred: the physician may not want to diagnose him- or herself for reasons of objectivity or self-sufficiency. Considering current societal views in Nigeria, for example, and the general comments by critics, a feeling by the universities that they are objective would be an illusion. [99] Similarly, reason of self-sufficiency would hardly stand any test of reality. The university is largely dependent on government funding and government directives. [100]

More plausible perhaps is the notion that researchers may not see "academic leaders" as managers. This, in our opinion, would be a mistaken view. A manager is "a person who controls". [101] The object of control could be a business, a farm, a university establishment, in fact, any organization. Stewart distinguishes between two common uses of the word manager. In the general sense of the word, a manager may be defined to relate to all persons who occupy positions above a certain level in an organizational hierarchy. In its restrictive sense, such people must also have subordinates whom they manage directly. [102] Even in the restrictive use of the word, academic leaders qualify as managers. To "manage" is to "take charge". The meaning and the use of the term cannot be restricted only to organizations that manufacture physical commodities. Mintzberg's view is explanatory and illuminating: managers are those people formally in charge of organizations or their subunits[. . .]. This includes people with titles such as president, prime minister, foreman, dean, department head and bishop. [103]

Even if academic managers are seen as "less practical" than their industrial counterparts, the former nonetheless are organizational managers wielding enormous influence. In the Nigerian example, they also face problems and challenges that are very practical indeed. [104] The actions or inactions of academic leaders the world over have profound effects on society's progress or lack of it. Therefore, it is felt that a study of this group is not only justified, but long overdue. The present study is an attempt to initiate researches into what academic leaders actually do.

It is felt that such information could have important implications for the future selection, training, and development of academic leaders, issues which are particularly relevant at a time when many academic leaders are facing new and increasingly severe problems due to the decrease in financial support for the universities.

3.9 Notes and References

[1] Fayol, H., *General and Industrial Management*, trans. Constance Storrs, London: Pitman, 1949. First Published in French in 1916. (Administration industrielle et generale, Paris).

[2] Koontz, H.J., The Management Theory Jungle, *Journal of the Academy of Management*, Vol. 4, No. 3, Decemeber, 1961, pp. 174–188.

[3] The Principle of the Universality of Managerial Functions states that: "Managers perform the same functions regardless of their place in the organization structure or the type of enterprise in which they are engaged. Acting in their managerial capacity, presidents, department heads, foremen, supervisors, college deans, bishops, and heads of government agencies all do the same thing[. . .]. It means that anything significant that is said about the functions of one manager applies to all managers." in: H. Koontz and C. O'Donnel, *Principles of Management: An Analysis of Managerial Functions*, McGraw-Hill, New York, 5th ed., 1972, p. 53.

[4] Wren, D.A., *The Evolution of Management Thought*, 2nd ed., Wiley, New York, 1979, pp. 538–548. In fact, the Fayolian view continues to be embraced until the present day. Wren is only an example of a recent writer, himself suggesting the inclusion of "leadership" and "control" into the Fayolian list of managerial functions.

[5] Mintzberg, H., *The Nature of Managerial Work*, Harper and Row Publishers, New York, 1973, p. 10.

[6] Carlson, S., *Executive Behaviour: A Study of the Work Load and the Working Methods of Managing Directors*, Strombergs, Stockholm, 1951, p. 24.

[7] Gulick, L.H., Notes on the Theory of Organization, in: Gulick, L.H. and Urwick, L.F. (eds.), *Papers on the Science of Administration*, Columbia University Press, New York, 1937, p. 13.
[8] Newman, W.H., *Administrative Action: The Technique of Organization and Management*, Prentice-Hall, Englewood Cliffs, N.J., 1951, p. 28.
[9] Terry, G.R., *Principles of Management*, Irwin, Homewood Ill., 1953, p. 9.
[10] Richman, B.M. and Farmer, R.N., *Leadership, Goals, And Power In Higher Education*, Jossey-Bass Publishers, San Francisco, 1974, p. 19.
[11] Mintzberg, H., op. cit., pp. 8–9.
[12] Stewart, R., *Contrasts in Management: A Study of Different Types of Managers' Jobs, Their Demand and Choices*, McGraw-Hill, London, 1976, p. 121.
[13] Carlson, S., op. cit., p. 24.
[14] Mintzberg, H., op. cit., p. 7.
[15] Koontz, H.J., op. cit., p. 174; The practitioners mentioned are Fayol, Mooney, Alvin Brown, Sheldon, Barnard, and Urwick.
[16] Mintzberg, H., op, cit., p. 21.
[17] Gibbs, S., The Role of the Manager, M.B.A. Dissertation, University of Bradford, 1982, p. 4.
[18] Taylor, F.W., *Scientific Management*, Harper and Row, New York, 1947, pp. 117–118. First Published in 1911.
[19] Mintzberg, H., op. cit., pp. 133–134.
[20] Gibbs, S., op. cit., pp. 4–5
[21] Carlson, S., op. cit., p. 55.
[22] Stewart, R., *Managers and their Jobs: A Study of the Similarities and Differences in the Ways Managers Spend their Time*, Macmillan, London, 1967, p. 24.
[23] Mintzberg, H., op. cit., p. 230.
[24] Gibbs, S., op. cit., p. 5.
[25] Carlson, S., op. cit., p. 10. The aim of the investigation was, according to the author, "neither to develop any normative rules as to how executives should behave, nor to describe their 'typical' or average behaviour".
[26] McCall, M.W., Morrison, M.A., Hannan, R.L., Studies of Managerial Work: Results and Methods, *Centre for Creative Leadership*, Technical Report No. 9, North Carolina, 27402, May 1978, p. 2.
[27] Burns, T., The Directions of Activity and Communication in a Departmental Executive Group, *Human Relations*, Vol. 7, 1954, pp. 73–97.
[28] Burns, T., Management in Action, *Operational Research Quarterly*, Vol. 8, 1957, pp. 45–60.
[29] Copeman, G., How British Executives Spend Their Day, in: Copeman, Luijk, and Hanika, *How The Executive Spends His Time*, Business Publications Limited, London, 1963, pp. 3–16.
[30] Dublin, R. and Spray, S.L., Executive Behavior and Interaction, *Industrial Relations*, Vol. 3, 1964, pp. 99–108.
[31] Horne, J.H. and Lupton, T., The work activities of 'middle' managers: An exploratory study, *The Journal of Management Studies*, Vol. 2(1), 1965, pp. 14–33.
[32] Thomason, G.F., Managerial Work Roles and Relationships (part I). *The Journal of Management Studies*, Vol. 3, 1966, pp. 270–284.
[33] Thomason, G.F., Managerial Work Roles and Relationships (part II), *The Journal of Management Studies*, Vol. 4, 1967, pp. 17–30.
[34] Marples, D.L., Roles in a Manufacturing Organization, *The Journal of Management Studies*, Vol. II, 1968, pp. 183–204.

[35] Brewer, E. and Tomlinson, J.W.C., The Manager's Working Day, *The Journal of Industrial Economics*, Vol. 12, 1964, pp. 191–197.
[36] Lawler, E.E., Porter, L.W., and Tennenbaum, A., Manager's attitudes toward interaction episodes, *Journal of Applied Psychology*,Vol. 52, 1968, pp. 432–439.
[37] Hinrichs, J.R., Communications Activity of Industrial Research Personnel, *Personnel Psychology*, Vol. 17, 1964, pp. 193–204.
[38] Hinrichs, J.R., Where has all the time gone? *Personnel*, Vol. 54(4), 1976, pp. 44–49.
[39] Brewer and Tomlinson, op. cit., p. 191.
[40] Stewart, R., (1967), op. cit.
[41] Blau, P.M., Patterns of interaction among a group of officials in a government agency, *Human Relations*, Vol. 7, 1954, pp. 337–338.
[42] Guest, R.H., Of Time and the Foreman, *Personnel*, Vol. 32, 1956, pp. 478–486.
[43] Jasinki, F.J., Foreman relationships outside the work group, *Personnel*, Vol. 33, 1956, p. 131.
[44] Ibid., pp. 134–135.
[45] Ponder, Q.D., The Effective Manufacturing Foreman, in: E. Young (ed.), *Industrial Relations Research Association Proceedings of the Tenth Annual Meeting*, Madison, Wisconsin, 1957, pp. 41–54.
[46] Dale, E. and Urwick, L.F., *Staff in Organization*, McGraw-Hill, New York, 1960.
[47] Landsberger, H.A., The horizontal dimension in bureaucracy, *Administration Science Quarterly*, Vol. 6, 1961, pp. 299–332.
[48] Luijk, H., How Dutch Executives Spend Their Day, in: Copeman, Luijk, and Hanika, *How The Executive Spends His Time*, op. cit., pp. 17–82.
[49] Kelly, J., The study of executive behaviour by activity sampling, *Human Relations*, Vol. 17, 1964, pp. 277–287.
[50] Kelly, J., *Organizational Behaviour*, Irwin-Dorsey, Homewood Ill., 1969.
[51] Ibid., p. 355.
[52] Mintzberg, H., op. cit.
[53] Mintzberg, H., The Manager's Job: Folklore and Fact, *Harvard Business Review*, July–August, 1975, pp. 49–61.
[54] Kurke, L.B. and Aldrich, H.E., Mintzberg was right! A replication and extension of the nature of managerial work, *Management Science*, Vol. 29, No. 8, August, 1983 pp. 975–984.
[55] McCall, M.W. and Lombardo, M.M., Looking Glass, Inc.: The First Three Years, *Centre for Creative Leadership, Technical Report No. 13, North Carolina*, 27402, 1979.
[56] Taylor, F.W., op. cit., pp. 117–118.
[57] Sayles, L., *Managerial Behaviour*, McGraw-Hill, New York, 1964.
[58] The publications from these researches are vast. They include those of Stogdill, Shartle, and Associates (1956), Mahoney, Jerdee, and Carroll (1965), Prince (1970), and Hemphill (1959).
[59] Shartle, C.L., Leadership and executive performance, *Personnel*, Vol. 25, 1949, p. 370.
[60] Fleischman, E.A., The Description of Supervisory Behaviour, *Journal of Applied Psychology*, Vol. 37, 1953, pp. 1–6.
[61] Ibid., p. 2.
[62] Hemphill, J.K., Job description for executives, *Harvard Business Review*, Vol. 37(5), 1959, pp. 55–67. See also, Hemphill, J.K., *Dimensions of Execu-*

tive Positions, Ohio Studies in Personnel, Research Monograph No. 98, Bureau of Business Research, Ohio State University, 1967.

[63] Ibid.

[64] Neustadt, R.E., *Presidential Power: The Politics of Leadership*, Wiley, New York, 1960.

[65] Homans, G.C., *The Human Group*, Harcourt Brace Jovanovich, New York, 1950.

[66] Stieglitz, H., The Chief Executive—And His Job, *National Industrial Conference Board*, Personnel Policy Study, No. 214, New York, 1969.

[67] Wikstrom, W.S., Managing at the Foreman's Level, *National Industrial Conference Board*, Personnel Policy Study, No. 205, New York, 1967.

[68] Walker, C.R., Guest R.H., and Turner, A.N., *The Foreman on the Assembly Line*, Harvard University Press, Cambridge, Mass., 1956.

[69] McCall, Morrison, and Hannan, op. cit., pp. 6–18.

[70] Ibid., pp. 19–25.

[71] Ibid., p. 6.

[72] Ibid.

[73] Cohen, M.D. and March, J.G., *Leadership and Ambiguity: The American College President*, McGraw-Hill, New York, 1974, pp. 253–261.

[74] Ibid.

[75] Dahl, T. and Lewis, D.R., Random Sampling Device Used in Time Management Study, *Evaluation*, Vol. 2(2), 1975, pp. 20–22.

[76] Lupton, T., *Management and the Social Sciences*, Penguin Education, Harmondsworth, Middlesex, 1983, p. 19.

[77] Birley, D., *The Educational Officer and His World*, Routledge and Kegan Paul, London, 1970.

[78] Hill, L., *The Local Government Officer*, George Allen and Unwin, London, 1983.

[79] Gibbs, S., The Role of the Manager, M.B.A. Dissertation, University of Bradford, 1982.

[80] Kogan, M. and Van der Eyken, W., *County Hall: The Role of the Chief Education Officer*, Penguin, Harmondsworth, Middlesex, 1973.

[81] McCorkle, C.O. and Archibald, S.O., *Management and Leadership in Higher Education*, Jossey-Bass Publishers, San Francisco, 1982.

[82] Jedamus, P., Peterson, M.W., and Associates, *Improving Academic Management: A Handbook of Planning and Institutional Research*, Jossey-Bass Publishers, San Francisco, 1980.

[83] Mintzberg, H., op. cit., pp. 221–229.

[84] McCall, Morrison, and Hannan, op. cit., p. 17.

[85] Mintzberg, H., op. cit., pp. 221–223.

[86] Stewart, R., (1967), op. cit., p. 11.

[87] Ibid.

[88] McCall, Morrison, and Hannan, op. cit., p. 28.

[89] Hemphill, J.K., op. cit., p. 56.

[90] McCall, Morrison, and Hannan, op. cit., p. 28.

[91] Ibid., p. 33.

[92] Burns, T., (1954), op. cit.; he studied 4 middle managers.

[93] Kelly, J., (1964), op. cit.; he studied 4 foremen.

[94] Mintzberg, H., (1973), op. cit.; he studied 5 chief executives.

[95] Dublin, R. and Spray, S.L., op. cit.; they studied 8 senior and middle managers.

[96] Brewer, E. and Tomlinson, J.W.C., The Manager's Working Day, *The Jour-*

nal of Industrial Economics, Vol. 12, 1964, pp. 191–197; They studied 6 senior managers.
[97] Marples, D.L., Studies of Managers—A Fresh Start?, *The Journal of Management Studies*, Vol. 4, 1967, pp. 282–299. He studied 8 low to middle-level managers.
[98] Landsberger, H.A., op. cit., He studied 3 middle managers.
[99] Ike, M.C., Manpower or Manhood?, *Management in Nigeria*, Jan., 1977, pp. 6–17.
[100] Fafunwa, B., Nigerian Varsities: Problems and Challenges, *National Concord*, 12, Jan., 1983. See also, Salami, A., Universities: Alternative Sources of Finance to Government Funding, *Sunday Standard*, October, 31, 1982.
[101] Hornby, A.S., *Oxford Advanced Learner's Dictionary of Current English*, London: Oxford University Press, 1982.
[102] Stewart, R., (1967), op. cit., p. 1.
[103] Mintzberg, H., op. cit., p. 3.
[104] Fafunwa, B., op. cit., p. 12.

Chapter 4
Research Design and Methodology

4.1 Introduction

This chapter presents a summary of the design and the methodology adopted in this study. The research questions towards which the design was directed concern the academic leader's work activities and characteristics and their opinions and perceptions about the same. Specifically, we are interested in how academic leaders spend their time and in the amount of time academic leaders spend on the various aspects of their jobs. We are also interested in the opinions, attitudes, and perceptions of academic leaders and the implications of all these for effective academic management.

The setting of this research, as the background material in Chapter One will suggest, and the overview of the Universities in Chapter Two will confirm, is on the Nigerian and the British academic scene. Therefore, all along, data from the British sample is used to compare and to contrast our findings in the Nigerian sample in an attempt to ascertain and to identify possible cultural variations. This approach is particularly useful because, as the literature review in Chapter Three shows, the vast majority of the researches and the publications of the work characteristics of industrial managers have been carried out in Western Europe and America, and not in developing countries such as Nigeria.

First, we define formally the "academic leader". Next, the processes undertaken in designing the research instruments are explained. This includes the pilot studies. Thereafter, the sampling procedure comprising of both the selection, distribution, and the administration of the research instruments is briefly discussed. Sampling responses are also stated. Finally, the data analyses methodology is presented as well as the steps taken to ensure the reliability and the validity of our findings.

4.2 Definition of the Academic Leader

In this study, "academic leaders" are defined as the academics occupying administrative positions such as heads of departments, deans, directors, and vice-chancellors. Important to our definition is the requirement that the academic leader must occupy a formal administrative position within the university organizational complex. He or she must also be directly in charge of some subordinates who are invariably both academic and administrative staff.

Therefore, in our definition, a pioneer researcher, a professor or a front line academic with some "followers" does not become an academic leader per se. Also, academic leadership, in our use of the term, has nothing to do with seniority or proficiency in research skills or breath and depth of knowledge in itself. If a senior lecturer is the head of an academic unit (say a department) and there are professors in that unit, the senior lecturer is the academic leader by our definition and the professors are not. The professors are still subordinate to the head of department insofar as leave and course arrangements, meetings, and other departmental activities and policies are concerned. This situation occurs in the Nigerian example where especially (but not exclusively) foreign professors may not want or would not be given administrative roles.

4.3 Designing the Research Instruments

Studying managerial jobs and behaviour is an important activity now blessed "with a rich methodological heritage". [1] The basic perspectives in the study of managerial work was presented in Chapter Three with a discussion of the merits and demerits of each method. However, variants of the basic research methods continue to be invented and used. For example, Shapira and Dunbar used an in-basket technique to study Mintzberg's proposed managerial roles, [2] while McCall and Lombardo did a simulation study of a glass company to show how environmental uncertainty affects managerial behaviour and effectivenesss [3]. McCall and Segrist also used Mintzberg's proposed roles to develop and refine an instrument to explore how managerial roles vary by level and function [4]. Nonetheless, the examples cited above are mere variants of the basic methodological options discussed in Chapter Three.

An earlier review of the methodologies and the literature on the study of managers' jobs show the desirability of using multiple research designs for more reliable results [5]. In this investigation, therefore, the diary and the questionnaire methods are jointly employed. It is hoped that this combination of a direct and an indirect method will lead to more reliable results, especially where the findings from the two methods are supportive.

In this research, we use the diary as the principal research method especially in obtaining data on the academic leader's work characteristics. The questionnaire method enables us to have a larger sample of respondents to give a picture of the academic leader's perception of their jobs and roles. The latter instrument has also been used to obtain data on such items as the university goals, and the academic leader's attitudes and opinions on a number of issues. In this study, therefore, the questionnaire is used not only to complement but also to supplement the diary in the hope that the whole shall be greater than the sum of its parts.

The research instruments (the diary and the questionnaire) for this study were initially designed and based on the author's experiences, from the literature on organizational behaviour, from the previous diaries and classifications of Carlson [6], Burns [7], and Stewart [8], and from the managerial work roles as defined by Mintzberg [9], and as used by Morse and Wagner [10]. This was modified and refined based on comments from some volunteer academic leaders in Nigeria and Britain.

A pilot study was conducted based on the refined research instruments. Data was collected and analysed with the aid of the computer, and a seminar was presented based on the written report. A number of academics in Britain attended the seminar. The seminar report was critically though warmly received, especially by the members of the Human Resources Research Group at the University of Bradford Management Centre. The report of this seminar was subsequently published in the Management Research News [11].

The comments and suggestions from the seminar participants provided fresh inputs which were used to further modify the research instruments. The diary was again piloted (on a smaller scale) two additional times before the final format, a copy of which is provided

Academic Leaders' Study (Diary Method)

Date (if on a new day): ____, ____, 1984.
Time at the beginning of the activity: ________

Activity?		Subject Matter?		Where?		With Whom?	
Deskwork	☐	Teaching	☐	Own Office	☐	Students	☐
Scheduled meetings	☐	Research	☐	Other Units	☐	Colleagues	☐
Unscheduled meetings	☐	Consulting	☐	Other Campuses	☐	Admin. Staff	☐
Telephoning in out	☐	Admin. and Mgt.	☐	Home	☐	External	☐
Travelling	☐	Personal	☐	Other Organizations	☐	Alone	☐
Computing	☐						
Practicals	☐						
Coffee/Tea break	☐						
Lunch	☐						
Miscellaneous	☐						

Approx. duration (minutes) 5 10 20 30 40 50 60 Otherwise, specify time:

Activity performed with: (No of people) 0(alone) 1 2–5 6–20 21–50 51+

Fleeting Contacts and Interruptions

	Personal	Telephone
Students		
Colleagues		
Administrative staff		
External person		
Self		

Figure 4-1: A Copy of the Diary Used in this Study

in Figure 4-1 and also in Appendix A, where the accompanying explanatory notes and illustrations of how to fill the diary are provided. A copy of the final version of the questionnaire is provided in Appendix B. It is the information obtained from the diary that is discussed in Chapters Five, Six, and Seven of this book.

The diary was designed to record the activities of the academic leader, the subject matter of these activities, where the academic leader was, with whom, the activity duration, and the number of people who was with the academic leader at any point in time. The diary was also designed to record the extent to which the academic leader's day was fragmented, hence the section on fleeting contacts and interruptions at the bottom of each page of the diary. The frequency, and not the time, of interruptions and contacts of less than 5-minutes' duration were to be recorded under this section. This design was also partly to make the recording job of the academic leader easier, as every single event would not necessarily constitute an "activity" to be separately recorded on another page. This provision, we observed, halves the number of "activities" as are obtained during the pilot work and the main study.

For most of the analyses in this study, however, it is the time that the managers spend on their activities rather than the frequency of those activities, that is used as a measure to describe the academic leaders' activities. [12] Time is also the main measure used by previous researchers and as Stewart explains, it seems more of a comprehensive measure than does the frequency [13] although as she admits, for some purposes, frequency may be the better measure [14]. In our analyses of individual diaries and the communication to individual academic leaders about the average figures of their activities, both frequency and time analyses were used (see Appendix C).

4.4 Sample Selection, Distribution and Responses

The 1982 Commonwealth Universities Yearbook was used to select our sample of academic leaders. [15] From this source, the number of estimated Nigerian academic leaders in all the 18 universities listed in the book was less than 600. This total targeted population was stratified into four: vice-chancellors, directors, deans, and head of departments or incumbents of equivalent positions. A total of 140 questionnaires was sent to a random sample of the potential respondents. The British sample comprised of 60 academic leaders who were similarly selected on a random basis from the 47 listed U.K. Universities. [16]

In the selection of the sample for the diary, academic leaders who were already sent questionnaires were excluded. This was to reduce bias and to enhance greater cooperation. Eighty-five diaries were printed in all. Out of these, 50 were despatched to Nigeria, and the remaining 35 distributed in the United Kingdom. Most of the Nigerian diaries were sent to individual academic colleagues in different Nigerian Universities. These people assisted in the administration of the diaries to willing academic leaders. However, a number of diaries were also sent direct to some randomly selected Nigerian academic leaders, especially in universities where the researcher does not have any acquaintances, and where responses were nonetheless desired. In the British sample, academic leaders were randomly selected, and diaries were sent to them by post.

The responses to the questionnaires as well as to the diaries are tabulated in tables 4-1 and 4-2.

Table 4-1: Sample Responses to the Questionnaire

	Nigeria	Britain	Total
Number despatched	140	60	200
Usable number returned	75	34	109
Percentage response rate	54	57	55

Table 4-2: Sample Responses to the Diary

	Nigeria	Britain	Total
Number despatched	50	35	85
Usable number returned	26	12	38
Percentage response rate	52	34	43
No. of participating university	08	09	17

The response rates were adjudged to be quite satisfactory. [17] This is especially so in the case of the diary where cooperation for filling-in such bulky papers over a duration of one week (seven days) is not easy to obtain. In fact, because of the difficulty of getting cooperation, Stewart suggested that only willing managers may participate in the diary methodology, leaving little room for the random selection of managers [18] which we adopted in the main. A detailed classification of the responses from the diary and the questionnaire on the basis of the position of the academic leaders is provided in Appendix E.

4.5 Data Analyses Methodology

The questions of reliability and validity are important points to consider in designing researches, and in their analyses. [19] As such, before the data from this study were obtained, a number of precautions were taken to reduce the possible sources of errors that would in turn have limited their reliability. Some of these precautions were incorporated into the design of the final instruments. When the completed research instruments were received, they were edited to ensure that they were properly filled in. Every page of the diary, for instance, was checked to ensure that it was correctly recorded and that all the manager's time was accounted for.

Some analyses were carried out on the basis of each day for which the diary was filled in. This was before the data was coded and input into the computer for analyses. The results of the computer analyses were later checked to ensure that they were consistent with the basic statistics earlier computed with the aid of the electronic calculator. Data emanating from this study were therefore analysed in stages, and with the aid of the computer. As evident from the discussion of the research findings, the Nigerian and the British data were separately analyzed. A classification and a description of the groupings of academic leaders on the basis of how they spend their time is given in Chapter Seven.

Academic leaders were given the opportunity to know the relative frequency of their activities and how they spent their time in comparison to our pilot results. Various measures were, as can be seen, taken to limit deliberate bias in recording or in computational errors. Therefore, while one cannot, perhaps, be absolutely certain that all the recordings were conscientiously made without biases, the incidence of deliberate falsification, if available, must be minimal. To enhance greater reliability of our results, recordings were made in as many universities as are possible. See table 4-2 for details. These were made during a continuous period of seven days during in-term months of March, April, May, June, and July, 1984.

Where there are comparable data, the analysis of the questionnaire was carried out to support that of the diary. In cases of differences, the results from the diary were considered superior as they are empirical and less amenable to biases and other errors. As Payne argues with respect to questionnaire responses, ". . . recall may differ from fact, and therefore should not be taken as fact". [20] Berdie and Anderson, writing on the same issue concur: subjects should not be given too much credit for good memory. [21] Furthermore, Hodgkinson and Edelstein suggest that even when numerical data are requested, the responses from study participants are often incorrect. [22] Therefore, the results from the diary are used basically for

Chapters Five, Six, and Seven while Chapter Eight discusses the differences between comparable data from the diary and the questionnaire.

4.6 Notes and References

[1] Kurke, L.B. and Aldrich, H.E., Mintzberg was right! A replication and extension of the nature of managerial work, *The Journal of Management Science*, Vol. 29, No. 8, August 1983, p. 975.

[2] Shapira, Z. and Dunbar, R.L.M., Testing Mintzberg's Managerial Roles: Classification Using an In-Basket Simulation, *Journal of Applied Psychology*, Vol. 65, 1980, pp. 87–95.

[3] McCall, M.W. and Lombardo, M.M., Looking Glass Inc.: The First Three Years, *Centre for Creative Leadership*, Technical Report No. 13, North Carolina, 27402, 1979.

[4] McCall, M.W. and Segrist, C.A., In Pursuit of the Manager's Job: Building on Mintzberg, *Centre for Creative Leadership*, Technical Report No. 14, North Carolina, 27402, 1980.

[5] McCall, M.W., Morrison, M.A., and Hannan, R.L., Studies of Managerial Work: Results and Methods, *Centre for Creative Leadership*, Technical Report No. 9, North Carolina, 27402, May 1978, pp. 28, 33. See also, Torrington, D. and Weightman, J., *The Business of Management*, Prentice-Hall International, Englewood Cliff, N.J., pp. 64–65, 1985.

[6] Carlson, S., *Executive Behaviour: A Study of the Work Load and the Working Methods of Managing Directors*, Strombergs, Stockholm, 1951, p. 46.

[7] Burns, T., The Directions of Activity and Communication in a Departmental Executive Group, *Human Relations*, Vol. 7, 1954, pp. 73–97.

[8] Stewart, R., *Managers and their jobs: a study of the similarities and differences in the ways managers spend their time*, Macmillan, London, 1967, pp. 162–163.

[9] Mintzberg, H., *The Nature of Managerial Work*, Harper and Row Publishers, New York, 1973.

[10] Morse, J.J. and Wagner, F.R., Measuring the Process of Managerial Effectiveness, *Academy of Management Journal*, Vol. 21, No. 1, 1978, pp. 23–35.

[11] Oshagbemi, T.A., The Job Characteristics of Academic Leaders: A Pilot Study, *Management Research News*, Vol. 7, No. 2, 1984, pp. 20–23.

[12] Time is one of the manager's most flexible resources which the manager spends as he or she wishes. Time is also used to activate other resources, and the time spent on activities are often indicative of the importance attached to those activities. An important organizational resource as the manager's time has not only cultural relevance, but also technological dimensions. See Oshagbemi, T.A., The Cultural Factor in Nigeria's Development Equation, *Journal of Social and Economic Studies*, Vol. X, Part 1 and 2, 1982, pp. 243–257. See also, Robert, D., Culture and the Management of Time: A Comparison of Japanese and American Top Management Practice, *Asia Pacific Journal of Management*, Vol. I, No. 1., Sept. 1983, pp. 65–71. Drucker discusses the uniqueness and the importance of time as a resource in: Drucker, P.F., *The Effective Executive*, Heinemann, London, 1967, pp. 21–43.

[13] Stewart, R., op. cit., p. 4.
[14] Ibid.
[15] The Association of C.U., *The Commonwealth Universities Yearbook*, 1982, Vol. III, pp. 2021–2111.
[16] Ibid., Vol. I., pp. 206–833. The 47 listed U.K. Universities include the Open University.
[17] Various measures were designed to increase the response rates. These include the following: (a) The diary was printed with a professional touch from the computer output which was used to design the format. (b) There was a colour appeal. The first 4 pages (the explanatory notes and the 3 sample illustrations of how to fill-in the diary) were of different colours from the rest of the 80-page diary which was white. The print in the illustration were also of smaller characters as they were photo-reduced to the same size as the diaries, a design appeal. See Appendix A. (c) The study group was identified and respondents were offered the opportunity to know more about the project (see the covering letter to Appendix A) in addition to being supplied with the comparative details of their work characteristics. See Appendix D. (d) Reminder letters were sent to non-respondents after about a month appealing for their cooperation and ensuring confidentiality. See Appendix D. (e) Finally, a stamped and addressed envelope was provided for the respondent's conveniences. See the covering letter to Appendix A.
[18] Stewart, R., The use of diaries to study manager's jobs, *The Journal of Management studies*, Vol. 2, 1965, p. 235.
[19] Goode, W. and Hatt, P., *Methods in Social Research*, McGraw-Hill, New York, 1962.
[20] Payne, S.L., *The Art of Asking Questions*, Princeton University Press, Princeton, N.J., 1951, p. 29.
[21] Berdie, D.R. and Anderson, J.F., *Questionnaires: Design and Use*, The Scarecrow Press, Inc., Metuchen, N.J., 1974, p. 12.
[22] Hodgkinson, H.L. and Edelstein, S., Questionnaires: In fact, there is error, *Educational Researchers*, Vol. 1(8), August 1972, pp. 9–10.

Chapter 5
The Nature of the Academic Leaders' Jobs I

5.1 Introduction

This chapter begins a discussion of the results of the research. First, it considers how long academic leaders work. Then, their activities—what they do—are examined as well as the subject matter of these activities. Later, it looks at where academic leaders perform their jobs and how long these activities take. All discussions are made from the point of view of how, where, with whom, etc. academic leaders spend their time.

5.2 How Long Academic Leaders Work

The average total hours worked by the 26 Nigerian academic leaders was 41. [1] This is the net sum of all the time and episodes recorded from Monday to Friday. This number of total working hours is slightly less than the corresponding figure for the 12 British academic leaders who recorded 43. These total working hours included the time spent in all social but official functions, such as entertaining an external examiner. It also included, of course, the time spent working at home and in other organizations. However, the hours excluded the time taken off for non-working lunches and for all the non-accounted for time spent between activities. If the lunch hours were included, the aggregate total hours spent by the Nigerian academic leaders will rise to 44 and that of the British academic leaders to 47.

Compared with previous studies, our results are within range. They suggest that, on the average, academic leaders work for at least as long as industrial managers. Stewart studied the total time spent by a sample of 160 senior and middle-level British managers and found out that they worked on the average for a net of 42 hours a week. [2]

A similar study by Copeman showed that British chief executives worked a net of 44 hours per week while their departmental managers averaged only 37 hours per week. [3] Another study carried out in Britain by Burns reported an average of 41.5 hours a week for the 76 senior managers sampled. [4] This study compares with Horne and Lupton's where an average of 44 hours was recorded during the one week that the 66 middle managers kept the diaries. [5] The figures quoted above show that the total hours spent by our samples of the Nigerian and the British academic leaders were reasonably in line with similar averages from studies of British industrial managers.

A study carried out in America by Mintzberg (1973) using the observational method gave a working average of 40 hours a week in respect of the five managing directors studied. [6] In a replication study of Mintzberg's work by Kurke and Aldrich, a total of 44 hours was recorded during the one week when the 4 top executives were observed. [7]

An earlier study (1956) of American managers showed the much longer time of about 60 average working hours a week. [8] However, the latter study was based on interviews and questionnaires, and the hours included short lunch periods. The explanation for these significantly higher average total working hours is probably the research methodology employed. Results from questionnaires tend to be biased in this type of studies. [9] However, we observe that the 9 Swedish managing directors studied by Carlson worked for very long hours, an average of 10 hours, with daily variations of between 8.5 to 11.5 hours. [10] Similarly, the 25 Dutch directors studied by Luijk worked very long hours, 60 or more hours a week. [11]

Average total working hours, even when defined rigorously, should be interpreted carefully as this may conceal a wide range of hours. Table 5-1 shows the variation in the total working hours of our sampled Nigerian and British academic leaders. The table shows that the average hours worked by the 26 Nigerian academic leaders varied between less than 30 to over 55, while that of the 12 British academic leaders ranged from less than 35 to over 55 hours a week. A wide range of total working hours from less than 35 to over 60 hours a week was recorded by Stewart. [12] Mintzberg's study showed a range from 53 by the manager who worked the longest to 28 by the manager who worked the shortest hours. [13]

Variations in total working hours are obviously due to several factors. Some studies, such as those of Copeman, Luijk, Burns, Horne

Table 5-1: The Distribution of the Total Hours Worked by the Academic Leaders

Hours per week	British	Nigerian
26–30	–	2
31–35	1	5
36–40	5	4
41–45	2	8
46–50	1	3
51–55	2	3
56–60	1	1
N*	12	26
Mean	43.17	41.35
C.V. %*	17.93	18.89

*N is used here, and will subsequently be used to refer to the sample size. Similarly, C.V. denotes the co-efficient of variation, and it is expressed in percentages. The coefficient of variation of a distribution is the standard deviation divided by the mean.

and Lupton, suggest that higher-level managers tend to work longer than lower-level ones. For example, Burns found that heads of units or their immediate subordinates worked significantly longer hours than the other managers. Copeman discovered that the chief executives in his sample averaged a gross of 53 and a net of 44 hours per week, while the departmental heads averaged only a gross 43 and a net of 37 hours a week. [14] Similarly, Horne and Lupton found that the nearer a manager is to the chief executive, the longer he tends to work.

Reliable comparisons cannot be made in our study, as the sample sizes of academic leaders on each level was small. Larger samples of academic leaders at each level in the same university would be necessary for vaild comparisons. That comment notwithstanding, tables 5-2 and 5-3 (but especially the former) seem to positively support the suggestion that higher-level managers tend to work longer than lower level ones. The conclusion from the tables is that differences in the levels of managers may be important in explaining variations in managers' working hours.

However, a cause of variations in working hours has been attributed to differences in organizations. In their study, Horne and Lupton found that the range of average hours worked varied between

Table 5-2: The Position of the British Academic Leaders and the Total Number of Hours Worked per Week

Position	Vice-chancellor	Director	Dean	Head of dept.
Hours worked	54	44	37	38
	–	33	44	52
	–	57	46	39
	–	–	–	38
	–	–	–	36
Average	54	44.7	42.3	40.6

companies of 39 to 54 hours per week. Burns also found similar range of differences in companies, from 37 hours per week in one company to 47 in another. It would have been useful, however, if these studies gave the differences in working hours, if any, within companies. This is because, as Stewart commented, even within some sample companies, variations in working hours between two managers could

Table 5-3: The Position of the Nigerian Academic Leaders and the Total Number of Hours Worked per Week

Position	Vice-chancellor	Director	Dean	Head of dept.
Hours worked	–	41	56	49
	–	49	30	44
	–	42	40	37
	–	31	34	43
	–	51	53	26
	–	43	–	37
	–	–	–	34
	–	–	–	31
	–	–	–	46
	–	–	–	34
	–	–	–	52
	–	–	–	43
	–	–	–	45
	–	–	–	40
	–	–	–	45
Average	–	42.8	42.6	40.4

often be substantial. Since our sample in each university is very small, generalizations between universities would not be reliable.

Stewart suggested that a further cause of variation in working hours is related to differences in the type of job. In her opinion, differences in the type of job is more important than differences between companies in explaining variations in working hours. She discovered that the sales managers on her sample, for example, worked longer than the other types of managers. Stewart's findings support the view that managers with fairly well-defined functions such as accountants tend to work the shortest hours, while those who travelled a lot worked the longest. Although our respondents are widely varied in their subject areas, demarcation in university disciplines is fluid and differences in functional specialization are not meaningfully related to variations in working hours. However, three of the academic leaders who were involved in on site experiments recorded an above average working hours of almost 50 hours a week. One of these was a director of an animal centre. The other two were heads of agricultural units who were involved in lots of experimentation. It was further observed that academic leaders work longer when they travel on conferences than when they are at their base universities.

Another possible cause of variations in working hours may be due to individual manager's work motivation. This may be especially true in academic organizations where lecturers see themselves more as colleagues and less in terms of subordinate-superior relationships. Beyond a minimum control, academic leaders determine their own jobs and their own working hours. This practice is unlike that in industry.

In summary, some factors seem important in explaining the range of differences in the hours worked by managers: (1) Individual manager's level of motivation and work habits in relation to the volume of work at hand. Some managers may be highly motivated and some delegate more, while others are more effective in the management of their time; (2) Differences between types of functions between say a works manager and a sales manager. Managers who travel a lot and those who spend time in practical jobs outside their offices tend to spend a higher total working hours than those who do not; (3) Differences between organizational levels as, for example, between a vice-chancellor and a head of department, or as between a senior and a junior manager. The senior managers tend to be more involved in meetings—committees, interviews, etc.; (4) Differences in the size of an organization, as a large organization necessitates more time in formal communications like scheduled periodic meetings and in more external contacts than a smaller organization. Larger universities, for example, tend to have more committees etc. than the smaller ones. These committees—whether established or ad hoc—often require members to work extra hours.

It is important to observe the fact that many academic leaders work on Saturdays and Sundays. In our Nigerian sample, the 14 academic leaders who recorded work during the weekend averaged a total of about 5.5 hours, while their 5 British counterparts who made similar entries in their diaries averaged 4.5 hours a week. It was not clear whether those who did not make entries did not work or they just refused to fill in more diaries. If the hours recorded during the weekend are added to their respective totals, the Nigerian academic leaders would have about 47 and the British about 48 total working hours a week. Studies of the hours of work by managers in industry (apart from that of Carlson) did not report additional hours by the managers during the weekends. In view of the fact that industrial managers work very little at home, [15] perhaps it will be true to guess that they do not generally work at weekends.

An average of about a 50-hour work week, which our samples seem to support, is a busy one. Academic leaders are working hard, and their work is demanding in time and energy. Undoubtedly, some of them are overworked. Using Perkin et al.'s figures, the College Presidents in New York work, on the average, for more than 60 hours a week, a figure regarded as a strong convention in the academic culture. [16] Cohen and March's estimates are that American College Presidents work for about 50–55 hours from Monday to Friday. Further assuming a 5 to 10 hours of the average working weekend, Cohen and March concluded that the College President works a total of about 60 hours a week. [17] From our data, a 50-hour work-week would appear more empirically defensible for both the Nigerian and the British academic leaders, than the 60-hour estimates. However, a study exclusively of vice-chancellors in Nigeria and Britain would be needed for a more valid comparisons with those of the American College Presidents.

Our results show that the British and the Nigerian academic leaders did not have significantly different working hours. Therefore, it is possible that academic jobs may be roughly similar in both countries.

In Nigeria, the official working hours for the other civil servants are 40 hours a week. This does not include overtime hours. But considering the fact that the 40 official hours most likely include non-working periods, perhaps Nigerian academic leaders, on the average, work a bit longer than their civil servant counterparts. It remains to be empirically ascertained how many working hours Nigerian managers in private industry put in a week.

5.3 Activities—What Academic Leaders Do

We describe in this section the various activities which academic leaders perform.

5.3.1 Deskwork

This activity was defined to refer to all paperwork including reading, writing, grading of scripts, and figure work. Table 5-4 shows a distribution of the proportion of total time which our sampled academic leaders spent on deskwork. The average of the percentage of total time spent by the Nigerian academic leaders in deskwork activities was 44, and the corresponding figure for the British sample was 43. This is the single activity for which the academic leaders spent most of their time, and there was no significant difference between the percentage time spent by both the British and the Nigerian academic leaders.

Our result is not surprising, for the academic leader's job involves, in the main, teaching and research, in addition to administration and management, and these necessitate excessive reading and writing. Industrial managers would not be expected to be involved in as much paperwork as the academic leaders who, indeed, have paperwork as their stock in trade. The proportion of total time which the academic leaders spent on deskwork is therefore understandably higher than similar figures recorded by industrial managers, as a comparative analyses in table 5-5 will reveal.

However, although the means differ, the range of variations in table 5-5 shows that some academic leaders did in fact spend less time on paperwork than some industrial managers.

Table 5-4: The Distribution of the Percentage of Total Hours Which the Academic Leaders Spent on Deskwork

Percentage	British	Nigerian
00–20	–	1
21–30	4	4
31–40	–	4
41–50	5	8
51–60	1	7
61–70	1	1
71–80	1	1
N	12	26
Mean	43.42	44.04
C.V. %	35.56	32.22

Table 5-5: A Distribution of the Percentage of Total Hours Which Managers Spent on Deskwork

Researcher	Date	Average	Range	Organization
Burns	1957	24	12–35	Industrial and commercial
Brewer and Tomlinson	1963–64	30	17–53	
Hinrichs	1964	26	16–29	
Horne and Lupton	1965	24	2–27	
Thomason	1966	25	12–51	
Stewart	1967	36	7–84	
Mintzberg	1973	22	16–38	
Kurke and Aldrich	1979	26	22–31	
Oshagbemi	1985	44	11–17	Universities
Oshagbemi	1985	43	25–73	

5.3.2 Scheduled Meetings

This activity was defined as planned or regular meetings, including time-tabled lectures and seminars. Table 5-6 shows that Nigerian academic leaders spent 29 percent, and their British counterparts 25 percent of their respective total hours on this activity. The Nigerian academic leaders spent a little more time on this activity because they were involved in more teaching than the British sample.

Mintzberg found that industrial managers spent a high proportion

Table 5-6: The Distribution of the Percentage of Total Hours Which the Academic Leaders Spent on Scheduled Meetings

Percentage	British	Nigerian
00–10	2	1
11–20	4	4
21–30	1	13
31–40	3	6
41–50	1	–
51–60	1	1
61–70	–	1
N	12	26
Mean	25.25	28.62
C.V. %	60.59	45.25

Table 5-7: A Distribution of the Percentage of Total Hours Which Industrial Managers Spent in Meetings

Researcher	Date	Scheduled	Unscheduled	Total
Luijk	1963	–	–	68
Brewer and Tomlinson	1963–64	–	–	51
Hinrichs	1964	–	–	50
Horne and Lupton	1965	–	–	54
Thomason	1966	–	–	48
Choran	1969	21	15	36
Mintzberg	1973	59	10	69
Kurke and Aldrich	1979	50	12	62
Gibbs	1982	38	18	56
Lawrence	1984	22	20	42
Lawrence	1984	30	18	48

of their time in scheduled meetings (59%), and this finding was supported by Kurke and Aldrich's figure of 50 percent. Other industrial managers obviously spent a high percentage of their total time in meetings, as is evident from table 5-7. However, unlike in our study, the time spent in meetings were not subdivided into scheduled and unscheduled sessions by all researchers. Stewart, for example, had the proportion of the total time spent in informal meetings and committee, but these like many other categories are hardly easily compared with our findings.

5.3.3 Unscheduled Meetings

This category of meetings is defined as impromptu or unplanned for. Table 5-8 shows that it consumed about 11 percent and 7 percent of the Nigerian and the British academic leaders' total working hours, respectively. The time of the British academic leaders did appear relatively more highly planned than the time of the Nigerian academic leaders. However, these differences are not statistically significant.

Table 5-8: The Distribution of the Percentage of Total Hours Which the Academic Leaders Spent in Unscheduled Meetings

Percentage	British	Nigerian
00–05	8	3
06–10	2	9
11–15	–	12
16–20	–	2
21+	2	–
N	12	26
Mean	6.83	10.50
C.V. %	123.87	40.00

5.3.4 Telephoning

Table 5-9 shows a distribution of the proportion of total time which the academic leaders spent on telephoning. In each of the Nigerian and the British sample, less than one percent of the academic leaders' working time was spent on this activity. Industrial managers spent more time than this figure, as a comparative analysis in figure 5-10 shows. A possible explanation for the difference is the fact that academic leaders interact more on a face to face basis with the students who can be regarded as their own "customers". [18] During working hours, students are also in much closer proximity to the academic leaders than the customers of most of the private industries. Indeed, in the Nigerian case, academic leaders tend to live in close proximity to the university staff, both administrative and academic, who often occupy university quarters.

Table 5-9: The Distribution of the Percentage of Total Hours Which the Academic Leaders Spent in Telephoning

Percentage	British	Nigerian
0	8	17
1	1	2
2	2	5
3	–	2
4	1	–
N	12	26
Mean	0.75	0.69
C.V. %	172.00	152.17

Table 5-10: A Distribution of the Percentage of Total Hours Which Managers Spent in Telephoning

Researcher	Date	Percentage	Organization
Luijk	1963	15	Industrial and Commercial
Copeman	1963	5	
Brewer and Tomlinson	1963–64	6	
Hinrichs	1964	6	
Horne and Lupton	1965	9	
Stewart	1967	6	
Choran	1969	17	
Mintzberg	1973	6	
Kurke and Aldrich	1979	8	
Gibbs	1982	5	
Lawrence	1984	11	
Lawrence	1984	7	
Oshagbemi	1985	0.75	Universities
Oshagbemi	1985	0.69	

Another explanation is the fact that most of the telephoning that occurred fell under fleeting contacts, as they were of less than five minutes' duration. For instance, Mintzberg's figure of 6 percent for this activity did not include a distinction between an activity and a fleeting contact. Nonetheless, academic leaders probably spend relatively less time on telephoning as compared to industrial managers.

5.3.5 Other Activities

Apart from deskwork, meetings, and telephoning, other activities detailed in the diaries are practicals, computing, travelling, and miscellaneous events in addition to lunch, coffee, or tea breaks. These activities taken together account for about 16 percent of the Nigerian academic leaders' time, and for 24 percent of the British. Individually, lunch, tea and coffee sessions, practicals, computing, and travelling respectively account for about 6, 2, 1, 0, and 2 percent of the Nigerian academic leaders' time. For the British, the activities, in order, account for 8.5, 2, 3, 1.5, and 5 percent of their total working time. Miscellaneous activities such as "taking children from the staff school", or "going to the postal agency to collect stamps", account for 5 and 4 percent of the Nigerian and the British academic leaders' working time, respectively.

5.4 The Subject Matter of Academic Leaders' Jobs

This section rests on the premise that the content or the subject matter of the activities which academic leaders perform can be usefully grouped into either teaching, researching, consulting, administration and management, and personal.

5.4.1 Teaching

Teaching was defined to include preparation time, and it encompasses all the activities related to the dissemination of knowledge. Table 5-11 details the distribution of the percentage total hours which our sampled academic leaders spent on teaching. An average of 17 percent was recorded by the Nigerian sample, while the British sample recorded 12 percent. The greater percentage rate (not statistically significant) obtained from the Nigerian sample is to be expected, and it is explained in terms of the paucity of qualified staff to lecture all relevant courses. Therefore, many heads of departments and deans often have to teach.

Table 5-11: The Distribution of the Percentage of Total Hours Which the Academic Leaders Spent on Teaching

Percentage	British	Nigerian
00–10	6	11
11–20	3	4
21–30	3	8
31+	–	3
N	12	26
Mean	12.42	16.54
C.V. %	88.73	77.09

5.4.2 Researching

Table 5-12 shows that the academic leaders spent a little more time on research than teaching, averaging 21 percent of the total time for the British, and 20 percent for the Nigerian sample. This finding is not surprising, as research is regarded as the "lifeblood" of the university system and as academic promotions depend substantially on the success of research in terms of publications. However, both teaching and research are important university functions. It was observed that the academic leaders vary widely in the amount of time which they recorded on research as the distribution on table 5-12 conveys. There was no important difference in the amount of time which both samples spent on research. It is believed that the Nigerian academic leaders who are yet to attain professorship will probably spend a considerable time on research. Also, academics who are not leaders, may typically spend a greater proportion of their time not only on research, but also teaching.

5.4.3 Consulting

This activity, until recently, has not been a popular one in Nigeria, and academics who engaged in it could be accused of divided interest. In these days, however, consultancy divisions have been established in many universities. These are aimed at generating funds to augment the worsening university finances.

Table 5-12: The Distribution of the Percentage of Total Hours Which the Academic Leaders Spent on Research

Percentage	British	Nigerian
00–10	3	4
11–20	3	12
21–30	3	6
31–40	2	2
41+	1	2
N	12	26
Mean	20.92	20.19
C.V. %	73.13	62.21

Table 5-13 shows that in both British and in Nigeria, the academic leaders spent a very small proportion of their time on consulting, averaging about 4 percent in the British case, and only 3 percent in the Nigerian sample. Out of the Nigerian sample size of 26, 15 academic leaders did not engage in consulting at all, the corresponding number being 7 for the 12 British academic leaders. The wide variations in table 5-13 is to be expected, as the services of all university disciplines are not equally being demanded by the private industries.

Table 5-13: The Distribution of the Percentage of Total Hours Which the Academic Leaders Spent on Consulting

Percentage	British	Nigerian
00–00	7	15
01–05	3	5
06–10	–	4
11–15	1	1
16–20	1	1
N	12	26
Mean	3.58	3.19
C.V. %	176.82	153.29

5.4.4 Administration and Management

Contrary perhaps to popular belief, academic leaders spend a greater proportion of their total time on administration and management. The time that our samples spent on administration and management was greater than the time spent on teaching, researching, and consulting combined. This finding is true in both the Nigerian and the British samples. Table 5-14 details the distribution of the proportion of hours which the academic leaders spent on this activity. It shows that the British academic leaders spent an average of 47 percent of their total time with a coefficient of variation of about 50. The corresponding figure for the Nigerian academic leaders was 48, with a lesser variation, the coefficient being only about 31.

Table 5-14: The Distribution of the Percentage of Total Hours Which the Academic Leaders Spent on Administration and Management

Percentage	British	Nigerian
00–30	3	1
31–40	3	6
04–50	–	8
51–60	2	5
61–70	3	5
71+	1	1
N	12	26
Mean	47.25	47.92
C.V. %	50.20	31.18

This finding is of interest because it shows that academic leaders are not technical, research officiers, but managers. With the bulk, and with upper ranges of 75 and 89 percent of their total time spent in administration and management, their jobs are the jobs of managers, however skilled they may be in their expert areas. As we observed earlier, in fact, some of them no longer teach, nor consult, nor conduct researches. Some of the details of the jobs they recorded under this activity include preparing faculty budgets, attending Council meetings, presenting proposals to Senate, participating in the interview of a prospective head of department, writing a reference on a former employee, and attending external examiners' meeting.

5.4.5 Personal

This section is the recognition that the content of some of the activities of academic leaders, such as writing personal letters, taking a lunch break, or telephoning a friend, cannot correctly be classified as either teaching, researching, consulting, or administration and management. Rather, these should be recorded more appropriately under personal matters. We recognize, however, that the distinction between personal and official jobs may not be very clear and obvious in all cases. Certainly, the distinction between reading for teaching, researching, or for consulting purposes, for example, is very thin. Table 5-15 shows the distribution of the percentage total hours which our sampled academic leaders recorded on personal activities, revealing averages of more than 10 percent of total time in both samples.

Table 5-15: The Distribution of the Percentage of Total Hours Which the Academic Leaders Spent on Personal Matters

Percentage	British	Nigerian
00–05	–	3
06–10	4	9
11–15	4	7
16–20	–	5
21–25	2	1
26+	2	1
N	12	26
Mean	15.83	12.23
C.V. %	59.42	54.05

5.5 Where Academic Leaders Perform Their Jobs

Academic leaders are an interesting lot. They vary widely not only in the functions they perform, but also where these take place. The diary had distinguished jobs performed in own offices, other units, other campuses, at home, and in other organizations. As we noted earlier, the time spent travelling was small, an average of only 2 percent for the Nigerian sample, and 5 percent of the total time for the

British sample. The time spent on journeys were added to the time spent in their respective destinations. It should be noted, however, that journey periods were most often idle hours, i.e. they did no other work whilst travelling.

5.5.1 Own Office

Table 5-16 shows that academic leaders perform most of their jobs in their own offices. The British academic leaders spent as much as 50 percent, and their Nigerian counterparts 45 percent of their total hours in their offices. This finding compares with Stewart's senior and middle managers who averaged 51 percent in their offices, a figure exactly identical with Mintzberg's sample of five chief executives. Other researchers such as Horne and Lupton, Kurke and Aldrich, where the sampled managers spent 52 percent and 68 percent of their respective total time, are supportive of the view that managers at all levels spend a considerable amount of their time in their own offices. Cohen and March's figure of 35 percent which the College Presidents spent in their own offices appears slightly low and Luijk's finding of 85 percent for his sample of managing directors is high, although it is in line with Burns and with Kelly's suggestion that the time spent at one's desk increases with rank. The latter proposition is, however, unsupported by our data, as there was no relationship between rank and the time spent on deskwork.

Table 5-16: The Distribution of the Percentage of Total Hours Which the Academic Leaders Spent in Own Office

Percentage	British	Nigerian
11–20	–	1
21–30	2	3
31–40	2	6
41–50	2	5
51–60	1	8
61–70	4	2
71–80	1	1
N	12	26
Mean	50.42	45.04
C.V. %	34.99	31.42

5.5.2 Other Units

The percentage of total hours which the academic leaders spent in the other units is presented in table 5-17. This distribution includes the time spent in other campuses of the same university, if any. It shows that the British academic leaders spent about 30 percent and the Nigerian academic leaders up to 36 percent in other university units. The higher figure in the Nigerian sample was explained by the extra hours which they spent in teaching which took place in the other units.

On the whole, each of the sampled group of academic leaders spent about 80 percent of their total hours in their own establishments, confirming the statement by McCall et al. that managers are "home-bodies". The managers in Stewart's sample spent 75 and those in Horne and Lupton's, 85 percent of their time in own establishment. However, the corresponding figure in Cohen and March's study was only 47 percent, as the presidents spent just 12 percent of their time elsewhere on campus, in addition to the 35 percent spent in their own office noted in the previous section. [19]

Table 5-17: The Distribution of the Percentage of Total Hours Which the Academic Leaders Spent in the Other University Units (Including Other Campuses, if Any)

Percentage	British	Nigerian
11–20	2	3
21–30	6	8
31–40	2	6
41–50	1	3
51–60	–	4
61+	1	2
N	12	26
Mean	29.67	36.19
C.V. %	49.78	42.58

5.5.3 At Home

Each of our British and Nigerian academic leaders spent about 10 percent of their working time at home, the details of the distribution of the hours spent at home being provided in table 5-18. Most of the academic leaders had their lunch at home, and there was often a blurring of the distinction between office and home hours. They did not observe rigid office hours as the other public servants would tend to. Sometimes, the academic leaders did not go to work early. On other occasions, they left early or stayed behind very late. A few of them went to their offices on Saturdays and Sundays.

Cohen and March found that the College Presidents spent as much as 16 percent of their working time at home, a figure obviously higher than the corresponding one reported by Horne and Lupton (4%), and Stewart (1.5%). Over half of the managers in Stewart's sample, for example, did not work at all at home during the four weeks when they recorded their diaries. This result compares with the distribution in table 5-18, where almost all the academic leaders in our sample worked for some period at home. The coefficient of variation of 89 and 79 percent in the distribution, however, show the high variance in the academic leaders' behaviour in the amount of time they spent at home.

Table 5-18: The Distribution of the Percentage of Total Hours Which the Academic Leaders Spent at Home

Percentage	British	Nigerian
00–05	5	7
06–10	2	8
11–15	2	4
16–20	–	3
21+	3	4
N	12	26
Mean	9.67	11.31
C.V. %	89.14	78.60

5.5.4 Other Organizations

Our sampled academic leaders spent about 11 percent and 8 percent each working in other organizations. See table 5-19. Academic leaders who spent a lot of time in other organizations were either those who went into the private companies to consult, or more often, those who went to other universities as external examiners or for seminars and conferences. Cohen and March found that the College Presidents spent 22 percent of their time out of town and 14 percent in other organizations in the same town. This gives a total of 36 percent of the total hours spent in other organizations, a figure which the authors themselves admitted as being rather high. Corresponding figures from Stewart's study (9%) and Horne and Lupton's (11%) compares with our findings.

In summary, the academic leaders, on the whole, spent about 80 percent of their time on campus, about 60 percent of that in their own offices. This gives an average of over 30 hours which the average academic leader spent within the university premises each week.

Table 5-19: The Distribution of the Percentage of Total Hours Which the Academic Leaders Spent in Other Organizations

Percentage	British	Nigerian
00–10	9	23
11–20	–	2
21+	3	1
N	12	26
Mean	10.50	7.65
C.V. %	131.43	125.23

5.6 The Duration of the Activities of Academic Leaders

The academic leaders who filled our diaries worked long hours on the same activity, many of them recording activity durations of two or more hours at a time. Most of the long sessions were spent on research and on the various meetings in addition to teaching, which normally lasts for a minimum duration of one hour. The academic leaders, however, spent some time on activities of short duration, averaging slightly less than 2 percent of the total time spent in each of the samples. The short sessions were spent mostly on deskwork and on unscheduled meetings. Tables 5-20 and 5-21 show the distributions of the proportion of time which the academic leaders spent on short and long-duration activities. Table 5-21 shows that the Nigerian and

Table 5-20: The Distribution of the Percentage of Total Hours Which the Academic Leaders Spent in Activities of Short Duration (i.e. Activities of 5 to 10 Minutes Inclusive)

Percentage	British	Nigerian
0–1	8	15
2–3	2	7
4–5	1	2
6–7	–	–
8–9	1	2
N	12	26
Mean	1.83	1.88
C.V. %	133.33	146.28

Table 5-21: The Distribution of the Percentage of Total Hours Which the Academic Leaders Spent in Activities of Long Duration (i.e. Activities Lasting 2 or More Hours)

Percentage	British	Nigerian
00–10	3	4
11–20	1	3
21–30	2	2
31–40	2	7
41–50	1	2
51–60	1	5
61–70	2	3
N	12	26
Mean	33.25	35.12
C.V. %	71.67	57.03

the British academic leaders spent approximately the same proportion of time on long-duration activities. This was about one-third of their respective total hours.

Mintzberg's observational study reported that his five chief excutives spent an average of 49 percent of their total time in activities of less than 9 minutes' duration and only 10 percent in activities lasting more than one hour. Corresponding figures from Kurke and Aldrich were 63 percent and 5 percent, respectively. However, the above available industrial figures are not exactly comparable to our study with regard to the time spent on short-duration activities. This is because, unlike in the above reported studies, most of our otherwise short-duration activities would have been recorded as fleeting contacts.

On the whole, the distribution of the average durations for all activities showed a mean of slightly higher than one hour. This is true whether the distribution is with or without fleeting contacts, and it is true for both the Nigerian and the British samples, as tables 5-22 and

Table 5-22: The Distribution of the Average Durations for all Activities—With Fleeting Contacts

Duration	British	Nigerian
21–40	2	2
41–60	2	9
61–80	4	11
81–100	2	4
101+	2	–
N	12	26
Mean	69.33	62.08
C.V. %	42.69	29.47

Table 5-23: The Distribution of the Average Durations for all Activities—Without Fleeting Contacts

Duration	British	Nigerian
21–40	3	3
41–60	1	10
61–80	6	9
81–100	1	4
100+	1	–
N	12	26
Mean	64.50	60.65
C.V. %	38.18	28.37

5-23 show. It is probably true, therefore, to say that academic leaders tend to work a bit longer on the same activity than their industrial counterparts. Such a pattern of activity duration seems necessary for the academic leaders to do their work more effectively. The modal value, for example, obtained from the overall activity duration from 16 of the 26 Nigerian academic leaders was 60 minutes. This result is not surprising, as lecture periods are often of one hour duration.

5.7 Summary

In summary, the activity analyses show that the academic leaders spent most of their time on deskwork, followed by scheduled and then unscheduled meetings. Telephoning was observed to account for less than one percent of the academic leaders' working hours. Very close average figures and similar variations were obtained in both the British and the Nigerian samples. However, comparative industrial figures were observed to be understandably different in most of the major activities. Explanations for observed differences were proferred.

The content or subject-matter analyses show that the academic leaders spent the greatest proportion of their time in administration and management, a function which accounted for almost half of their total time. The analyses also reveal the superior importance which academic leaders accord to research vis-à-vis teaching in the allocation of their time. Furthermore, it shows that personal activities accounted for about 10 percent, and consulting for less than 4 percent of the academic leaders' total time.

The academic leaders spent about half of their time in their offices, and, on the average, about 80 percent of their total time within the university premises. The analyses of the time spent at different locations show that they spent about the same proportion of time at home as in other organizations—about 10 percent.

Academic and industrial managers showed similar characteristics in the analyses of the locations of their jobs, with the exception that academic leaders tend to do relatively more work at home than industrial managers. However, academic leaders seem to spend more time on long-duration, and less time on short-duration activities. The average activity duration for the academic leaders was slightly above one hour, with or without fleeting contacts. Various distributions were presented in the chapter to show the detailed findings in respect of these job characteristics.

5.8 Notes and References

[1] All figures are rounded up to the nearest whole number. Unless otherwise stated, total working hours refer to the net figures, i.e. after subtracting the time taken for personal lunch.

[2] Stewart, R., *Managers and their jobs: A study of the similarities and differences in the ways managers spend their time*, London, Macmillan, 1967, p. 29.

[3] Copeman, G., Luijk, H., and Hanika, F. deP., *How The Executive Spends His Time*, Business Publications Limited, London, 1963, p. 7.

[4] Burns, T., Management in Action, *Operational Research Quarterly*, Vol. 8, No. 2, 1957, p. 48.

[5] Horne, J.H. and Lupton, T., The Work Activities of 'Middle' Managers, *The Journal of Management Studies*, Vol. I, No. 2, 1965, p. 30.

[6] Mintzberg, H., *The Nature of Managerial Work*, Harper and Row, New York, 1973, p. 197.

[7] Kurke, L.B. and Aldrich, H.E., Mintzberg was right! A replication and extension of the nature of managerial work, *Management Science*, Vol. 29, No. 8, August 1983, pp. 975–984.

[8] The Editors of Fortune, *The Executive Life*, Garden City, N.Y., Doubleday, 1956, reported in Stewart, Rosemary, op. cit., p. 30. See also, Mansfield, R., et al., where over 40% of the 1058 British managers surveyed reportedly worked for longer than 50 hours a week; Mansfield, R., et al., The British Manager in Profile, *British Institute of Management Foundation*, London, 1981, p. 11 (Table 15).

[9] McCall, M.W., Morrison, M.A., and Hannah, R.L., Studies of Managerial Work: Results and Methods, *Centre for Creative Leadership*, Technical Report No. 9, North Carolina, 27402, May 1978, p. 42.

[10] Carlson, S., *Executive Behaviour: A Study of the Work Load and the Working Methods of Managing Directors*, Strombergs, Stockholm, 1951.

[11] Copeman, Luijk, and Hanika, op. cit., p. 22.

[12] Stewart, R., op. cit., p. 31.

[13] Mintzberg, H., op. cit., p. 242.

[14] The gross hours was defined to include the time spent on private activities including lunch.

[15] Reference to studies reported in Chapter 6.

[16] Cohen, M.D. and March, J.D., *Leadership and Ambiguity: The American College Presidents*, MaGraw-Hill, New York, 1974, p. 126.

[17] Ibid.

[18] The individuals or groups who buy and make use of the academic leaders' products and services.

[19] It is assumed that "elsewhere in town" did not include any time spent in other campuses of the same university.

Chapter 6
The Nature of the Academic Leaders' Jobs II

6.1 Introduction

This chapter continues the discussion of the nature of the academic leaders' jobs which was begun in Chapter Five. It examines in detail the various forms and types of contact which academic leaders make, the varieties in, and the fragmentation of their jobs. As in Chaper Five, all discussions are made from the point of view of how academic leaders spend their time.

6.2 Contacts With People I: Types

This section examines the percentage of total time which academic leaders spend with students, colleagues, administrative staff, and non-members of the university community.

6.2.1 Students

Table 6-1 details the proportion of time which the academic leaders spent with their students. This includes the time spent with students in and outside the lecture halls. Surprisingly, perhaps, it shows that academic leaders do not spend as much time with their students as is popularly believed. The Nigerian academic leaders spent less than one-fifth of their time with students, and their British counterparts recorded less than ten percent of their time with their own students. While the proportions of total time spent by the two groups are low, there is a difference between them. The Nigerian academic leaders spent about 16 percent of their total time with their students in contrast to the corresponding figure of 7 percent spent by the British academic leaders. The difference in the average total time spent by the two groups is significant at the 99 percent confidence level. [1]

One reason for this difference is the earlier on identified higher number of scheduled and unscheduled meetings which the Nigerian academic leaders had with their students. In fact, in the Nigerian case, the academics often act as "school teachers" rather than lecturers, and this state of affairs is a result of the generally poor quality or non-existence of teaching aids, low-level of library stocks, and the other paraphernalia of effective teaching.

Another possible reason why British academic leaders tend to spend less contact time with their own students may lie in the more frequent use they make of the telephone as a medium of interacting with their students. In fact, the results of the analyses of the academic leaders' fleeting contacts seem to support this thinking. Whereas 90 percent of all fleeting contacts by Nigerian academic leaders was by person while only 10 percent was by telephone, the fleeting contacts by the British academic leaders were 55 percent by person and 45 percent by telephone. There may also be some significant underlying cultural differences in attitude in both countries regarding student—staff personal contacts. However, there are no empirical data to substantiate this speculation.

Table 6-1: The Distribution of the Percentage of Total Hours Which the Academic Leaders Spent with Students

Percentage	British	Nigerian
00–10	7	11
11–20	5	8
21–30	–	3
31–40	–	3
41+	–	1
N	12	26
Mean	7.08	16.04
C.V. %	92.94	85.72

6.2.2 Colleagues

Academic leaders spend more of their time with colleagues than with their students. This fact is revealed in table 6-2, where the Nigerian academic leaders record about 22 percent, and the British almost 26 percent of their time with their colleagues. Next to being alone, their colleagues is the group with which academic leaders spend most of their time. Academic leaders perform miscellaneous functions with their colleagues which consume time. These include having coffee or tea together, writing joint books, or attending unit meetings and seminars.

Table 6-2: The Distribution of the Percentage of Total Hours Which the Academic Leaders Spent with Colleagues

Percentage	British	Nigerian
00–10	3	5
11–20	1	7
21–30	4	11
31–40	2	1
41+	2	2
N	12	26
Mean	25.83	22.31
C.V. %	68.18	54.73

6.2.3 Administrative Staff

Despite the fact that academic leaders spend most of their time in administration and management, they do not spend most of this time with members of the adminstrative staff. The time which the academic leaders spent with members of the administrative staff was less than that spent with their colleagues, a conclusion arising from the data presented in table 6-3. Here, the academic leaders each spent about 15 percent of their time with the administrative staff. Most of this time was spent with secretaries in administrative routines and in the official communication networks.

6.2.4 Non-Members of the University

The proportion of time which the academic leaders spent with non-members of their universities is presented in table 6-4. It shows that the Nigerian academic leaders spent least of their time with this group, a result arising, perhaps, from the relatively small percentage of time which they spent in consulting. British academic leaders spent

Table 6-3: The Distribution of the Percentage of Total Hours Which the Academic Leaders Spent with Members of the Administrative Staff

Percentage	British	Nigerian
00–10	6	9
11–20	3	11
21–30	–	6
31–40	2	–
41+	1	–
N	12	26
Mean	15.42	14.50
C.V. %	92.74	58.62

Table 6-4: The Distribution of the Percentage of Total Hours Which the Academic Leaders Spent with Non-Members of the University

Percentage	British	Nigerian
00–10	8	19
11–20	1	4
21–30	2	2
31+	1	1
N	12	26
Mean	11.33	7.69
C.V. %	90.11	128.22

about 11 percent of their time with non-members of their universities, an average higher than the time which they spent with their own students. However, both groups recorded high degrees of variation in the time spent with non-members of the university. This variation is shown in table 6-4.

6.3 Contacts With People II: Numbers

Rather than the particular class of people, the size of the group which academic leaders interact with is discussed in this section. The proportion of time which the academic leaders spent alone, with one person, with a small group (2–5 people), and with large groups of six or more people are detailed in tables 6-5, 6-8, 6-9, and 6-10, respectively.

6.3.1 Time Alone

Academic leaders perform most of their jobs in solitude. This finding is revealed in table 6-5 where both the Nigerian and the British academic leaders spent about 40 percent of their time alone. [2] Stewart reported that the industrial managers in her sample spent 34 percent of their time alone. Actually, one would expect research managers and academic leaders to spend relatively more time alone than typical industrial managers. This is because writing and reading which form the bulk of the academic leaders' job, require a high degree of reflection and concentration. It was observed that during the examinations, the academic leaders who were involved in the grading of scripts spent a higher percentage of time alone than the majority who recorded the diaries during in-term full teaching period. It would be expected that academic leaders would spend a greater percentage of time alone during the vacations when the students are no longer around. However, we did not record any diaries during the holidays.

Cohen and March recorded that American College Presidents spent only about 25 percent of their time alone. The vice-chancellor

Table 6-5: The Distribution of the Percentage of Total Hours Which the Academic Leaders Spent Alone

Percentage	British	Nigerian
11–20	3	4
21–30	–	2
31–40	3	9
41–50	3	5
51–60	1	4
61–70	–	2
71–80	2	–
N	12	26
Mean	40.75	39.27
C.V. %	47.93	34.30

Table 6-6: The Rank of Nigerian Academic Leaders and the Percentage of the Total Time Spent Alone

Rank	Vice-chancellor	Director	Dean	Head of dept.
The percentage of total hours worked	–	16	39	46
	–	28	25	49
	–	44	35	51
	–	20	35	58
	–	35	38	19
	–	–	–	35
	–	32	–	19
	–	–	–	39
	–	–	–	64
	–	–	–	41
	–	–	–	45
	–	–	–	54
	–	–	–	65
	–	–	–	37
	–	–	–	52
Average	–	29.17	34.4	44.9

Table 6-7: The Rank of British Academic Leaders and the Percentage of the Total Time Spent Alone

Rank	Vice-chancellor	Director	Dean	Head of dept.
The percentage of total hours worked	15	42	17	45
	–	36	45	32
	–	37	20	51
	–	–	–	73
	–	–	–	76
Average	15	38.3	27.3	55.4

in our sample spent only 15 percent of his time alone. It is therefore probable that rank may affect the percentage of time which managers spend alone, as the data on tables 6-6 and 6-7 seem to convey. However, the deans in the British Universities spent a smaller percentage of time alone than the directors. Actually, in the organization of some universities, the rank of some deans may not be lower than that of some directors. What seems more reliable is the fact that both the deans and the directors on the one side spent a much lower percentage of time alone than the heads of units.

The rate of change in or the size of an organization are also possible explanations for the differences in the percentage of time which managers spend alone. However, we do not have evidence in this study, either to support or to refute any of these possibilities.

6.3.2 Time With Others

Academic leaders spend about 60 percent of their total time with others, either singly or in groups. Tables 6-8 and 6-9 show that our sampled academic leaders spent about one-fifth of their time with one person, and they spent about the same proportion of time with groups of 2–5 people. Table 6-10 shows that the Nigerian academic

Table 6-8: The Distribution of the Percentage of Total Hours Which the Academic Leaders Spent With one Person

Percentage	British	Nigerian
00–10	4	4
11–20	3	8
21–30	3	11
31+	2	3
N	12	26
Mean	22.25	19.81
C.V. %	75.24	41.24

Table 6-9: The Distribution of the Percentage of Total Hours Which the Academic Leaders Spent With 2–5 People

Percentage	British	Nigerian
00–10	2	12
11–20	4	3
21–30	2	9
31+	4	2
N	12	26
Mean	22.42	16.73
C.V. %	51.92	67.60

Table 6-10: The Distribution of the Percentage of Total Hours Which the Academic Leaders Spent With 6 or More People

Percentage	British	Nigerian
00–10	5	4
11–20	4	5
21–30	2	12
31–40	1	3
41+	–	2
N	12	26
Mean	14.58	24.12
C.V. %	74.21	52.78

leaders spent an average of over 24 percent of their time with groups of six or more people, while the British sample spent a corresponding figure of less than 15 percent. The difference in the average of the total time spent by the two samples is significant at the 95 percent confidence level. [3] This result is consistent with the finding that the Nigerian academic leaders spent significantly more time with students, the latter being normally more than five in number.

6.4 Fleeting Contacts

The diary had defined fleeting contacts and interruptions as incidents of less than 5-minute duration. No attempt was made to distinguish between fleeting contacts and interruptions, as the academic leaders may not have the patience or the time for such detailed recordings. Furthermore, only the frequency of fleeting contacts was recorded and not the actual time spent on it. Table 6-11 is a distribution showing the total fleeting contact by method, while table 6-12 shows the same distribution by the person involved.

Table 6-11 shows that, allowing for the different sample sizes, the Nigerian sample had a slightly higher average number of fleeting contacts than the British academic leaders. The vast majority of these fleeting contacts was by person rather than by telephone. For every fleeting contact by telephone, the Nigerian academic leader had about ten by person. This result differs significantly from the situation in Britain where the academic leaders had almost as many fleeting contacts by telephone as they did by person. The explanation for this difference is the frequent lack of functional telephone facilities in many Nigerian university campuses. Indeed, an effective telephone system has not yet become widespread in the country as a whole.

Table 6-12 shows the frequency of the academic leaders' fleeting contacts by person. It shows that the majority of the fleeting contacts

Table 6-11: The Distribution of the Total Fleeting Contacts by Method

Method	Number	Percentage of Total*	Country
Person	350	55	Britain
Telephone	287	45	
Total	637	100	
Person	1424	91	Nigeria
Telephone	133	9	
Total	1557	100	

*The percentage figures are rounded up to the nearest whole number.

Table 6-12: The Distribution of the Total Fleeting Contacts by Persons

Persons	Number	Percentage of Total*	Country
Students	75	12	Britain
Colleagues	213	33	
Adm. staff	237	37	
External	107	17	
Self	5	1	
Total	637	100	
Students	347	22	Nigeria
Colleagues	554	36	
Adm. staff	409	26	
External	169	11	
Self	78	5	
Total	1557	100	

*The percentage figures are rounded up to the nearest whole number.

which the academic leaders had were from their colleagues and the administrative staff, and not from the students. British academic leaders had a higher percentage fleeting contacts from their administrative staff than their Nigerian counterparts, the latter recording a higher number of relative fleeting contacts with their own students. Both samples recorded low fleeting contacts by themselves.

The discussions above relate to the total picture in respect of fleeting contacts. During an activity, however, fleeting contacts, when they occur, could be by person, by telephone, or by both methods. The distribution of such occurrence is almost even between the three possibilities in the British sample. In the Nigerian case, there were both relatively very low fleeting contacts that were by telephone alone or by both telephone and person, while contacts exclusively by person were very high.

6.5 Job Fragmentation

The academic leaders' jobs, like those of most managers, is highly fragmented. The academic leaders in our sample experienced many fleeting contacts, and they performed many activities in a typical day. Furthermore, although the table 6-5 showed that they were alone for about 40 percent of their total time, the duration of such "alone" periods were short, and they were interrupted by fleeting contacts. This hampers continuous concentration.

Table 6-13: The Distribution of the Number of the Average Daily Activities (Diary Entries)

Number	British	Nigerian
00–05	1	4
06–10	8	14
11–15	1	7
16–20	2	1
N	12	26
Mean	9.75	9.35
C.V. %	43.76	35.54

Tables 6-13, 6-14, 6-15, and 6-16 present various distributions measuring the extent of job fragmentation which the academic leaders experienced. Tables 6-13 and 6-14 show that the academic leaders

Table 6-14: The Distribution of the Number of the Average Daily Fleeting Contacts

Number	British	Nigerian
00–05	3	3
06–10	3	8
11–15	2	8
16–20	4	4
21+	–	3
N	12	26
Mean	10.58	11.92
C.V. %	56.47	48.84

Table 6-15: The Distribution of Alone Periods of one Hour or Longer Broken by Fleeting Contacts and Interruptions

Number	British	Nigerian
00–05	5	7
06–10	5	5
11–15	2	10
16–20	–	4
N	12	26
Mean	6.75	9.89
C.V. %	52.90	53.02
1* Number	14	19
2* %	27.58	31.15
3* Hours	12.56	14.34

1* is the average whole number of such brief interruptions during such periods for each academic leader.
2* is the average percentage of the total time of such alone periods for each academic leader.
3* is the average number of hours per week of such alone periods for each academic leader.

had about 11 fleeting contacts during an average of almost 10 activities every day. It follows that, on the average, the academic leaders experienced one fleeting contact during the course of every activity.

Table 6-16: The Distribution of Alone Periods of one hour or Longer Without any Interruptions

Number	British	Nigerian
00–05	10	10
06–10	2	13
11–15	–	3
N	12	26
Mean	3.17	5.92
C.V. %	68.44	65.46
2* %	10.83	17.19
3* Hours	5.25	7.88

2* is the average percentage of the total time of such alone periods for each academic leader.

3* is the average number of hours per week of such alone periods for each academic leader.

For the academic leader to do a meaningful work beyond signing routine papers, it would be desirable to have at least an hour of undisturbed peace. Table 6-15 shows that the academic leaders had an average of less than 10 of such periods each week, i.e. when they were alone for periods of one hour or longer, allowing the occurrence of fleeting contacts during such periods. This was about 28 percent of the British academic leaders' total time and about 31 percent of that of the Nigerian. The number of fleeting contacts and interruptions which featured during such periods averaged about 14 for the British, and 19 for the Nigerian sample. Table 6-16 further shows that the Nigerian academic leaders were in fact only truly alone for about 17 percent of their total time, the corresponding figure being 11 percent for the British sample. In terms of the number of the actual hours involved, this is less than 8 hours for the Nigerian, and about 5 hours for the British sample, for the whole week.

6.6 Job Variety

Academic leaders vary greatly in the jobs they perform. This variety is reflected not only in the number of their daily working hours, but also in the fleeting contacts which they experience, and in their diary entries. Tables 6-17, 6-18, and 6-19 show the distribution of some of these measures of variety.

Table 6-17: The Distribution of the Differences in the Maximum and the Minimum Daily Hours Worked

Number*	British	Nigerian
1	3	4
2	2	6
3	2	4
4	2	3
5	1	3
6	2	3
7	–	1
8	–	2
N	12	26
Mean	3.17	3.69
C.V. %	58.44	58.73

*The number of hours (i.e. the difference between the maximum and the minimum daily hours worked) was rounded up to the nearest whole number.

In table 6-17, the hours worked by the academic leaders were recorded on a daily basis. The minimum daily hours was subtracted from the maximum daily hours during the week for each academic leader. It is the difference, rounded up to the nearest whole number which is presented in the distribution in table 6-17. It shows that the difference between the maximum and the minimum daily hours which was recorded during the week was as high as 6 in the British sample and even 8 in the Nigerian sample. The diaries revealed that on some days, the academic leaders worked for more than 12 hours while on other days, they hardly recorded 5 hours.

In tables 6-18 and 6-19, we had similarly subtracted the differences between the maximum and the minimum daily figures during the week for the fleeting contacts and the diary entries (activities), re-

Table 6-18: The Distribution of the Differences Between the Maximum and the Minimum Daily Fleeting Contacts

Number	British	Nigerian
00–05	3	3
06–10	3	8
11–15	1	10
16–20	2	2
21+	3	3
N	12	26
Mean	12.42	12.19
C.V. %	65.20	57.77

Table 6-19: The Distribution of the Differences in the Maximum and the Minimum Daily Diary Entries

Number	British	Nigerian
0–2	2	3
3–4	5	5
5–6	3	8
7–8	–	3
9+	2	7
N	12	26
Mean	4.83	6.15
C.V. %	55.68	45.89

spectively. Again, the distributions show that the difference between daily fleeting contacts could be as high as 20, and the corresponding number for the diary entries as many as 9.

In addition to these enumerated varieties in the academic leaders' job characteristics, other varieties were exhibited in the location, the type and the nature of contact, and the duration of an activity. Previous distributions have shown this all along. Because our diaries were completed only during the session, we cannot comment on the cyclical variations in the job characteristics of academic leaders. However, the picture of the variety presented above is likely to be richer were additional data collected during the vacations.

6.7 Summary

In summary, Chapter Six discussed the contacts which the academic leaders made with various groups and numbers of people. It noted that the academic leaders spent most of their time with their colleagues and the administrative staff, spending relatively little time with students and with non-members of the university community.

Fleeting contacts and interruptions were analyzed by person and by telephone. About 90 percent of the Nigerian academic leaders' total fleeting contacts were by person. This was unlike the British academic leaders who experienced almost an equal number of contacts by phone as by person. Again, it was found that academic leaders had more fleeting contacts from their colleagues and the administrative staff than from the students.

The academic leaders' jobs were fragmented with an average of one fleeting contact per each activity. As many as an average of 10 activities occurred daily. Alone time with or without fleeting contacts up to and beyond one hour were analyzed, and the results show that the academic leaders were truly alone for less than 18 percent of their total time.

The analyses of the variety exhibited by the academic leaders were made, and they reveal a rich pattern of variations in the daily hours worked, fleeting contacts made, and the diary entries (activities) recorded.

6.8 Conclusions on the Job Characteristics of Academic Leaders

Chapters Five and Six have summarized the results of this research on the nature of the job characteristics of academic leaders.

The general conclusions showed that the academic leaders' job characteristics were similar to those of the industrial managers. For example, the total hours worked, as well as the percentage of time spent within organizational premises were quite close as between our study of academic leaders and other studies of managers within the industries. In addition, all managers, whether industrial or academic, exhibited rich varieties in their jobs which were, in both cases, highly fragmented.

There were important exceptions, however. For example, the academic leaders spent more of the percentage of their total time alone or on deskwork than comparable figures from managers in the industries would suggest. Academic leaders also tend to differ in the extent of the proportion of their time which is spent in meetings and telephone, since they tend to spend less than industrial managers on these activities. Furthermore, the activity duration of academic leaders tends to be longer than that of industrial managers—i.e. episodes do not appear to be as brief.

Another general conclusions of this study is on the similarities between the jobs of the Nigerian and the British academic leaders. With the exception of the time spent with students and with groups of 6 or more people, the two groups of academic leaders showed similar job characteristics. These similarities were evident in the jobs they performed, the subject of these, the location, and the duration of their activities. Therefore, academic jobs are roughly similar in both countries, and cultural differences do not appear to affect the nature of academic jobs significantly.

This study is also a contribution to the notion that the nature of managerial work is a necessary qualification to the concept of the universality of managerial functions. Academic leaders are managers, but their job characteristics are not identical in all aspects with those of industrial managers. They cannot reasonably be expected to be.

6.9 Notes

[1] (t-value = 2.71; degrees of freedom = 35.88; 2-tail probability = 0.010)

[2] Fleeting contacts or interruptions (i.e., events of less than 5 minutes' duration) were disregarded in the computation of this figure for the time spent alone. In addition, the academic leader was not considered alone if he was on the phone with someone else.

[3] (t-value = 2.38; degrees of freedom = 25.04; 2-tail probability = 0.025)

Chapter 7
Job Profiles of Academic Leaders

7.1 Introduction

Chapters Five and Six have shown that academic leaders vary widely in the proportion of time which they spend on their activities. Variations in the proportion of time were also revealed in the location of these activities, with whom they were performed, and so on. The coefficient of variation obtained in respect of some of the distributions of the job characteristics of academic leaders were higher than 100 percent. It is useful to ask, therefore, whether in view of these variations, academic leaders [1] can be meaningfully classified on the basis of how, where, with whom, etc. they spend their time.

A meaningful grouping may have implications in the training or development programmes designed to assist academic leaders in the performance of their jobs. It will also show whether there is an alternative and possibly a more useful way of classifying academic leaders apart from the traditional approach based on the criterion of rank alone. Perhaps, discussions or studies on managerial effectiveness may also be more usefully tackled in relation to fairly comprehensive yardsticks of job characteristics, i.e. whether some groups in the classified sample will reveal some relative ineffective management practices vis-à-vis other groups.

This chapter confirms that academic leaders can be usefully grouped on the basis of how they spend their time. It describes the method for the classification, the criteria used, and the results.

In the classification that follows, the British and the Nigerian academic leaders have been grouped together. It may therefore be useful to explain why the two groups of academic leaders were not classified separately. There are three explanations to this. First, the sampled academic leaders from Nigeria and Britain exhibited similar job characteristics. This similarity was evident in the activities that the two groups of academic leaders performed, the subject of these, where they took place, the time taken, and so on. In essence, therefore, it was only logical to keep together the two sampled results that we have discovered to possess insignificant differences. Our decision was justified in the resulting five groupings each of which has at least a member from both countries. In fact, group three, the Educational Leaders Type 1, has equal numbers from Nigeria and Britain.

Second, separately clustering only twelve academic leaders which was the sample size from Britain may not really be meaningful. The number is too small for useful interpretation. At any rate, it would have been difficult to compare the resulting two classes of clusters from both countries, and the whole exercise would have served little or no purpose. The third reason is closely related to the second one. Our results show that, individually, academic leaders vary widely in the practice of their jobs. That is indeed the reason for the classification—to see whether in spite of this variety, meaningful groupings will emerge. The clustering methodology works such that, given this significant variety in job characteristics, the more members are in the group to be classified, the greater the chance of having more homogenous groupings emerging. This aids clearer interpretation. Furthermore, grouping the two sets of academic leaders together for classification purposes has further demonstrated the similarity in the two groups of academic culture, especially how academic leaders spend their time.

7.2 The Criteria Used for Classification

It is obvious that the nature of the groupings obtained will be a partial function of the criteria used and the methodology employed. Different criteria from ours and or different methodology may produce different results. However, in order to produce a useful grouping, "comprehensive" criteria incorporating the major elements of the activities, locations, contacts, etc. should be made. A selection of such criteria which was used in our classification is listed in Appendix F. It contains 24 variables.

7.3 The Methodology Employed

There is nothing new in attempting to group objects or to classify people. For example, the Hindus, the early Greek, and the Romans developed several typologies based on variations in human physical and behavioural characteristics. [2] In fact, as far back as the 18th Century, Linnaeus was concerned with classification in the plant and animal kingdom, stating the general justification of his attempts in the following words:

> All the real knowledge which we possess, depends on methods by which we distinguish the similar from the dissimilar. The greater the number of natural distinctions this method comprehends, the clearer become our idea of things. The more numerous the objects which employ our attention, the more difficult it becomes to form such a method and the more necessary. [3]

Similarly, it was from Adanson's 18th Century ideas on classification that the methods of numerical taxonomy later developed. [4] More recently, mathematicians and statisticians have made attempts to develop more formal and precise statistical and mathematical models to cluster analysis. Because the number of variables (criteria) and the cases involved in classification problems are often numerous, computer specialists now design and refine computer programs to eliminate the drudgery and the error level in the otherwise very cumbersome computations involved.

Although the goals of users are often dissimilar, [5] the basic problem and theory in cluster analysis remains the same: essentially, given a sample of X objects, each of which is measured on each of Y variables, cluster analysis is concerned with grouping the objects into N classes, where within group similarities across the Y variables are maximised, while between group dissimilarities are also maximised.

In grouping the academic leaders, hierarchical clustering using Ward's method with Euclidean distance measure was used. [6] Hierarchical clustering has the advantage of allowing the researcher to choose the level of clustering that group the respondents in the way that best suits his or her purpose. The computer procedure for this method is fully described in the cluster analysis package by Wishart. [7] Data in respect of the academic leaders were processed on the University of Bradford Cyber 170-720 Computer. The program was requested to generate 2 to 8 clusters for inspection. We decided on the number of clusters by examining the dendrograms (see Appendix

G) and by noting the changes between fusions. This procedure is recommended by Everitt, [8] especially for hierarchical techniques which we employed. The process identified five clusters.

Several authors, for example Friedman and Rubin, suggested that a plot of the criteria against the cases may help to decide the best number of clusters. [9] However, this suggestion was not helpful in our case, as there were 24 variables against which each of the 38 academic leaders were measured. Actually, Thorndike found that the latter suggestion is generally not satisfactory, especially when either the number of criteria, or the cases are too many. [10]

It should be mentioned that in our classification scheme, the 24 variables were not weighted, although Morrison in discussing the use of cluster analysis in market research takes the view that managers should be free to assign weights to variables arguing that objectivity should not be sacrificed for "managerial meaningfulness". [11] Sokal and Sneath, however, question the validity of assigning weights to variables based on intuitive judgments of what is important, contending that clustering attempts to reveal "natural" groups and not artificial ones. [12] We take the view of Burnaby who argues that including a variable while excluding some others, in effect, means assigning weights: equal weights to the variables chosen and zero weights to those not selected. [13]

Our study is an exploratory one. The objective of our classification is to evolve natural clusters of the academic leaders based on the set of the original data provided. Resulting clusters are then examined for meaningful interpretation based on the criteria on which the groups differ.

7.4 The Groups of Academic Leaders

From the results of the cluster analysis, we identified five groups of academic leaders. These are described below.

7.4.1 Administrators Type 1

The first group, Administrators Type 1, got their name from the fact that they spent, on the average, a higher percentage of total working time on administration and management and with the administrative staff members than any of the other groups. There were 10 members on this group, and they were further distinguished by the fact that they worked the longest hours (47 hours) during the week, and they spent the highest percentage of time on deskwork, and at home. However, they spent the least, and a remarkably low percentage of time on teaching. They also spent the least percentage of total time on scheduled meetings and with large groups of people (6 or more). Of the 10 members, there were 3 deans, 1 director, and 6 heads of departments.

7.4.2 Administrators Type 2

The second group, Administrators Type 2, exhibited similar characteristics to the first group, differing only slightly in the percentage of their total working time which they spent in most of the activities that distinguished Administrators Type 1. For example, the Administrators Type 2 came next to those in Type 1 in the percentage of their time which was spent on administration and management, on deskwork, and at home. Administrators Type 2 got their name from these features, and for spending the highest percentage of their time in the office. The Administrators Type 2, in addition, spent a lower percentage of time on research and consulting than any of the other groups. There were 12 members making up this group, and they comprised of 3 directors, 1 dean, and 8 heads of departments.

The Administrators Types 1 and 2 are distinguished in Two important respects: The administrators Type 2 spent about half of their working time alone, and they experienced the highest rate of fleeting contacts, characteristics where Administrators Type 1 did not feature as prominently. The Administrators Type 2 are further distinguished from the Administrators Type 1 in their average total working hours. Administrators Type 2 did not work as long, recording only about the average total working hours for the overall sample. In addition, the Administrators Type 2 spent considerably much lower percentage of time with members of the administrative staff than did Administrators Type 1. In fact, the Administrators Type 2 spent less than half of the percentage of time which the Administrators Type 1 recorded with members of the administrative staff. Finally, teaching and research roles seem to have been interchanged by the two groups. While the Administrators Type 1 spent a relatively high proportion of their time on research but did least teaching, the Administrators

Type 2 did relatively substantial teaching, but spent the least percentage of time on research.

The picture created by an examination of their respective diaries, and the percentage of time which the two groups spent on each of the 24 criteria is this: The academic leaders in Type 1 are strategic administrators who worked long hours and who interacted on a one to one basis, and apparently very well, with the members of their staff. On the other hand, members of the Administrators Type 2 are tactical trouble shooters, who preferred to be alone for most of the time. However, perhaps because they did not seem to delegate enough, they were most often interrupted by members of the organization who wanted to clarify issues or obtain authorization for miscellaneous activities. These distinctions, in our opinion, seem to justify separating into two the otherwise single group of administrators.

7.4.3 Educational Leaders Type 1

The Educational Leaders Type 1 worked for an average of only 38 hours a week, a figure which was next only to the shortest hours recorded by the Educational Leaders Type 2 described later. There were only 4 members of this group, and they were therefore the smallest of all the groups. Their members were made up of a director, a head of department, and two deans. Educational Leaders Type 1 spent the highest percentage of time on teaching and on unscheduled meetings. They also came second in the percentage of total time which the five groups each spent with students and colleagues, hence their name.

Two features seem to particularly distinguish this group. They spent the highest percentage of time on short-duration activities, with a figure which was more than triple the corresponding figure obtained by any of the other groups. In addition, the Educational Leaders Type 1 recorded by far the highest number of activities during the week. These characteristics seem to separate them not only from the next group, but in fact from all the other groups. See later tables for comparative analyses of the groups.

7.4.4 Educational Leaders Type 2

This group of academic leaders, who were 7 in number, worked the shortest number of hours. Like the Educational Leaders Type 1, they attended meetings a great deal, spending the highest percentage of time on scheduled meetings which in the present context were usually lectures. Educational Leaders Type 2 stand out prominently in one feature: the percentage of time spent in the other units. Here, they not only spent the highest percentage of time, but recorded a percentage figure which was almost double that obtained by Group 2 who came next. The Educational Leaders Type 2 also spent more percentage of time with students and with colleagues than any of the other groups. Of the 7 members in this group, there were 3 directors, 2 deans, and two heads of departments.

The Educational Leaders Type 2 are distinguished from those in Type 1 on the following very important characteristics: quite unlike the Educational Leaders Type 1, Educational Leaders Type 2 spent the lowest percentage of time on short-duration activities, and they recorded the least number of activities during the week, obtaining a figure which was much less than half that obtained by Type 1. Additionally, the Educational Leaders Type 2 also interacted much more with large groups of people than those in Type 1.

The general picture of the two groups obtained by a further examination of their respective diaries is this: Educational Leaders Type 1 are small-group academic leaders who are very accessible to students on short-duration and on unscheduled basis. They tend to lecture fairly small class sizes, especially post-graduate students. On the other hand, Educational Leaders Type 2 spend more time in the other units with students of large class sizes. They tend to have more scheduled and long-duration classes, interacting very little with one person, but quite a great deal with their colleagues. They appear to be teachers of a kind who do their work and leave the scene, and are not easily accessible to students on short time basis. To treat the educational leaders as one big group will blur these very important distinctions.

7.4.5 Research Leaders

The fifth and the last group of academic leaders are Research Leaders who got their name from the relatively high percentage of time which they spent on research, consulting, and on long-duration activities. The Research Leaders recorded the highest percentage of time in these activities. Because they are involved in consulting a great deal, they spent the highest percentage of time in the other organizations, and with non-members of the university. These were often in small groups of 2–5 people.

The Research Leaders recorded the lowest fleeting contacts. They also recorded the least, and remarkably very low percentage of time on unscheduled meetings, administration and management, and with students. However, they spent a moderately high percentage of time with their colleagues.

There were 5 members of this group. One of them was a vice-chancellor. Another was a director while the rest were heads of departments. It is useful to observe that this group came second only to the first group in the number of hours they spent working, spending more than the average time for the overall sample.

7.5 Comparisons of the Groups of Academic Leaders

The five groups of academic leaders are now compared with detailed illustrative tables which are designed to show not only comparisons among groups, but also within groups. The first table (table 7-1) summarizes the description of each group and how long they work.

Table 7-1: A Comparison of the Total Working Hours Spent by Each Group

Group	Description	Total hours*
One	Administrators Type 1	47
Two	Administrators Type 2	42
Three	Educational leaders Type 1	38
Four	Educational leaders Type 2	36
Five	Research leaders	44
Mean	Overall sample	42

* Please, note that all the figures in this table and in subsequent tables in this chapter are rounded up to the nearest whole number.

Table 7-2 presents the percentage of the total working time spent by each group on different activities. It shows that group 1 spent the highest percentage of time on deskwork but this was only slightly higher than the percentage of time spent by group 2. Group 4 who spent the least percentage of time on deskwork averaged only about half of the time spent by group 2. However, group 4 spent the highest percentage of time on scheduled meetings, recording markedly higher percentage of time on this activity than any of the other groups. The percentage of time spent by all the groups on unscheduled meetings were roughly even with the exception of the figure recorded by group 5 which was very low. However, group 5 seems to compensate for this by spending the highest percentage of time on miscellaneous activities.

Table 7-2: The Percentage of the Total Working Time Spent by Each Group on Different Activities

Activity	Group 1	Group 2	Group 3	Group 4	Group 5	Mean
Deskwork	55	52	32	26	38	44
Scheduled Meetings	22	24	23	46	25	28
Unscheduled Meetings	10	8	15	11	4	9
Other Activities	13	16	30	17	33	19
Total	100	100	100	100	100	100

Table 7-3 shows the percentage of the total working time spent by each group in the subject matter of their activities. It reveals that group 1 spent very little time on teaching where group 3 recorded the highest percentage of time. Group 5 spent the highest percentage of time on research, but this was only slightly higher than the percentage of time spent by group 1. However, group 5 recorded a percentage of total time on consulting which was at least double the corresponding percentage obtained by any other group. Groups 1 and 2 spent higher percentage of time on administration and management than the other groups. All the groups spent more or less the same proportion of time on personal matters.

Table 7-4 details the percentage of the total working time spent by each group at different locations. It can be seen that groups 1, 2, and 3 spent roughly the same proportion of time in their own office. Group 4, who spent the least percentage of time in their own office recorded the highest percentage of time in the other units, spending a percent-

Table 7-3: The Percentage of the Total Working Time Spent by Each Group in the Subject Matter of Their Activities

Subject-Matter	Group 1	Group 2	Group 3	Group 4	Group 5	Mean
Teaching	5	19	27	19	12	15
Research	27	13	17	21	28	20
Consulting	2	1	3	5	10	3
Administration and management	56	54	37	43	31	48
Personal	10	13	16	12	19	14
Total	100	100	100	100	100	100

age of time which was almost double that spent by any of the other groups. The other groups recorded roughly similar percentages in the other units. While group 5 spent the least percentage of time in the other units, it recorded an exceedingly high percentage of time in other organizations, spending a higher percentage of time in the other organizations than all the other four groups combined. Group 1 recorded the highest proportion of time at home.

Table 7-4: The Percentage of the Total Working Time Spent by Each Group at Different Locations

Location	Group 1	Group 2	Group 3	Group 4	Group 5	Mean
Own office	53	55	53	26	39	47
Other Units	26	31	30	61	22	34
Home	16	10	8	7	9	11
Other Organizations	5	4	9	6	30	8
Total	100	100	100	100	100	100

The time which the groups spent with different categories of people are summarized in table 7-5. It can be observed that group 5 spent the least proportion of time with students followed by group 1. Group 4 spent the highest percentage of time not only with students, but also with colleagues. However, the distribution of time which was spent with colleagues by the five groups did not reveal high variations.

Group 1 spent a much higher percentage of time with members of the administrative staff, while group 5 spent significantly much higher proportion of time with non-members of the university. Apart from these two isolated cases, the other groups did not show much variation in the time spent with these two groups of people. With the exception of group 4 who spent relatively little time alone, all the other groups recorded almost about the same average percentage of time alone.

Table 7-5: The Percentage of the Total Working Time Spent by Each Group With Different Categories of People

Category of People	Group 1	Group 2	Group 3	Group 4	Group 5	Mean
Students	7	15	17	23	3	13
Colleagues	21	18	26	35	22	23
Administrative Staff	25	11	11	11	14	15
External	5	6	8	10	23	9
Alone	42	50	38	21	38	40
Total	100	100	100	100	100	100

The distribution which the 5 groups spent with different size numbers of people is presented in table 7-6. It shows that group 1 spent more time with one person, while group 4 spent more time with six or more people. Groups 5 and 4 spent about the same proportion of time with 2–5 groups of people.

Table 7-6: The Percentage of the Total Working Time Spent by Each Group With Different Size Numbers of People

Number of People	Group 1	Group 2	Group 3	Group 4	Group 5	Mean
1 person	31	17	24	13	16	21
2–5 people	14	13	20	28	28	18
6 or more people	13	20	18	38	18	21
Alone	42	50	38	21	38	40
Total	100	100	100	100	100	100

Table 7-7 shows that group 3 is clearly distinguished by the proportion of time which the members, on average, spent on activities of short (less than or equal to 10 minutes) and long-time (greater than or equal to 2 hours) durations. The same group clearly exhibits clear distinctive features in the average entries or the activities recorded during the week. See table 7-8 where the distribution of some measures of job fragmentation is shown.

Table 7-7: The Percentage of the Total Working Time Spent by Each Group in Different Activity Durations

Activity duration	Less than or equal to 10 minutes	Greater than or equal to 2 hours
Group 1	2	32
Group 2	1	42
Group 3	8	3
Group 4	1	35
Group 5	1	47
Mean	2	35

Table 7-8: A Comparison of the Groups of Academic Leaders on Some Measures of Job Fragmentation

Measures of Job fragmentation	Average fleeting contacts per week	Average diary entries per week
Group 1	64	51
Group 2	68	42
Group 3	41	83
Group 4	60	34
Group 5	31	39
Mean	58	47

7.6 Summary

In summary, Chapter 7 presented a meaningful grouping of academic leaders on the basis of how academic leaders spend their time. Using 24 different criteria of their job characteristics, and applying Ward's clustering method, using the procedure described in the cluster analysis package by Wishart, five distinct groups of academic leaders were formed. These were labelled Administrators Type 1, Administrators Type 2, Educational Leaders Type 1, Educational Leaders Type 2, and Research Leaders.

A description of the 5 groups of academic leaders was made, and it revealed that Administrators Type 1 spent the highest percentage of time on administration and management and with members of the administrative staff. They also worked the longest hours and recorded the highest percentage of time on deskwork. While generally exhibiting similar work characteristics to Administrators Type 1, Administrators Type 2 distinguished themselves by spending the highest percentage of total working time alone, and by recording the greatest number of fleeting contacts. In general, these characteristics are symptomatic of administrators who are strategic planners versus those who are tactical troubled shooters.

The Educational Leaders Type 1 were small group academic leaders who spent the highest percentage of time on teaching, and who interacted with students on a short-time, unscheduled basis. As interaction contacts were of very short durations, their average number of activities was higher than that of any of the other groups. Educational Leaders Type 2 spent the highest percentage of time with students and colleagues and, unlike the Educational Leaders Type 1, they spent the highest percentage of time on scheduled meetings. Educational Leaders Type 2 were most often in the other units interacting with large groups of students. Both groups of academic leaders worked for short number of hours, each recording total average working hours well below the overall average.

Group 5 were Research Leaders, and this group spent a greater percentage of time on research and consulting than any of the other groups. The Research Leaders worked very long hours, often in organizations outside their universities, and they recorded the lowest fleeting contacts.

Various detailed distributions were presented to compare the 5 groups of academic leaders.

7.7 Implications of the Groupings of Academic Leaders

Chapter Seven has shown that a meaningful classification of academic leaders is possible, notwithstanding the picture conveyed in Chapters

Five and Six that academic leaders vary widely in the practice of their jobs. Furthermore, it has demonstrated that academic leaders in both Britain and Nigeria can be grouped together and classified usefully on the basis of how they spend their time. In the resulting classification, for example, each group has at least one member from both the Nigerian and the British samples of academic leaders. Indeed, group 3 has an equal number of members of British and Nigerian academic leaders.

The cluster analysis in Chapter Seven has also shown that there is an alternative way of classifying academic leaders into intelligible group apart from the conventional classification based on position alone. Instead of using only one criterion, rank, our classification was based on 24 criteria which are various measures of the job characteristics of academic leaders, especially those based on how academic leaders spend their time.

In this regard, it is interesting to observe that in the resulting classification, the deans were not in one exclusive group, nor were the directors, nor were the heads of departments. Rather, the academic leaders were all represented in the various groups. For example, each of the five groups had, at least, a head of department and a director. The only group without a dean had a vice-chancellor. This alternative method of classifying academic leaders appears very useful, as it uses fairly comprehensive criteria of job characteristics.

Another implication of our classification is that training programmes should, perhaps, be focused on groups of academic leaders with similar work characteristics, and attendance on management development programmes should not be made a function of one's rank alone. In our classification, for example, the Administrators Type 2 may benefit from a course on delegation and human relations, while the Research Leaders may gain from a course emphasizing the importance of effective management in the determination of an organizational success. Our classification seems to suggest that effectiveness in managerial practices can be increased by tailor-made development programmes based on managers' work characteristics.

However, nothing in this research suggests that one group of our classified academic leaders was necessarily less effective than the other. We merely say that because each group exhibited different job characteristics, they would need different assistance programmes to increase their effectiveness levels. One problem of the concept of effectiveness relates to organizational goals. If university goals were only research and consulting excellence, for example, it is clear that one of our groups will tend to be more effective than the others. But in the real world of multiple goals and multiple measures, discussions on the effectiveness of groups can only be relative. It would be interesting and useful to know, however, the one of the five groups that would tend to be the most effective in relation to the overall university goals.

Lastly, one other implication of the grouping of academic leaders is that the majority (about three-fifth) of the academic leaders were classified as administrators, either strategic or tactical. [14] This further reinforces one of the conclusions made in Chapter Five that the jobs of academic leaders are administration and management, and that academic leaders' expert knowledge in their various disciplines did not becloud this fact.

In comparison to the number of academic leaders who were classified as administrators, only half were grouped as Educational Leaders, and about half of the Educational Leaders were in turn classified as Research Leaders. It follows, therefore, that academic and research competence alone may not be the best and the sole criterion for appointing academic leaders, whose jobs are in the main, administration and management. Notwithstanding the difficulty of assessment, perhaps, some measure of competence in administration and management may also be considered useful in selecting academic leaders. Alternatively, perhaps, universities should consider assisting academic leaders in performing their management and administrative jobs more effectively. This may be approached through occasional tailor-made development programmes based on the need resulting from an examination of their job characteristics.

In conclusion, it should be restated that our grouping of academic leaders was based on a sample of 38 academic leaders from Nigeria and Britain. These people filled our diaries for one week. The small sample size, and the duration of the time during which they filled the diaries are limitations to the conclusions made in this chapter. It is hoped that more senior academics could, in future, be persuaded to take part in this type of research, and filling diaries for a longer time. This would provide an opportunity to test the validity of our findings, and of our classification which was not, in any case, intended to be definitive.

Finally, the naming of the groups should not give the wrong impression away from the fact that 24 variables were actually used for the classification of the academic leaders, and that only the average data for the various groups were compared. It is possible, therefore, that a given academic leader in a group may not necessarily feature prominently on the criteria from where his group name apparently emanated.

7.8 Notes and References

[1] Both the Nigerian and the British academic leaders were combined for this classification since the academic leaders from both countries exhibited very similar job characteristics. The combination was justified as each of the resulting group has, at least, a member each from both countries. In fact, one group (group 3) has equal number of members from Nigeria and Britain. See later sections of this chapter.

[2] Everitt, B., *Cluster Analysis*, Heinemann Educational Books, London, 1974, p. 2.

[3] Ibid., Quoted from *Genera Plantarum*, first published in 1737.

[4] Everitt, B., op. cit., p. 3. See also, Lorr, M., *Cluster Analysis for Social Scientists*, Jossey-Bass Publishers, San Francisco, 1983, pp. 7–8.

[5] Ibid.; See for example, Ball, G.H., *Classification Analysis*, Stanford Research Institute, 1971, where the author lists seven possible uses of clustering techniques. These are, namely, data exploration and data reduction, hypothesis generation and hypothesis testing, prediction based on groups, finding a true typology, and model fitting.

[6] Readers interested in the details of this method should consult, Ward, J.H., Hierarchical grouping to optimise an objective function, *Journal of the American Statistical Association*, Vol. 58, 1963, pp. 236–244.

[7] Wishart, D., *Clustan User Manual*, Inter-University Research Council Series, Report No. 47, (3rd Ed.), January, 1978; and the Supplement to this Edition by the same author, April, 1982.

[8] Everitt, B., op. cit., p. 57.

[9] Friedman, H.P. and Rubin, J., On some invariant criteria for grouping data, *Journal of American Statistical Association*, Vol. 62, 1967, pp. 1159–1178.

[10] Thorndike, R.L., Who belongs in a family? *Psychometrika*, Vol. 18, 1953, pp. 267–276.

[11] Morrison, D.G., Measurement problems in cluster analysis, *Management Science*, Vol. 13, 1967, pp. 775–780.

[12] Sokal, R.R. and Sneath, P.H.A., *Principles of Numerical Taxonomy*, Freeman, London, 1963.

[13] Everitt, B., op. cit., p. 50.

[14] It is of interest to note that the Administrators Type 2 were actually more in number than the Administrators Type 1. Could this mean that in reality administrators who are tactical trouble shooters outnumber those who are strategic planners?

Chapter 8
The Perceptions of Academic Leaders

8.1 Introduction

Chapters Five and Six have examined, in detail, the job characteristics of academic leaders, while Chapter Seven has classified academic leaders into job profiles on the basis of how they spend their time. These chapters were based on the empirical results from the diary recordings. However, it is important to ascertain how academic leaders perceive their jobs. An understanding of how academic leaders perceive their jobs is useful in appraising their attitudes towards these jobs and in explaining their behaviour in their jobs.

It is also useful to ascertain academic leaders' perceptions of how they spend their time. For example, to what extent do academic leaders' estimates differ from the recorded data in respect of how they apportion their time amongst the various aspects of their jobs? This information may give us an estimate of the extent to which academic leaders know their jobs. In this chapter, therefore, we shall not only examine academic leaders' perceptions of aspects of their jobs, we shall also consider their perceptions of how they spend their time. Furthermore, since it is of value to know the differences and similarities in managerial perceptions, we shall examine and compare the perceptions of British and Nigerian academic leaders and the perceptions of academic leaders on the one hand with those of industrial managers on the other.

In order to examine whether academic leaders know how they spend their time, we compare their estimates from the questionnaire with their recordings on the diaries. It will be recalled that in order to reduce bias in the entries to both the questionnaire and the diaries, academic leaders who filled in questionnaires were not given diaries to complete. It will also be recalled that 34 and 75 academic leaders, from Britain and Nigeria respectively, completed our questionnaire. The corresponding number of those who filled in the diary (over a period of one week) in both countries were 12 and 26. See Appendix E for details on the responses to the research instruments.

We shall now discuss academic leaders' perceptions on how long they work, where they spend their working time, with whom, what they do, and how long their average activity lasts. The latter part of this chapter shall concentrate on their perceptions of the elements affecting their jobs more directly.

8.2 Academic Leaders' Perceptions of how They Spend Their Time

The questionnaire was designed to have 17 items on estimates of how academic leaders spend their time that were directly comparable to the recorded data from the diaries. The mean of each estimate was then compared with the corresponding mean of the diary recordings and a statistical test was made to show significant differences, if any. Tests were conducted for the Nigerian and the British samples separately. A summary of the results of these tests in respect of how both the British and the Nigerian academic leaders perceive that they spend their time in comparison to how they actually recorded spending their time is produced on table 8-1.

8.2.1 How Long Academic Leaders Work

It can be seen in table 8-1 that the Nigerian academic leaders, on average, estimated that they spent about 52 hours working from Monday to Friday, while they actually recorded an average of 41 working hours during this period. Similarly, the British academic leaders estimated 53 and recorded 43 working hours during the corresponding period. The differences between the means in the estimated and the recorded total time, were in both the Nigerian and the British samples, statistically significant.

However, the differences between the time reported by our questionnaire and the diary must be settled in favour of the diary. The results of the questionnaire (in respect of the allocation of time) whilst highly valuable, may only be a reflection of academic leaders' perceptions as to how they spend their time or the actual hours they would like to spend in contrast to the actual hours worked. Indeed,

Table 8-1: A Summary of the Results of the Tests of Differences Between Means in Respect of How Academic Leaders Spend Their Time

Activities	Nigerian Estimated	Recorded	T-Value	British Estimated	Recorded	T-Value
Total working hours (Monday to Friday)	51.93	41.35	5.30***	52.50	43.17	3.52**
Average activity duration in minutes	33.40	62.08	−5.73***	27.65	69.33	−4.57***
Percentage of total time spent in own office	53.17	45.04	2.44*	48.82	50.42	−0.27
Percentage of total time spent in other units	18.44	34.42	−4.91***	21.53	27.42	−1.07
Percentage of total time spent in other campuses	3.95	5.58	−0.42	1.53	2.25	−0.42
Percentage of total time spent in other organizations	9.05	7.65	0.67	13.21	10.50	0.59
Percentage of total time spent at home	15.35	11.31	1.87†	14.91	9.67	1.76†
Percentage of total time spent alone	23.25	39.27	−5.11***	28.68	40.75	−1.99†
Percentage of total time spent with students	24.97	16.04	2.86**	20.47	7.08	4.29***
Percentage of total time spent with colleagues	21.12	22.31	−0.45	22.06	25.83	−0.71
Percentage of total time spent with administrative staff	20.96	14.50	3.30**	19.88	15.42	0.93
Percentage of total time spent with external members	9.49	7.69	0.86	10.38	11.33	−0.27
Percentage of total time spent on research	21.09	22.81	−0.55	22.12	24.83	−0.50
Percentage of total time spent on administration and management	42.20	54.54	−3.17**	46.74	56.17	−1.14
Percentage of total time spent on consulting	10.20	3.38	5.05***	7.59	4.25	1.32
Percentage of total time spent on teaching	26.64	18.81	2.49*	23.32	14.75	1.84†

† = $P < 0.10$ (two-tailed) ** = $P < 0.01$ (two-tailed)
* = $P < 0.05$ (two-tailed) *** = $P < 0.001$ (two-tailed)

from the experiences gained during the pilot study, the exercise of filling the diary revealed that academic leaders (like other managers) may not know how they spend their time. [1]

It is of interest to note that in both the British and the Nigerian case, there was an over-estimation of the total working hours. See table 8-2, where the summary of the nature of the academic leaders' perceptions are provided.

Table 8-2: The Nature of the Errors Committed by the Academic Leaders in Estimates of How They Spent Their Time

Activities	Nature of errors
Total working hours (Monday to Friday) Percentage of total working time spent on teaching Percentage of total working time spent with students Percentage of total working time spent at home	Overestimation
Average activity duration Percentage of total working time spent alone	Underestimation
Percentage of total working time spent in own office Percentage of total working time spent in other units Percentage of total working time spent with administrative staff Percentage of total working time spent on consulting Percentage of total working time spent on administration and management	Inconsistency

The academic leaders were reasonably accurate on the estimate of the following activities:—
Percentage of total working time spent in other campuses,
Percentage of total working time spent in other organizations,
Percentage of total working time spent with colleagues,
Percentage of total working time spent with external members,
Percentage of total working time spent on research.

There was thus an apparent consistent tendency for academic leaders to overstate or overestimate their total working hours. However, since the hours recorded by our diaries refer to net figures, perhaps, academic leaders' estimates referred to their gross working hours (without subtracting the time for lunch and idle periods between activities). Even then, their figures would still have been slightly exaggerated. It is also of interest to note that the mean total time estimated by both the British and the Nigerian academic leaders were very close and were both in line with Cohen and March's estimates of 50–55 working hours for the American College Presidents. [2]

Although the figures are not included in table 8-1, the academic leaders were also asked to estimate the hours they spent working on Saturday and Sunday. On this, the mean estimate from the Nigerian sample was 7.48 hours and 7.26 hours for the British academic leaders. Again, these results were consistent with Cohen and March's estimates of between 5–10 working hours during the weekend which was obtained for the American College Presidents.

Of the 26 academic leaders who completed the Nigerian diaries, only 14 actually recorded working during the weekend. Similarly, of the 12 British academic leaders who completed the diaries, only 5 filled in the pages of the diaries on Saturday and Sunday. If we assume that the academic leaders who did not fill the pages of the diaries on Saturday and Sunday did not work during the weekend, the average total hours recorded during the period would have been 3.04 hours for the Nigerian academic leaders, and 1.83 hours for the British. In each case then, the differences between the estimated mean time versus the recorded time during the weekend would be statistically significant at the 99.9 percent confidence level.

If, however, we assume that the academic leaders who did not fill in the diaries over the weekend might have actually worked, but would not be bothered filling in more diaries, (i.e. treat responses from them as missing data, instead of zero as in the former case) then the average total hours spent by the British academic leaders would rise to 4.40 during the weekend, while that of the Nigerian academic leaders would also rise to 5.64 hours during the same period. Based on this assumption, the mean difference between the British academic leaders' working time during the weekend ceases to be statistically significant, while the Nigerian case continues to be significant although at a lower level of 95 percent confidence level.

8.2.2 Where Academic Leaders Spend Their Time

The diary and the questionnaire had distinguished the time spent in the own office, other units of the same campus, other campus or campuses, other organizations, and at home for comparative purposes.

As can be seen in table 8-1, there were no significant statistical differences between the estimated and the recorded time spent in the other campuses and in the other organizations by both the British and the Nigerian academic leaders. The British academic leaders also did not reveal significant differences in their estimated and recorded time in their own office and in the other units. However, the Nigerian academic leaders showed significant differences between their estimated and the recorded averages in these two locations. The tests of significance showed a higher level of difference between the estimated and the recorded time in the other units than the one obtained for the own office.

There were significant differences for the British and the Nigerian samples between the estimated and the recorded time spent at home. However, these differences were significant only at a rather low confidence level of 90 percent. While the academic leaders probably worked a little longer at home in comparison to the industrial managers, the academic leaders themselves tended to exaggerate the time they spent working at home. Significant differences at the 90 percent confidence level were included in the results of the analyses, as our study was merely an exploratory one designed to find out general trends and situations about the job characteristics and perceptions of the academic leaders, and it was not one set out to rigorously test, accept, or reject statistical hypotheses as such.

8.2.3 With Whom Do Academic Leaders Spend Their Time?

In addition to being alone, four different categories of people were identified in the research instruments with whom academic leaders could possibly work. These are students, colleagues, administrative staff, and non-members of their university system. Table 8-1 shows that there were no significant differences between the estimated and the recorded time spent either with colleagues or with non-members of the university in the Nigerian and in the British samples. While the Nigerian sample revealed significant differences in the estimated versus the recorded time spent with members of the administrative staff, the British sample did not show corresponding significant difference with that category of staff. However, both groups of academic leaders showed significant differences in the estimated compared with the recorded time spent with students and alone.

8.2.4 What Academic Leaders Do

The academic leaders were asked to estimate the percentage of their total time spent on teaching, researching, consulting, and on administration and management. A comparison of these with the corresponding recordings on the diaries showed that no significant differences existed between their estimates and the diary findings in respect to the time spent on researching. However, significant differences were obtained on teaching, consulting, and on administration and management.

Table 8-3: A Summary of The Estimated Versus the Actual Percentage Time Spent by Managers on Different Activities

Activity	Estimated Percentage	Actual Percentage	Source	Nature of Error
Production	53–55	34	Burns, 1954, 1957	Overestimation
Reading and	32	25	Hanika, 1963	
Writing	30–39	24–29	Hinrichs, 1964	
Phone calls	9	4	Dahl and Lewis, 1975	
Phone calls	9–11	6–8	Hinrichs, 1964	
Thinking and Calculating	6	2	Dahl and Lewis, 1975	
Thanking and Calculating	19	5	Hanika, 1963	
Meetings and/or Informal Discussions	47 44 16–46	69 54 22–54	Dahl and Lewis, 1975 Hanika, 1963 Hinrichs, 1964	Underestimation
"Research"	17	9	Dahl and Lewis, 1975	Inconsistency
"Research and Development"	5	16	Burns, 1957	

Source: Adapted from: McCall, Morrison, and Hannah 1978, p. 17.

Table 8-3 presents comparative data concerning the accuracy of industrial managers' estimates of how they spent their time. This shows that managers overestimated the time they spent on production, reading and writing, phone calls, and thinking and calculating, but underestimated the time they spent on meetings and or informal discussions. The results concerning the time which managers spent on research are inconsistent. Whereas Burns reported that managers underestimated the time spent on "research and development", [3] Dahl and Lewis found out that their sampled managers overestimated the time spent on "research". [4]

8.2.5 The Average Activity Duration of Academic Leaders

Table 8-1 shows that the academic leaders grossly underestimated their activity duration. Consistent underestimation to only about half of the actual activity duration were obtained in both the Nigerian and the British samples. Whereas the academic leaders estimated that their activities last, on the average, for about 30 minutes, the recordings from the diaries showed that average activity duration of about an hour might be nearer to reality.

8.3 Comments on Academics' Perceptions of How They Spend Their Time

In general, it can be seen from table 8-1 that the Nigerian academic leaders did not know how they spent their time in more than half of the cases examined. Although somewhat better estimators, the British academic leaders were also wrong in about 40 percent of the cases tested. In this, our study appears to substantiate Ritchey's, which found major discrepancies between the estimated and the measured time allocation among university faculty members. [5]

It is clear from table 8-1 that the academic leaders consistently overestimated how long they worked, and the time spent with students and on teaching. Why would academic leaders overstate the time spent on teaching and with students? One explanation is that they believe that they should spend more time with students and on teaching. Another explanation is that they believe that the society expects them to spend more time on these activities. So, in their estimates, they may unconsciously respond to these beliefs. With regards to the other errors, academic leaders may simply not know how they spend their time, since the likelihood of a deliberate bias was low. It should be observed that as in the case of the diaries, there were wide variations in the responses to the questionnaire. While academic leaders have varied working patterns, they also seem to possess different perceptions as to how they spend their time.

8.4 Industrial Managers Perceptions of How They Spend Their Time

If academic leaders do not know how they spend their time, industrial managers seem to be no better. As noted earlier in discussing what academic leaders do, some of the findings of industrial managers' perceptions of how they spend their time is reported in table 8-3. Here, Hanika's, [6] Hinrichs', [7] Burns', [8, 9] and Dahl and Lewis' [10] contributions are summarized.

In general, the available data seem to suggest that industrial managers perceive themselves as spending more time than they actually do on technical and individual activities and less time on interactions, especially informal ones. That is why McCall et al. conclude that:

> All that can be counted on is that managers make errors—sometimes quite large errors—when they try to estimate how they spend their time. [11]

8.5 Academic Leaders' Perceptions of Aspects of Their Jobs

In this section, we examine academic leaders' perceptions of their primary jobs of teaching, researching, consulting, and administration and management more closely. In doing this, we asked the academic leaders to score the activities in terms of (1) the extent to which they considered them to be their primary responsibilities, (2) the extent to which they enjoyed doing them, (3) their estimate of their competence in executing them, (4) their estimated percentage of total working time spent among them, (5) and the extent to which competence on activity affected career prospects or promotional success in the university.

The academic leaders were asked to rate the main aspects of their jobs with respect to these variables on a scale measuring from 1 (signifying low rating) to 10 (signifying high rating.) Table 8-4 presents the summary of the ratings of aspects of these jobs by both the Nigerian and the British academic leaders. It should be recalled that 75 academic leaders from Nigeria responded to the questionnaire, while 34 academic leaders similarly responded from Britain.

In the discussions which follow, we give an overview of the academic leaders' perceptions, beliefs, and attitudes on the main aspects of their jobs. We identify cultural differences where these are manifested, and we compare the job areas as well as the dimensions enumerated. It must be appreciated, however, that our discussion is necessarily interrelated and interwoven.

8.5.1 The Overall Picture of The Academic Leaders' Ratings

Tables 8-4, 8-5, 8-6, and 8-7 are provided to give a comprehensive view of the academic leaders' perceptions of the main aspects of their jobs. The tables are intended to be used together for complete information.

It can be seen from table 8-4 that the mean ratings were generally very high on research and on administration and management, high on teaching, and low on consulting. To get a fuller picture of the academic leaders views on these jobs, a ranking of the jobs in order of the perceived importance, level of enjoyment, the percentage of time spent, etc. is provided on table 8-5. It can be observed from the ranking that research was generally ranked first, consulting was consistently ranked last, while teaching and administration and management were mostly ranked in between.

8.5.2 Cultural Differences

It can be observed in table 8-5 that the rankings between the Nigerian and the British academic leaders were consistent with respect to the perceived importance of these jobs, the level of their enjoyment of the jobs, and the percentage of time spent on them. As far as estimates of their competence in performing the jobs were concerned, the Nigerian academic leaders judged that they were most competent at teaching and much less so at administration and management. The British counterparts, on the other hand, rated compe-

Table 8-4: A Summary of the Academic Leaders' Ratings of Aspects of Their Primary Jobs

	Teaching			Researching			Consulting			Admin. & Mgt.		
	Brit.	Nig'n	T-Val	Brit.	Nig'n	T-Val	Brit.	Nig'n	T-Val	Brit.	Nig'n	T-Val
The extent to which the academic leaders considered their jobs to be their primary responsibilities	7.12	7.25	0.23	8.31	8.20	−0.20	3.51	5.11	2.87**	8.29	8.15	−0.31
The extent to which the academic leaders enjoyed doing their jobs	7.62	8.58	2.20*	9.41	9.03	−1.66	5.48	6.16	1.03	5.79	6.59	1.43
The estimate of the academic leaders' competence in performing the jobs	7.39	8.57	2.75**	8.42	8.49	0.21	5.91	6.81	1.46	7.55	7.30	−0.68
The estimate of the academic leaders' percentage of total working time spent among the jobs	23.32	26.64	1.03	22.12	21.09	−0.40	7.59	10.20	1.72	46.74	42.20	−1.09
The extent to which competence on activity affected career prospects or promotional success in the university	4.79	6.22	2.51*	8.99	8.64	0.89	2.64	3.78	2.36*	6.38	5.43	−1.82

* = $P < 0.05$ (two tailed) ** = $P < 0.01$ (two tailed)

Table 8-5: A summary of the Rankings of the Ratings of Aspects of the Academic Leaders' Primary Jobs

The extent to which the academic leaders considered the jobs to be their primary responsibilities		The extent to which the academic leaders enjoyed doing the jobs		The estimate of the academic leaders' competence in performing the jobs		The estimate of the academic leaders' percentage of total working time spent among the jobs		The extent to which competence on activity affected career prospects or promotional success in the university	
Nigeria	Britain	Nigeria	Britain	Nigeria	Britain	Nigeria	Britain	Nigeria	Britain
Research	Research	Research	Research	Teaching	Research	Admin. & Mgt.	Admin. & Mgt.	Research	Research
Admin. & Mgt.	Admin. & Mgt.	Teaching	Teaching	Research	Admin. & Mgt.	Teaching	Teaching	Teaching	Admin. & Mgt.
Teaching	Teaching	Admin. & Mgt.	Admin. & Mgt.	Admin. & Mgt.	Teaching	Research	Research	Admin. & Mgt.	Teaching
Consulting	Consulting	Consulting	Consulting	Consulting	Consulting	Consulting	Consulting	Consulting	Consulting

tence at research first, followed by administration and management, and only then teaching.

The two groups of academic leaders also differed slighly in their ranking of the extent to which competence at an activity affected career prospects or promotional success. While they both agreed that research affected their promotional success most, they were not agreed on what came next, teaching or administration and management. The Nigerian academic leaders said it was teaching, while the British academic leaders seem to believe that it was competence on administration and management. It is of interest to note that consulting was consistently rated the least in all the five considerations by both the Nigerian and the British academic leaders. Consulting was, accordingly, ranked the lowest on table 8-5. The interpretation of this is obvious.

Another interesting finding is revealed on table 8-5 in terms of the relationship between administration and management and research. Whereas the academic leaders spent the highest percentage of time on administration and management, the rankings of the other activities suggest that research contributed more to the academic leaders' career prospects, that they enjoyed research more, and that they regarded research more as their primary responsibility. Additionally, and rather ironically, the rankings also indicate that the Nigerian academic leaders believed they were more competent in the areas of teaching and research than administration and management, while their British counterparts believed themselves to be more competent at research as compared to administration and management.

However, since inferences made from the rankings alone may be deceptive, other tables are provided for more detailed examinations. For example, table 8-4 shows not only the absolute ratings, but also significant differences (where these occur) between the Nigerian and the British academic leaders' ratings on each of the primary jobs of teaching, consulting, researching, and administration and management. Similarly, table 8-6 presents a summary of the tests of differences between the academic leaders' ratings of aspects of their primary jobs.

8.5.3 Comparison by Job Area

In table 8-6, it can be seen that when the British and the Nigerian academic leaders' ratings of research versus administration and

Table 8-6: A Summary of the Results of the Tests of Differences Between the Academic Leaders' Ratings of Aspects of Their Primary Jobs

Jobs	The extent to which the academic leaders considered the jobs to be their primary responsibility		The extent to which the academic leaders enjoyed doing the jobs		The estimate of the academic leaders' competence in performing the jobs		The estimate of the academic leaders' percentage of total working time spent among the jobs		The extent to which competence on activity affected career prospects or promotional success in the university	
	Nigeria	Britain	Nigeria	Britain	Nigeria	Britain	Nigeria	Britain	Nigeria	Britain
Teaching & Research	−3.41***	−2.98**	−2.26*	−4.70***	0.41	−2.82**	2.31*	0.37	−9.72***	−6.90***
Teaching & Consulting	5.31***	5.99***	6.73***	2.69**	6.16***	2.34*	8.73***	4.84***	7.36***	2.80**
Teaching & Admin. & Mgt.	−2.22*	−1.72	5.82***	3.09**	5.01***	−0.40	−4.44***	−3.96***	2.36*	−2.68*
Research & Consulting	8.75***	9.14***	8.31***	6.60***	5.44***	4.08***	6.30***	6.05***	17.10***	9.57***
Research & Admin. & Mgt.	0.16	0.00	7.76***	6.53***	4.22***	2.89**	−6.31***	−4.81***	11.32***	3.40**
Consulting & Admin. & Mgt.	−9.22***	−7.42***	−1.13	−0.21	−1.90	−2.55*	−12.46***	−9.59***	−6.08***	−6.93***

* $P < 0.05$ (two tailed)
** $P < 0.01$ (two tailed)
*** $P < 0.001$ (two tailed)
N.B. All the figures in this table are the t-values of the resulting tests of differences

management were tested, significant differences between the ratings of the two jobs were obtained on all the scales by both groups of academic leaders with the exception of the extent to which they considered these aspects of their jobs to be their primary responsibility. This (when interpreted in conjunction with table 8-4) means that both the British and the Nigerian academic leaders rated research significantly higher than administration and management in terms of the extent to which they enjoyed doing the jobs, the extent to which they believed that they were competent for the jobs, and the degree to which they believed competence for the jobs affected their career prospects. This is notwithstanding the fact that the academic leaders spent a significantly greater percentage of their total time on administration and management than research. The two groups of academic leaders rated the two jobs of research and administration and management more or less equally in terms of the extent to which they considered them as their primary responsibilities. This is to say that the slightly higher ratings on research were not statistically significantly different from the ratings on administration and management in terms of the extent to which they considered the jobs to be their primary responsibilities. This finding is very useful in complementing the views held from the analyses of the rankings which were discussed earlier.

It is important to observe the non-significant differences in the level of enjoyment which both groups of academic leaders reported on the differences between consulting versus administration and management. This means that the academic leaders did not enjoy doing administration and management significantly more than they enjoyed consultancy. The import of this finding will be appreciated more when it is remembered that the academic leaders consistently rated consulting lowest on all the scales, and on all the aspects of the jobs.

Furthermore, as can be observed in table 8-4, there were no significant differences of opinion between the Nigerian and the British academic leaders' ratings of research and of administration and management (considered individually) on each of the five earlier stated scales used for the scoring. This result gives confidence to the consistency of the academic leaders' estimates on these two jobs and suggests that both groups of academic leaders do not differ significantly in their estimates regarding the importance or non-importance of these two functions considered individually.

With respect to teaching, however, there were significant differences of opinion between the Nigerian and the British academic leaders' estimates with respect to their level of enjoyment, their competence in execution, and the extent to which competence in job affected their promotional success. On each of these three considerations, the Nigerian academic leaders rated teaching significantly higher than the British. This signifies that the Nigerian academic leaders enjoyed teaching more, believed themselves to be relatively more competent at it, and believed that it affected their career success more than did the British academic leaders.

There were also two significant differences of opinions on the consulting function. The ratings on table 8-4 suggest that the Nigerian academic leaders claimed that consulting was more of their primary job than the British academic leaders accepted. Perhaps, this revelation was in response to the current very low university funding in Nigeria where the government has directed each university to be revenue earning through consultancy services. Surprisingly, perhaps, there was also a significant difference of estimates on the extent to which consulting affected career prospects, the Nigerian academic leaders again suggesting that competence on consulting affected their promotional prospects more than that of the British academic leaders. Possibly, this is in relation to the current importance attached to success in consulting referred to earlier. Some academic leaders now fear the possibility of redundancies, and some of the potential groups most affected have, not surprisingly, started warning on the dangers of commercialising education!

Lastly, table 8-4 also reveals that the British and the Nigerian academic leaders estimated that they apportioned their time among the four main aspects of their jobs in about the same ratio. However, the two groups differed significantly on each of the other four scales with respect to at least one of the four major job responsibilities.

In summary, the comparison of the academic leaders' perceptions of the main aspects of the jobs (which can be obtained from table 8-4) revealed that (1) the British academic leaders regarded consultancy to be of lower priority than the Nigerian, (2) the Nigerian academic leaders enjoyed teaching more and thought themselves more competent at it than the British, and (3)the Nigerian academic leaders thought competence at teaching and consultancy affected their career prospects more than did the British.

8.5.4 Comparison Between Jobs

In this section, the estimates on two of the primary jobs of teaching, researching, consulting, and administration and management were compared in turn in both the Nigerian and in the British samples (separately) to show significant differences in their ratings, if any. The results of these are, as we already know, summarized on table 8-6. It can be observed on this table that there were significant differences between the ratings of consultancy and teaching and between consultancy and research, on all the five scales. It can also be seen in table 8-6 that the extent to which competence in a job affected career progress was rated significantly differently on all possible combinations of the four major jobs. [12] Of interest also was the consistent ratings by both groups of academic leaders on the extent to which they enjoyed doing all the combinations of their four main jobs.

There is a simple way to interpret table 8-6. For example, consider any 2 of the primary jobs, say, teaching and research (row 1), in any of the 5 scales, say the extent to which they affected the academic leaders' promotional success (the last 2 columns). The three stars below the Nigerian and the British academic leaders' columns (the last 2 columns on row 1) signifies that both the Nigerian and the British academic leaders rated one of the two jobs, teaching or research, significantly different than the other—at the 99.9 percent confidence level. From table 8-4, it would be found that research was actually rated higher than teaching. It is therefore important to use table 8-4 in conjunction with table 8-5, table 8-6, or table 8-7 for a complete interpretation of the latter tables.

It is of interest to note once again that research versus administration and management was rated consistently high by both the Nigerian and the British academic leaders on all the five scales. While the academic leaders rated research and administration and management about the same in the extent to which they considered them as their primary responsibilities, they rated research significantly higher than administration and management in terms of the levels of enjoyment, competence on execution, and the extent to which they believed the jobs affected their promotional success. However, the academic leaders spent significantly more time on administration and management than on research—a conclusion which was arrived at previously.

In general, there were consistent ratings between the Nigerian and the British academic leaders. The vast majority of the combinations of these four primary jobs were also rated significantly different, as can be seen in table 8-6. This is consistent with our earlier finding that research and administration and management were generally rated very high, (research rated generally higher than administration and management) teaching high, and consulting low, and it further confirms the general interpretation made from the rankings of these jobs.

8.5.5 Comparison by Dimension

From the pattern of the results discussed so far, it seems useful to find out the relationships, if any, between the academic leaders' responses to the five questions posed. This was done, and the results of the chi-square tests are presented in table 8-7, where it can be seen that except for administration and management, there was a very strong association between the academic leaders' enjoyment of their primary jobs and their competence for those jobs. Perhaps they enjoyed the jobs because they were competent for them. On administration and management, however, the level of their enjoyment was below the level of their stated competent in performing the jobs, and no association between the two existed.

The other relationships were not very clear. Apparently there was none between the allocation of the academic leaders' time on an activity and either their level of enjoyment of it or their estimated competence on the job. This finding is not surprising because, while the academic leaders spent most time on administration and management, for example, they agreed that they enjoyed research more.

Weak relationships were observed between what the academic leaders considered as their primary jobs and their level of enjoyment of these. There was also a weak relationship between the time spent on a job versus the expected benefit (career progress) from the job. It must be admitted though that the findings on most of the relationships were not consistently reassuring in both the British and the Nigerian samples—an indication of the wide and varied perceptions with which the academic leaders viewed the jobs in relation to the considerations enumerated.

Table 8-7: A Summary of the Results of the Chi-Square Tests to Show the Association Between the Variables Considered

	Teaching Nigeria		Britain		Researching Nigeria		Britain		Consulting Nigeria		Britain		Admin. & Mgt. Nigeria		Britain	
	X^2	d.f. Prob.	X^2	d.f. Prob.	X^2	d.f. Prob.	X^2	d.f. Prob.	X^2	d.f. Prob.	X^2	d.f. Prob.	X^2	d.f. Prob.	X^2	d.f. Prob.
Perceived job importance versus Level of enjoyment	106.92	54***	79.32	64 NS	45.41	35 NS	58.96	28***	117.13	81**	66.58	54 NS	89.97	63*	81.98	63 NS
Perceived job importance versus Estimated competence in job	69.65	45*	84.89	72 NS	42.89	36 NS	40.67	28 NS	88.76	81 NS	46.93	48 NS	51.63	56 NS	72.66	49*
Perceived job importance versus % time spent on job	211.79	117***	118.39	104 NS	55.03	77 NS	82.11	77 NS	64.98	63 NS	44.39	30*	132.77	98**	58.77	84 NS
Perceived job important versus Expected benefit	98.09	81 NS	51.63	56 NS	40.65	49 NS	62.95	42*	69.23	64 NS	86.31	42***	83.81	63*	64.60	63 NS
Level of enjoyment versus Estimated competence in job	68.46	30***	131.60	72***	66.71	30***	38.29	16**	143.36	81***	109.92	72**	84.50	72 NS	63.33	63 NS
Level of enjoyment versus % of time spent on job	65.71	78 NS	97.21	104 NS	48.24	55 NS	40.90	44 NS	77.50	63 NS	76.25	45**	116.27	126 NS	118.38	108 NS
Level of enjoyment versus Expected benefit	78.39	54*	59.49	56 NS	45.80	35 NS	16.74	24 NS	69.96	72 NS	58.78	63 NS	90.04	81 NS	124.44	81***
Estimated competence in job versus % of time spent on job	55.23	65 NS	120.28	117 NS	48.46	66 NS	39.40	40 NS	64.96	63 NS	57.24	40*	135.44	112 NS	74.86	84 NS
Estimated competence in job versus Expected benefit	60.84	45 NS	63.60	63 NS	72.36	42**	14.08	20 NS	54.44	72 NS	44.33	48 NS	92.39	72 NS	66.80	63 NS
% of time spent on job versus Expected benefit	146.81	117*	88.33	91 NS	63.38	77 NS	114.42	66***	75.34	56*	40.32	35 NS	183.42	126**	125.82	108 NS

* = $P < 0.05$ ** = $P < 0.01$ *** = $P < 0.001$ NS = Not significant

8.6 Summary

The first part of this chapter discussed academic leaders' perceptions of how they spend their time. The basis for this discussion was a comparison of the academic leaders' estimates of how they apportioned their time which were made on the questionnaire with the empirical findings on their time allocation obtained from the diary.

It was revealed that both the Nigerian and the British academic leaders consistently overestimated their total working hours from Monday to Friday. They also overstated the time they spent working on Saturday and Sunday if we assume that the academic leaders who did not fill in the diaries on these days did not work during the weekend.

It was further revealed that the academic leaders tended to exaggerate the time they spent working at home, and that the Nigerian academic leaders estimated spending significantly more time in the office and in the other units than was recorded in the diary study. Apart from these, no other significant differences between estimated and recorded time were observed in the locations of where the academic leaders worked. Our analyses showed that the academic leaders tended to understate the time they spent alone and definitely overstated the time spent with students. However, their estimates were reasonably close on the time spent with colleagues and the non-members of their respective universities.

Concerning the question on what the academic leaders spent their time, it was found that they estimated almost correctly the time spent on research. However, they exaggerated the percentage of time spent on teaching. Finally, the academic leaders grossly underestimated their average activity duration to a figure of only about half of the recorded data. Table 8-2 was presented to summarize the nature of the academic leaders' errors on how they spent their time. Some explanations were given for possible reasons for these errors.

The discussion which followed on the industrial managers' perceptions of how they spend their time showed that most managers, whether academic or industrial, are poor estimators of how they spend their time. In order words, managers do not know how they spend their time, and perhaps they tend to respond to conscious or unconscious rationalizations in their estimates of how they spend their time.

The second part of the chapter examines, in detail, academic leaders' perceptions of their primary jobs of administration and management, teaching, researching, and consulting. The examination was made from five basic considerations which the academic leaders rated on a scale measuring from 1 (signifying low rating) to 10 (signifying high rating). These considerations were: (1) the extent to which the academic leaders considered the jobs to be their primary responsibilities, (2) the extent to which they enjoyed doing them, (3) their estimate of their competence in executing them, (4) their estimated percentage of total working time spent among them, and (5) the extent to which competence for the activity affected career prospects or promotional success.

By simply ranking the academic leaders' ratings of the main aspects of their jobs, an interesting relationship between the academic leaders' jobs of research and administration and management was revealed. Whereas the academic leaders spent most of their working time on administration and management, they appeared to enjoy research more, felt that they were more competent at it, and agreed that it contributed more to their career prospects. This conclusion was supported by other more detailed analyses, including tests of significant differences between ratings and chi-square tests showing relationships between the variables considered. All the possible combinations of the four jobs and the five considerations were also made to reveal, indeed, a very comprehensive treatment of the academic leaders' perceptions of their jobs.

In general, the academic leaders appeared to be more committed to success at research than effectiveness in administration and management. This is to say that the role and importance of research seem to continue to predominate academic leaders' minds notwithstanding the fact that their jobs were, or at least were supposed to be, administration and management. In general also, the consulting function was, not surprising perhaps, rated the lowest of all the jobs and considerations. Differences and similarities between the Nigerian and the British academic leaders' ratings were, as much as possible, highlighted, while different tables were provided to show the detailed findings on this important and complex subject of the academic leaders' perceptions of their jobs.

8.7 Implications of the Perceptions of Academic Leaders

There are important implications of academic leaders' perceptions of their jobs and of academic leaders' perceptions of how they spend their time. For example, this chapter has shown that one cannot rely much on managers' estimates of how they spend their time. This is true of academic or industrial managers, as all managers tend to make errors in estimates of how they spend their time.

This revelation has a more serious implication on the methodology employed when designing researches to study managerial jobs. It reveals the weaknesses of the questionnaire methodology, as managers' estimates may be wrong, and the researcher may not know the nature and the extent of the error involved. The diary provides a more direct approach to studying managerial jobs, and it should be much less susceptible to deliberate structuring than the questionnaire approach.

In essence, this chapter has demonstrated the inadequacy of the questionnaire methodology when used alone to study the job activities of managers. It provides a strong support for the use of a multiple methodology that combines direct and indirect measures. In such a research design, the questionnaire would still be useful both as a supplement and a complement to the diary. In our study, for example, the questionnaire complements the diary findings on the fact that the academic leaders spent most of their time on administration and management. It also supplements the diary findings, for example, on the academic leaders' perceptions of the relative importance of research versus administration and management to them. These give greater depth and breath of knowledge of the academic leaders' jobs.

One other implication of this chapter is that the Nigerian and the British academic leaders did not only have similar job characteristics, but also showed similar perceptions of their jobs and of their time allocation. These findings in turn strengthen the notion of the similarity of the academic culture.

Finally, this chapter has serious implications for the selection, training, and development of academic leaders, topics that will be considered in greater detail in Chapter 9. The findings in the present chapter suggest that for greater effectiveness, only professors who enjoy administration and management should be selected as academic leaders and not, as one of the respondents put it, those who "accept administration as a cost to be borne as part of holding chairs". The selection of those who would regard administration and management as their primary job should also be sought in appointing academic leaders. The latter people would tend to be more committed to the job of effectively administering and managing their universities. Furthermore, only academics who demonstrates fair competence on administration and management (with successful administrative experience to back this up) should be made academic leaders. Alternatively, academics who are appointed leaders should not only accept that management skills can be learnt, but be willing to improve on their management skills through training and exposure at management development programmes.

On the nature of training, our analyses show clearly that while the demands of the academic leaders' job are in administration and management, the preferences of most of the academic leaders and or their abilities seem to be on research. The most appropriate training would therefore be one that is designed to assist academic leaders to improve on their management and administrative skills.

Lastly, some measure of managerial success, however crude, should be devised to assess the promotion of academic leaders to higher managerial levels. For example, a head of department who cannot manage his department well should not be a candidate for consideration as a dean. A corollary of the above suggestions is that only academics who are already very successful (preferably professors) should be appointed academic leaders—so that the distraction of the effort on research may be lessened. Implementing this suggestion may be more of a problem in Nigeria (where many academic leaders are yet to attain professorship) than in Britain. Another corollary is that "political factors" should as much as possible be replaced in favour of demonstrated merit in selecting academic leaders. Only academic leaders who are competent on administration and management and who enjoy the job should be selected to head universities. In this way, universities would tend to face squarely the challenges confronting them.

8.8 Notes and References

[1] Oshagbemi, T.A., The Job Characteristics of Academic Leaders: A Pilot Study, *Management Research News*, Vol. 7, No. 2, 1984, p. 22.

[2] Cohen, M.D. and March, J.G., *Leadership and Ambiguity: The American College President*, McGraw-Hill Book Company, New York, 1974, p. 126.

[3] Burns, T., Management in Action, *Operational Research Quarterly*, Vol. 8, No. 2, June 1957, pp. 45–60.

[4] Dahl, T. and Lewis, D.R., Random Sampling Device Used in Time Management Study, *Evaluation*, Vol. 2(2), 1975, pp. 20–22.

[5] Ritchey, J.A., Activity Patterns of an Engineering Faculty. *Unpublished Ph.D. Thesis*, University of Chicago, 1958, reported in: Hinrichs, J.R., Communications Activity of Industrial Research Personnel, *Personnel Psychology*, Vol. 17, 1964, p. 203.

[6] Hanika, F. deP., How to study your executive day, in: Copeman et al., *How the executive spends his time*, Business Publications Limited, London, 1963, pp. 85–90; see in particular, Table A on page 88.

[7] Hinrichs, J.R., op. cit.; see in particular, Table 3 on page 200.

[8] Burns, T., The directions of activity and communication in a departmental executive group, *Human Relations*, Vol. 7(1), 1954, pp. 73–97; see in particular, Table 3 on page 80.

[9] Burns, T., (1957) op. cit.; see in particular, Table II on page 51.

[10] Dahl, T. and Lewis, D.R. op. cit.

[11] McCall, M.W., Morrison, M.A., and Hannan, R.L., Studies of Managerial Work: Results and Methods, *Center for Creative Leadership*, Technical Report No. 9, North Carolina, 27402, May 1978, p. 18.

[12] Please, note that table 8-4 already has the absolute mean ratings of all the jobs on all the scales by both the British and the Nigerian academic leaders. The tables provided in this section are complementary, and should be used together for complete interpretation.

Chapter 9
The Selection, Training, and Management Development of Academic Leaders

9.1 Introduction

The focus of this book has been on the group referred to as the academic leaders. The intention has been to see the ways in which these principal actors in university administration could contribute towards a more effective academic management.

So far, we have examined in detail their work characteristics based on how they spend their time. We have not only outlined the jobs of academic leaders, we have also discussed the academic leaders' perceptions of and attitudes towards these jobs. In addition, academic leaders have been classified into job profiles based on their job characteristics. All along, the implications of the research for improved academic management have continually been highlighted.

One important dimension of the academic leaders' job remaining to be discussed relates to the issues of the selection, training, and management development for academic leaders. A consideration of these issues is important because they affect academic leadership and management practices more directly.

In this chapter, therefore, we now turn to a further consideration of these elements. Specifically, we seek to know whether the selection processes of academic leaders can be improved, and ask for the training programmes that can usefully be introduced or the managerial skills that can beneficially be developed among academic leaders. As was explained in Chapter One, the objective of all these is to contribute towards a greater awareness and a better understanding of the activities and perceptions of academic leaders and to identify the implications of these for effective university administration and management.

But what are the university goals which academic leaders pursue and which by implication are used as partial if not whole measures for academic leaders' effectiveness? What particular problems or constraints hamper the realization of these goals? What are the difficulties which academic leaders encounter in the course of carrying out their responsibilities? As a prelude to the main issues of this chapter, we shall discuss the answers to these questions of relevance to academic leadership and management practices.

9.2 What Are Universities For?

The question of what university goals are has been a subject of discourse since over a century. For example, Cardinal Newman published his book, "The idea of a university," as early as in 1852. [1] Yet, a review of the current opinions on university purpose still shows that the literature is replete with opposing views and controversies. In a speech delivered in 1972, Lord Annan still asked the basic question: "What are universities for, anyway?" [2] Surprisingly, perhaps, there are various answers to this supposedly simple question, and an interesting debate of the university purpose now exists. A summary of the major approaches to answering this question was presented in the form of models by Lynch. [3]

9.2.1 Models of University Purpose

There appears to be four popular models of the university purpose. These are the teaching, vocational, research, and the societal models.

9.2.1.1 The Teaching Model

This school of thought sees the university as an institution for the dissemination of knowledge. Newman, a powerful advocate of this point of view, associates research with some seclusion and argues that if the university goal were research, he could not "see why a university should have students". [4] In his book, Newman argues that:

> The common sense of mankind has associated the search after truth with seclusion and quiet. The greatest thinkers have been too intent on their subject to admit of interruptions. They have been men of absent minds and idiosyncratic habits, and have more or less shuned the lecture room and the public school. Pythagoras, the light of Magna Greetia, lived for a time in a

cave. Thales, the light of Ionia, lived unmarried and in private, and refused the invitations of princes. Plato withdrew from Athens to the groves of Academus. Aristotle gave twenty years to a studious discipleship under him. Friar Bacon lived in his tower upon the Isis. Newton indulged in an intense severity of meditation which almost shook his reason. The great discoveries in Chemistry and Electricity were not made in universities. [4b]

The author continued his exposition that:

Observations are more frequently out of universities than in them, and even when within their bounds need have no moral connexion with them. Porson had no classes. Elmsley lived in a good part of his life in the country. I do not say that there are no great examples the other way, perhaps Socrates, certainly Lord Bacon; still, I think it must be allowed on the whole that while teaching involves external engagements, the natural home for experiment and speculation is retirement. [4c]

Thus, in his numerous publications, Cardinal Newman expressed the view most forcibly that a university is "a place of teaching universal knowledge" and that its object is "the diffusion and extension of knowledge" rather than its "advancement". [4d]

9.2.1.2 The Vocational Model

This approach to university purpose sees the university as more or less a manpower training centre for various vocations. The vocational model sees the university as the supplier of competent and skilled labour in a particular field of need and relevance to the nation. In this function, the university would merely be fulfilling its role in the society's division of labour. This point of view is strongly held in many developing countries who see education as a vehicle for their "economic takeoff". For example, Ishaya Audu argues that universities should use education positively for development and welfare purposes. [5] Roger Ascham, a proponent of this model, articulated this view when he said that universities should be established "so that the realm may be served with preachers, lawyers and physicians". [6]

9.2.1.3 The Research Model

The research approach to university purpose is, perhaps, the most popular one. One of its proponents, Abraham Flexner, advocates that universities should be research orientated. [7] Writing about 60 years after Cardinal Newman, Flexner was convinced that universities should concern themselves "whole-heartedly and unreservedly" with the advancement of knowledge. [7b] It is arguable that if universities fail in their research propagation function, to that extent will they also be deficient in their other functions of the dissemination and the application of knowledge. Ishaya Audu also represented this school of thought when he said: "research is the lifeblood of a university and the university cannot be an excellent teaching institution without it". [8] In the same vein, Truscot observes: "a university is a corporation or society which devotes itself to a search after knowledge for the sake of its intrinsic value". [9]

The research model apparently has many followers and these people see students and teaching, as Lynch puts it, as "necessary evils". [10] It thus would be observed that the research model is diametrically opposed to the teaching model.

9.2.1.4 The Societal Model

Whereas research may be carried out for its intrinsic values (and some researches are carried out for the benefit of mankind in general) and while an assembly of students may come from different countries, the societal model of university purpose sees the role of a university in terms of serving a particular society. This model opposes the "ivory tower" concept of univeriities, i.e. of universities being isolated from the society, and advocates that for relevance of functions, universities must involve themselves in the aims and aspirations of their immediate societies. Searle summarises this approach in his view of the university purpose which is: "to benefit the community which created and maintains it". [11] In essence, this means that the objectives of universities are supposed to reflect the objectives of the immediate society of which they are a part. In this regard, the Robbins Report (in Britain) tacitly accepted that the Universities role is not simply of an inward nature, but that "universities and colleges have an important role to play in the general cultural life of the communities in which they are situated." [11b]

9.2.2 A Unifying Model of University Purpose

It would be easily observed that in the preceding discussion, knowledge is the marketable commodity in the universities. While the research model emphasizes propagating it, the teaching model stresses its dissemination, and the vocational and societal models argue that universities should apply knowledge in a particular society or in a particular desired area.

Furthermore, there is the complementary nature of the above four models. For example, some researchers are stimulated by teaching intelligent students who ask probing questions, some of which could provide basis of research studies. Researchers, in turn, may bring new and current ideas to improve the quality of their teaching, and they may pass first-hand research experiences over to their students. There is thus, for example, a symbiotic relationship between teaching and research. Similarly, the application of knowledge is the test ground of the utility of research. A research study is useful when it can be applied beneficially.

Thus recognising that the advocates of each of the above models were wrong in taking a partial view of the university purpose, we here support the *pluralistic model* of the university goal. Essentially, the pluralistic model argues that universities are multi-purpose organizations and that they are legitimate centres for the simultaneous pursuit of each of the above goals of teaching, research, manpower development, and services to a given society. Kerr has pointed out, for example, that in contrast to situations in the medieval period, modern universities now harbour several communities with often divergent interests. [12]

A pragmatic concept such as the *pluralistic model* of the university goal appears to have the advantages of accommodating other points of view. As such, it is flexible and comprehensive. A university may pursue each and all of the stated major goals. What a university emphasizes at a particular point in time may be a result of the prevailing circumstances.

It should be mentioned, in conclusion, that another comprehensive model was proposed by Lynch. [13] Developing the views of Fielden and Lockwood, [14] Lynch's unifying model suggests that a university may be considered from three separate but interrelated perspectives—the university as an organization, as an institution, and as a community. [15] However, the pluralistic model would appear more appropriate in discussing the university purpose as it focuses on the goals.

9.2.3 The Goals of Complex Organizations

Establishing the goals of an organization such as the university may often present a difficult task. [16] This is notwithstanding the fact that all organizations have formal, explicitly written goals at their incorporation or inception. The problem is that some of these legal or formal goals may be stated in very general terms. [17] Worse still, they may bear no relationship to the activities which the organizations pursue, i.e. actual or real goals may be different from formal or legal goals. To compound the confusion, what organizational members profess the goals of their organization to be may present yet a variation from both the formal and the real goals.

Formal goals are matters for the record. Real goals may be gathered from an examination of an organization's records of activities, and the allocation of resources, (including human beings) the suggestion being that real goals are regarded as those activities which an organization spends most of its resources in pursuing. [18] Perceived or stated goals can be gathered from the organization members, especially the organization's principal officers.

The formal goals of each university are written in the particular law establishing the university. Their actual goals can be obtained from an examination of their record of activities and the pattern of the deployment of their resources. While actual goals may differ widely from one university to the other, formal goals are not likely to differ as much.

9.2.4 Empirical Verification of University Goals

In a limited attempt to ascertain the perceived goals of universities, we obtained the views of over one hundred academic leaders in Nigeria and Britain concerning what they regarded as the university goals. Their answers, summarised in table 9-1 below, shows that academic leaders regard the university as a multi-purpose organization.

We identified research excellence, teaching excellence, services to the community (societal model), and competence and skill in a particular field (vocational model) as possible goals, and we requested the academic leaders to rate the importance attached to each of these goals by the university. The rating was on a scale measuring from 1

Table 9-1: Academic Leaders' Mean Ratings of Some University Goals

Goals	British	Nigerian
Research excellence	9.91	9.47
Teaching excellence	8.57	8.83
Services to the community (Societal Model)	6.62	7.69
Competence and skill in a particular field (Vocational model)	7.63	8.07
Sample size	34	75

Note: The scale used for the rating in this table and in the subsequent tables in this chapter was measured from 1 (signifying low rating) to 10 (signifying high rating).

(signifying low rating) to 10 (signifying high rating). The academic leaders responses (in table 9-1) ranked in the order of importance show that research was rated consistently as the most important university goal by both the Nigerian and the British academic leaders. This was followed by teaching, vocational, and societal goals, in that order. However, research was emphasized relatively more by the British academic leaders, while the Nigerian academic leaders seem to emphasize the importance of teaching relatively more.

In both cases, the academic leaders rated services to the community, societal goal, the least in the enumerated possible goals of the university. In part, this may be a result of the fact that this goal does not appear to be particularly focused. Nonetheless, the ratings on each of the goals were high enough to reflect the multi-faceted nature of academic institutions.

In summary then, universities appear to be centres of higher learning established generally for the propagation, dissemination, and the application of knowledge. In the multiple and complementary goals being pursued by the universities, research appears to occupy a place of pride being generally regarded as the "lifeblood" of the university. For example, the emphasis on research is well reflected in the promotion system of the academics. And that is why, as it will be recalled from the discussions of the previous chapter, the academic leaders rated research a little bit higher than even administration and management as their primary responsibility.

9.3 Problems of University Administration and Management

Having identified the major university goals, we now consider the problems and constraints to the realization of these goals. Chapter Two has already detailed the peculiar problems facing universities in Nigeria. That presentation was essentially a macro view of the problems facing the universities, although a discussion of some micro elements was also made.

In this section, we emphasise the management problems affecting the effectiveness of academic leaders in the execution of their jobs. In the latter part of this section, we also identify the important academic leaders' job elements on which the academic leaders experience their problems. First, we asked the academic leaders to rate some problems which affect the smooth running of their functions on a scale measuring from 1 to 10. The responses from the academic leaders are presented in table 9-2 where it can be seen that the three most highly rated management problems are dwindling resources, excessive work, and academic shortages.

Table 9-2: Academic Leaders' Mean Ratings of the Serious Management Problems Facing Them

Nature of problem	British	Nigerian
Communication problems	4.49	3.91
Excessive work (lack of time)	7.94	8.12
Colleagues do not cooperate	2.82	3.62
Subordinates are not effective	2.91	5.74
Students are troublesome	1.49	3.65
Dwindling resources	7.67	8.57
Academic staff shortages	6.06	7.80
Sample size	34	75

9.3.1 Academic Shortages

It can be seen from table 9-2 that both groups of academic leaders rated the problem of academic shortages third in rank as one of their most important management problems. In the British case, perhaps this problem of academic shortages is related to the problem of dwindling resources. That is, the universities do not have money to fill academic vacancies although qualified British academics could be recruited. In the Nigerian case, however, the problem of academic shortages may be more pronounced. Even with the availability of money, for instance, qualified staff, at least the Nigerian staff, would still be scarce, especially in the higher academic echelon.

This point was borne out in the analysis of the nationality of the academic leaders who responded to our questionnaire. Whereas virtually all the responding academic leaders in Britain were British, only 65 percent of the responding Nigerian academic leaders from Nigeria were Nigerians. The remaining 35 percent were made up of other nationalities. These were academics from other African countries (12%), Europeans (9%), Asians (8%), Americans (4%), and one Canadian (1%). [19]

9.3.2 Dwindling Resources

Another serious problem in both the British and the Nigerian universities is the one of dwindling resources. While universities in both countries have proliferated until recently, government subventions continue to decrease in both countries. It is in fact no wonder that the Nigerian academic leaders rated it as the most important management problem. The implications of financial shortages are evidenced everywhere—e.g., in the library stock, equipment acquisition or replacement, and in the allocation of money for research purposes.

In Britain, some university libraries complain that unless their allocations are increased, they may no longer be able to subscribe to some new journals. Foreign students now pay the full cost of tuition in British universities, while the fees for foreign as well as home students continue to increase. Because of financial shortages, some academic vacancies cannot be filled, resulting in the next management problem of excessive work for the academic staff.

9.3.3 Excessive Work

Excessive work as a management problem is perhaps a general one for all managers, whether academic or industrial. That managers generally have a lot of work to do is no news. Academic leaders in particular may have a lot of research commitments in addition to their administrative and management activities.

However, the incidence of excessive work may be related to how each academic leader manages his or her time. In this regard, the elements of effective delegation, conducting meetings, etc. may be issues of relevance in the academic leaders' management of his or her time. As we found in Chapter Seven, for example, some academic leaders appeared to delegate very little. Yet, effective delegation is one of the hallmarks of a good manager. As we also found in Chapter Eight, many academic leaders do not even know how they spend their time. How can such people be expected to manage the use of their time effectively?

9.3.4 Other Management Problems

Other management problems which the academic leaders rated as inhibiting the effective operation of their jobs include communication difficulties, lack of cooperation by colleagues, the ineffectiveness of subordinates, and the troublesome nature of students. However, judging by the ratings on the latter problems, it would appear that they do not constitute particularly serious problems.

9.3.5 Academic Leaders' Job Elements

In order to find out the areas in which academic leaders experience problems, we asked of the importance of some elements in the execution of the academic leaders' jobs. Ostensibly, it is on these elements that the academic leaders experience their problems. As usual, we requested the academic leaders to rank these job elements on a scale measuring from 1 (signifying low rating) to 10 (signifying high rating).

The responses from the academic leaders are presented in table 9-3 from where it can be seen that *staff selection and development, policy formulation*, and *extension of the frontiers of knowledge* seem to be the more important elements in the academic leaders' jobs. This conclusion is true for both the responses from the Nigerian as well as the British academic leaders. The high rating on these elements is not surprising, as the elements appear to be more academic matters in relation to the other enumerated elements. The latter elements include conflict resolution, external representation, internal resource allocation, and admitting students. These were rated as of less importance in the academic leaders' jobs.

It is important to observe that the rating of the element of the extension of the frontiers of knowledge is consistent with the high rating on research discussed earlier. Judging from the comments of some academic leaders in the questionnaire, conflicts occur rarely among the academics. However, conflicts are usually of a serious nature when they do occur. Internal resource allocation was also not rated particularly highly because that function is normally largely undertaken by the bursary departments of most universities. Similarly, while the academic leaders feature prominently in the admission process, the registry departments of most universities still handle the details of the communications. The external representation of units by the respective academic leaders would probably be higher for deans, directors, and vice-chancellors than for heads of departments. The ratings made by the academic leaders suggest that occasions for external representation were more numerous in the British than in the Nigerian situation.

Table 9-3: Academic Leaders' Mean Ratings of the Important Elements in Their Jobs

Elements	British	Nigerian
Conflict resolution	6.58	5.75
External representation	7.85	5.97
Internal resource allocation	7.64	7.22
Extension of the frontiers of knowledge	8.06	8.23
Staff selection and development	8.39	8.35
Policy formulation	8.82	8.19
Admitting students	7.34	7.63
Sample size	34	75

9.4 The Selection of Academic Leaders

The selection processes of Nigerian academic leaders are detailed in Chapter Two. As we stated in that chapter, Nigerian deans are elected by faculty staff, while heads of departments are appointed by the vice-chancellors. The directors are nominated by the vice-chancellors and confirmed by the Senate of the university of which the vice-chancellor himself is the chairman. Vice-chancellors in Nigerian universities are currently appointed by the Visitor to the university (the head of State or the president of the country) on the recommendation of the University Council who in turn gets suggestions from the Senate.

The processes for the selection of British academic leaders are fairly similar to the Nigerian practice. For example, in Britain, the Dean of each Board of Studies is normally appointed by the Senate from among the members of the Board of Studies concerned and on the nomination of that Board. However, there is an important exception in the appointment of vice-chancellors. In Britain, unlike in Nigeria, the University Councils have the final say in the appointment of their vice-chancellors. The position of vacant vice-chancellors is normally advertized, and University Councils may appoint a professor who is not necessarily from the particular university.

9.4.1 Criteria for Selection

It would be gathered from the above discussions that the criteria for the selection of academic leaders, other than some level of academic attainment, are fairly subjective. Much depends on the opinions of the vice-chancellors, although they may solicit for recommendations from relevant quarters. In the appointment of a head of department, for example, the vice-chancellor may ask for the recommendation of the dean—but this is only advisory. Invariably, academic leaders below the post of vice-chancellor are normally selected based on their academic seniority and demonstrated competence—defined in terms of research publications. This is not to deny, however, that academic leaders may be appointed on some other considerations. For example, in some Nigerian universities, academic leaders' selection may depend on one's state of origin. In British Universities, however, merit would appear to be the guiding consideration.

It is of interest to note that in both the British and the Nigerian Universities, the possession of administrative and management skills is not often an element of great importance in the selection process. Perhaps, the relative non-importance attached to the administrative and management skills criterion may be due to the difficulty of assessing this, whereas academic competence can be more readily ascertained. However, as Singleton argued, there appears to be "a potent, if unstated, belief that such skills are either trivial or unnecessary". [20]

Whatever the explanation or the reasoning behind the relative neglect of the use of administrative and management criteria in appointing academic leaders, it is important to observe that the selection criteria are, in the main, unsupported by the nature of work which academic leaders perform. Whereas academic leaders are often selected based on their research publications, the empirical study of the work characteristics of academic leaders documented in this study shows that academic leaders perform more management and administrative functions than the research activities. For example, the percentage of total working time spent on administration and management functions was more than double the corresponding time spent on research work. [21] In this, the academic leaders' work characteristics appear to conform to Fayol's dictum that as a manager moves up the organizational ladder, the less the technical work he performs and the more the administrative jobs.

A corollary arising from this observation (i.e. the incongruence between the selection criteria and the nature of work) is the recognition of the need to review the selection criteria of academic leaders (not the criteria for promoting academics) to reflect the importance of the administrative and the managerial nature of their work. A related corollary is the need for some form of management training to assist academic leaders if they are to perform their duties more effectively.

9.4.2 Who Heads the Universities?

Because of the administrative nature of the typical vice-chancellor's duties, and because of the logic of the universality of managerial functions, some commentators have argued that universities are better headed by lay administrators (administrators who have no training in serving the major goal activities of the organization). [22]

Traditionally, with very few exceptions, only professors have been appointed as vice-chancellors. These are individuals who normally hold strong professional commitment and share the values of academe. Their subject areas are of no relevance, and mathematicians, medical doctors, historians, chemists, lawyers, engineers, etc. have been appointed vice-chancellors. The only requirement has been that they should be academics first and foremost.

The call for professionalism in management and administration argues that if professionally trained and practically experienced administrators had been in charge of universities, perhaps some workers' strike or some student union demonstrations on the internal problems of the university might have been avoided, or their consequences considerably lessened. And that in general, the universities might have been more efficiently run and effectively operated.

9.4.2.1 Dilemma

Heading a professional organization such as the university or the hospital constitutes a special dilemma. According to Etzioni, it "is a typical case of institutionalized role conflict". [23]

> On the one hand, the role should be in the hands of a professional in order to ensure that the commitments of the head will match organizational goals. A professional at the head of the authority structure will mean that professional activity is recognized as the major goal activity, and that the needs of professionals will be more likely to receive understanding attention. [24]

On the other hand, Etzioni further explained that organizations have needs that may be unrelated to their specific goals, but which are nonetheless important. For example, organizations have to obtain funds, recruit personnel of all sorts, and manage the organizational resources well—and the typical professional may not be skilled in these management functions. Besides, a professional who is in charge of the organization may overemphasize professional commitment to the neglect of his major management and administrative duties. As an illustration, the writer is aware of an example of a flight captain who headed an airline and who, in part because he did not know what to do with the job of a head, but possibly also because of his professional interests, took to flying most of the time. In the same vein, there are some academic leaders who do not know what to do with the job of a leader. Some managers or heads of units lack skill in human relations, and in all these illustrations, the organization experiences a reduction in the levels of efficiency and effectiveness.

Because the role of a head of a professional organization seems to require two incompatible sets of orientations, personal characteristics, and aptitudes, one set of considerations is likely to be emphasized to the neglect of the other if the role is performed by either a lay administrator or a typical professional. [25]

9.4.2.2 Solution to the Dilemma

While there are several possible solutions to the dilemma of who heads the universities, it would appear reasonable to suggest that having academically oriented administrators as vice-chancellors would be the best. Such administrators would combine academic background with managerial training and practice. As such, they would easily be accepted by their academic colleagues.

In addition, heads who combine research competence with managerial expertise would not only ensure the commitment of the university to its major goals, but also, they would pay due attention to maintenance and supportive goals. Skilled in this way, they would tend to ensure better handling of the needs of their universities.

In practical terms, it is suggested that vice-chancellors be selected from among the professors who are competent and skilled in management and administration. That is, while academic competence would still be regarded as necessary attributes of vice-chancellors, they would no longer be regarded as sufficient condition for appointing academic leaders. Unless the universities pursue merit in this fashion, it should be expected that the governments and society would continue to erode the high confidence and esteem placed on the role of the university system.

9.4.2.3 Academic Leaders' Own Solution

In order to find out the academic leaders' own reactions and solutions to the dilemma of who heads the universities, our sampled academic leaders were asked to rate the extent to which they agree to the suggestion that administrators other than academics should be in charge of managing the universities on a scale measuring from 1 (low rating) to 10 (high rating). A distribution of the ratings by the British and the Nigerian academic leaders is provided in table 9-4. It can be seen that a mean rating of 4.45 from the Nigerian academic leaders, and a corresponding mean of 2.67 from the British academic leaders suggest that academic leaders would not accept lay administrators to head them. Some professors who commented on their forms argued that the specialized job of managing the universities can only be performed by the academics. Some other professors would want the administrators to be in charge of routine administrative functions while leaving strategic issues to them. They complained that it is often the lapses from routine administrative duties that waste much of their time.

While the response of the academic leaders is understandable, their interests would seem to be better protected if, in addition to academic qualifications, academic leaders also have some management training and experience, especially on skills development.

Table 9-4. The Distributin of the Ratings of the Extent to Which Academic Leaders Believe That Administration and Management in Universities Should Be Handle by Professional Managers and not by Themselves

Scale	British	Nigerian
1	16	12
2	4	14
3	4	6
4	4	6
5	1	13
6	0	5
7	1	3
8	3	6
9	0	7
10	0	2
Mean	2.67	4.45
Sample size	33	74
C.V. %	84.72	62.20

9.5 Training and Management Development for Academic Leaders

From the previous section, we have argued that in order to be more effective in their jobs, academic leaders would tend to benefit from some form of management training. This they do not presently have, as we explained earlier in Chapter Two. In this section, therefore, we attempt to identify the skills that would usefully be developed among academic leaders and discuss the nature and type of possible training and management development programmes that may be beneficial to the academic leaders. But first, we wish to find out the academic leaders' own reaction to the idea of management training, and the academic leaders' motivation towards effective management.

9.5.1 Academic Leaders' Reaction to Management Training

We asked the academic leaders two questions: (1) To what extent do you believe that some form of management training would be useful to you in performing your jobs better? (2) To what extent are you willing to accept management training as a prerequisite to or accompanying the appointment of academic leaders? As usual, the academic leaders were requested to rate their responses on a scale measuring from 1 (low rating) to 10 (high rating).

Table 9-5. The Distributin of the Ratings of the Extent to Which Academic Leaders Believe That Some Form of Training Would Assist Them in Being More Effective Managers

Scale	British	Nigerian
1	4	0
2	2	2
3	3	5
4	4	1
5	5	9
6	2	6
7	2	7
8	3	14
9	1	10
10	7	11
Mean	5.67	7.53
Sample size	33	75
C.V. %	55.04	30.97

The academic leaders' reactions to the above two questions are detailed in tables 9-5 and 9-6. The mean ratings were 5.7 for the British sample and 7.5 for the Nigerian sample. This indicates a moderate belief in the value of management training on the part of British academic leaders and a moderately high belief in the value of such training on the part of Nigerian academic leaders. In both cases, however, there were wide variations in ratings. While some academic leaders believe that management training is extremely beneficial, others doubt the gains to be derived from management training sessions. Nonetheless, the general interpretation seems to be that management training is regarded useful.

However, the responses in table 9-6 would appear to mean that academic leaders do not favour making management training a prerequisite to their appointments as academic leaders. Some of the academic leaders commented in part that they resent training. Perhaps, this is the force of tradition. Obviously sceptical of possible management training schemes, one of the respondents asked, "who are those to train us?" A few academic leaders indicated, however, that they would not mind accepting management training as a package accompanying their appointment as academic leaders.

Table 9-6. The Distributin of the Ratings of the Extent to Which Academic Leaders Are Willing to Approve of a Management Trainging Programme as a Prerequisite to or Accompanying Their Appointment as Academic Leaders

Scale	British	Nigerian
1	11	6
2	2	6
3	6	7
4	2	8
5	2	13
6	3	6
7	2	4
8	3	8
9	1	11
10	2	7
Mean	4.00	5.75
Sample size	34	75
C.V. %	74.11	48.73

9.5.2 Academic Leaders' Motivation to Manage

In this section, we ask the fundamental question of the extent to which academic leaders are motivated to effective management. An answer to this question is particularly valuable in view of the academic leaders' apparent resentment to training. Stated in other words, the question is: are the academic leaders attracted to management positions? Are they not? An answer will help us to further understand the academic leaders' disposition to management training which is intended to increase their effectiveness levels. Again, we

Table 9-7. The Distributin of the Ratings of the Extent to Which Academic Leaders Are Motivated Towards or Interested in Being Effective Managers

Scale	British	Nigerian
1	5	1
2	4	9
3	5	9
4	4	8
5	10	13
6	3	11
7	1	7
8	1	10
9	0	4
10	0	2
Mean	3.85	5.32
Sample size	33	74
C.V. %	48.67	42.64

requested the academic leaders to rate their opinions on our scale to sec the extent to which their motivation to manage correlates with their disposition to training. Table 9-7 summarises the responses from the academic leaders.

With a mean rating of slightly higher than 5 from the Nigerian academic leaders, and a mean rating of less than 4 from the British academic leaders, the interpretation from table 9-7 is that academic leaders do not appear to be particularly motivated towards management. However, the responses were greatly varied. While some academic leaders appeared to just manage to keep up with the demands of their offices, others seem to be very attracted to these positions.

This finding on the degree of the academic leaders' motivation to manage seems to be a reflection of the general motivational patterns of professionals. Whereas most successful professionals are not motivated to become administrators, [26] those who feel that they have little chance of becoming outstanding professionals in their fields often gravitate towards administrative and managerial jobs. [27] Etzioni observes that they may do this by serving on committees and by assuming minor administrative roles.

The apparent lack of strong motivation to manage by the typical academic leader must be treated with caution. Individual academic leaders' opinions may change with age and with promotions on the organizational ladder. In addition, our figures may serve as mere estimates of the academic leaders' motivation to manage. A projective and an indirect measure such as that devised by Miner (the Miner Sentence Completion Scale, MSCS) should perhaps be used for a more accurate estimate. [28] Nonetheless, our estimate of the academic leaders' motivation to manage seems to be consistent with their apparent resentment to training. Ironically, one of the reasons why academic leaders may not be particularly motivated to manage may be a result of the fact that effectiveness in administration and management do not seem to count in assessing their promotability even to higher managerial levels.

9.5.3 The Nature of Possible Management Training

Given that management training will be useful and will be accepted at least by some academic leaders, we hereunder discuss the nature of such possible training. First, it is important to emphasize that the nature and type of management training that would be beneficial to the academic leaders will de-emphasize the presentation of conceptual materials (which the majority of the academic leaders are very good at anyway) in favour of skills development. Mintzberg suggested that an orientation towards skills development should in fact be followed by management schools in the training of their managers. [29] An example of operationalizing such a training scheme involving skills development can be gathered from Wright and Taylor's book aimed at improving leadership performance through skills development. [30]

As opposed to generalized training programmes, academic leaders will, perhaps, benefit more from specialized training based on the identification of their management deficiencies—an exercise where the academic leaders themselves should be able to have some useful opinions based on the analysis of the nature of their work. If a newly appointed academic leader lacks administrative knowledge in a particular area, he should be assisted. If a vice-chancellor does not know how to conduct meetings, he should be trained in this art so that he would not waste other people's time during the many university meetings. Because of the high organizational levels which academic leaders occupy, it is common knowledge that unless a training programme designed for them is high-status, it cannot be successful.

While a specialized nature of training is advocated for academic leaders, empirical studies of the work activities of industrial managers reveal that managers in general may benefit from programmes with the following themes: how to handle a two-minute interaction; how to handle ceremonial events; how to decide when a meeting is necessary and who should attend; how to plan in the midst of chaos; how to delegate in an oral environments, etc. [31]

The comparability of functions between the private industries and the universities, a theme developed by Lynch [32] and which is largely supported in this research, means that some training programmes such as the ones indicated above may be applied usefully in university management.

However, in general, the findings of this study would seem to suggest that the areas of useful training needs for academic leaders may include the following: the clearing of academic leaders' deskwork speedily and satisfactorily; helping academic leaders to conduct meetings—making them short, focused, and effective; assisting academic leaders in effectively delegating functions to administrative assistants and secretaries, and becoming more democratic in the handling of unit affairs, i.e. involving other members of staff; clarification of organizational goals and objectives, procedures, etc. to new academic leaders; introducing academic leaders to elementary principles in the handling of student and staff grievances; and improving both the diagnostic and interactive interpersonal skills of academic leaders.

There is, of course, a vast literature in any of the above mentioned training need areas, and various methods such as lectures, seminars, role playing, discussions, and case studies are available for training purposes. For example, in-tray-exercises are training devices that can be usefully applied to clearing academic leaders' deskwork speedily. [33]

However, we must state that our objective in this regard does not extend to the designing of a training programme for academic leaders. Although this will be a natural development from this aspect of the study, our concern is really limited to the justification of training for academic leaders (arising from an examination of both the nature and the characteristics of academic leaders' work, and the current management and administrative practices in the academia) and the identification of the nature and the areas of training needs and skills development that will be beneficial to academic leaders. Training consultants are, however, encouraged to mount appropriate training programmes, taking into consideration both the nature and the characteristics of work, the perceptions, attitudes, and the job profiles of academic leaders that we have identified.

9.5.4 Management Skills Regarded as Useful

In order that any training programmes developed for academic leaders would be useful, we asked the academic leaders to identify the area of skills development that would be relevant to them and to rate the importance of these. The academic leaders' responses are summarized in table 9-8 where it can be seen that there were high ratings on the enumerated skills. This suggest that academic leaders' skills can usefully be developed in the areas of decision making, interpersonal relations, information management, leadership, and in fact general management.

However, leadership and interpersonal skills were rated higher than other skill areas by both groups of academic leaders. This suggests that training programmes in these two areas may be particularly valuable in assisting academic leaders in the performance of their jobs.

Table 9-8: Academic Leaders' Mean Ratings of the Skills Regarded as Useful in the Performance of Their Jobs

Skills	British	Nigerian
Decision-Making	8.59	7.16
Interpersonal	9.12	7.55
Information management	7.15	7.48
Leadership	9.03	8.92
General management	7.85	7.16
Sample size	34	75

9.6 Summary

This chapter has concentrated on the issues affecting academic leadership and management practices more directly. Continuing the focus on the academic leader, and building on the discussions in the earlier chapters, this chapter emphasized the issues of the selection, training, and management development for academic leaders. As a prelude to the consideration of these issues, the goals of universities and the peculiar management problems facing academic leaders were examined.

The bases for the discussions in this chapter were the responses to a survey from over one hundred academic leaders in Nigeria and Britain. These responses were detailed in several tables presented in the chapter. However, published materials were also used to buttress the opinions held and the suggestions made. As in the earlier chapters, the objective of this chapter continues to be the identification of ways in which the academic leaders can contribute towards a more effective academic management.

This chapter was divided into four sections. The first section attempted to establish the goals of universities. It reviewed the models of university purpose, and identified the teaching, research, vocational, and societal models. Recognising the complementarity of these models, a unifying model of the university purpose, the pluralistic model, was presented and discussed.

The latter part of the first section examined, in general, the goals of complex organizations such as the university. It distinguished between formal or legal goals, actual or real goals, and stated or perceived goals. Finally, an empirical verification of the university's stated or perceived goals was discussed based on the academic leaders' responses to our survey. This confirmed the multiple-purpose nature of universities and established the superiority of the research goal over other university goals.

The second section of the chapter discussed the management problems affecting the effectiveness levels of academic leaders in the performance of their jobs. The academic leaders' responses to our survey revealed that academic shortages, dwindling resources, and excessive work constituted the major management difficulties to both the British and the Nigerian academic leaders. The latter part of the second section also identified academic leaders' important job elements on which, presumably, they experience their problems. Again, the academic leaders' responses to the survey identified as major academic matters the extension of the frontiers of knowledge, staff selection and development, and policy formulation. The consistent ratings between the British and the Nigerian academic leaders on these job elements and problems give greater reliability to the findings.

Section three is on the selection of academic leaders. It explains the current selection processes in both the Nigerian and the British universities and observed that the selection criteria are based essentially on academic seniority and research publications. It noted, therefore, in consonance with our earlier findings, that the selection criteria of academic leaders are, in the main, unsupported by the nature of work which academic leaders perform. While academic leaders perform administrative and management functions, they are selected based on academic competence. It was therefore suggested that in order that academic leaders might be more effective in their jobs, the selection criteria should be reviewed to require more management and administrative skills on the part of academic leaders. Since the academic leaders do not favour making management and administrative competence a prerequisite to their appointment, it was suggested that specialized management training should be made available to academic leaders.

The latter part of section three posed and attempted to resolve the dilemma of who heads the universities. It considered the advantages and the disadvantages of a lay administrator versus a pure professional (an academic), and settled for the professional administrator who seems to combine the advantages of both a lay administrator and a pure professional. Finally, the academic leaders' own solution to the dilemma of who heads their universities was sought. The results of the survey revealed that the academic leaders would resent very much the idea of the lay administrators heading them.

The last section of the chapter was devoted to the issues of training and management development for academic leaders. First, the academic leaders' reaction to the idea of training was sought. Our investigations revealed that while most academic leaders seem to believe that some form of training would be beneficial to them, they would oppose making management training a prerequisite to their appointment as academic leaders. When an estimate of their motivation to manage was made, it showed that academic leaders may not be particularly motivated to effective management, and this explains in part their resentment to training. However, judging by some of the comments made in the questionnaire by the academic leaders, making management training a package to accompany their appointment would be better accepted.

It was argued that the nature of possible management training would emphasize skills development, be specialised, and be high-status to be successful. The areas of relevant skills which the academic leaders agreed would be beneficial to them include decision-making and information management, but especially inter-personal and leadership skills.

9.7 Implications of Academic Leadership and Management Practices

This chapter offers important implications on the leadership and management policies and practices in the universities.

One of these implications is that since the primary goal (not the only goal) of universities seems to be research excellence, any head of the university system who himself may not be or have been a successful researcher is not likely to be accepted, however good his or her skills in administration and management may be. However, the nature of the work which academic leaders do, and the nature of the problems and difficulties which they encounter in their jobs would suggest that academic leaders' effectiveness levels can be increased by recourse to management skills development programmes to complement their research skills.

Another implication is the identification of the academic leaders' important job elements which reveals that academic leaders tend to be more concerned with "academic matters". The implication is that overall university effectiveness can be improved if academic leaders have competent administrators and secretaries to take care of routine administrative functions, leaving strategic issues to the academic leaders.

One of the findings in this chapter is that the selection process of academic leaders is not consistent with the nature of work which academic leaders perform. While academic leaders perform administrative and managerial work mostly, they are selected based on their research competence. The implications of the finding are that if academic leaders are to do their work more effectively, the selection criteria should either be modified to incorporate the requirement of more management training and experience, or some form of management training should be instituted to assist academic leaders. Perhaps, a combination of both methods should be used.

Notwithstanding the doubts sometimes expressed on the gains to be derived from management education even by some management scholars, [34] one of the suggestions of this chapter is that academic leaders' managerial performances can be improved by recourse to management training. The academic leaders themselves seem to confirm that management training would be generally useful to them. However, to be successful, such a training programme must have a skills orientation and be high-status. Furthermore, to be relevant, the training should be specialised and related to the needs of the individual academic leaders.

In matters of training, however, one observation is that academic leaders, perhaps like some other managers, seem to be conservative. Universities everywhere seem to be strong in tradition and tend to overlook or underplay important changes that have occurred in the society. Surprisingly, this attitude of pro-conservatism in the matters of the practice of administration is unlike the academic leaders' attitude to research activities where changes in substance and methodology are easily accepted if found to be better than earlier ideas and/or practices. Academic leaders should realise that unless they improve on the general administration and management of the universities, intervention by the governments and the society on university affairs may increase. This trend would not be beneficial either to the universities or to the larger society.

In this regard, Singleton has argued that because of the growth in size and expenditure, the universities can no longer be left to themselves, and the outside world is increasingly critical of the values and achievements of universities. [35] This is so much so that the expansion of the university system in the western world has, according to Singleton, been almost eliminated over the last few years. Unfortunately, the experience of current academic leaders seems to be limited almost entirely to the era of phenomenal growth and expansion. Worse still, the new management skills which are now being required and which will increasingly be required in the future of stagnation or decline are not been now developed.

Academic leadership and management practices in the universities can be improved. It is hoped that some of the ideas expressed in this work will contribute towards this improvement.

9.8 Notes and References

[1] Newman, C.J.H., *The Idea of a University*, Longman, London, 1852, as referenced in: Lynch, J.E., Strategic Marketing Planning in UK Universities, University of Bradford, Ph.D. Thesis, 1981, p. 347.

[2] Annan, L.N., Lecture extract (1972), Quoted in: Lynch, J.E., op. cit., p. 2.

[3] Lynch, J.E., op., cit., pp. 2–7.

[4] Newman, C.J.H., *The Idea of a University*, Image Books, A Division of Doubleday and Company, Inc., Garden City, New York, 1959, preface, pp. 7–11; The view taken of a university in these discourse is that the university is a place for teaching universal knowledge.

[4b] Ibid.

[4c] Ibid.

[4d] Ibid.

[5] Audu, I., The functions of a university, in: Adaralegbe, A. (ed.), *A Philosophy for Nigerian Education*, Report of the National Curricula Conference, 8–12 Sept., 1969, Heinemann Educational Books, Ibadan, 1972. See also, Biobaku, S.O., The Purpose of University Education, and Hicks, S.I.'s introduction to chapter III on: The Purpose of a University; also included in Adaralegbe, A., 1972.

[6] Ascham, R., Quoted in Lynch, J.E., op. cit., p. 4.

[7] Flexner, A., *Universities: American, English, German*, Oxford University Press, London, 1930, pp. 102–105

[7b] Ibid., p. 24

[8] Audu I., op. cit., p. 61.

[9] Truscot, B., *Redbrick University*, Faber, London, 1943, p. 45.

[10] Lynch, J.E., op. cit., p. 5.

[11] Scarle, J. *The Campus War*, Pelican, London, 1972, p. 170.

[11b] Robbins, L. *Report of the Committee on Higher Education*, Cmnd. 2154, Her Majesty's Stationery Office, London, 1963.

[12] Kerr, C., *The Uses of the University*, Harvard University Press, Cambridge, Mass., 1963, pp. 18–19. See his full general exposition in: The idea of a multiversity, on pp. 1–45.

[13] Lynch, J.E., op. cit., pp. 7–13.

[14] Fielden, J. and Lockwood, G., *Planning and Management in Universities*, Chatto and Windus, London, 1973.

[15] Lynch, J.E., loc. cit.

[16] Cyert, R.M. and March, J.G., *A behavioural theory of the firm*, Prentice-Hall, Englewood Cliffs, N.J., 1963.

[17] There is a trend for new business owners to request their lawyers to draft articles of incorporation in such a way that their organization could almost pursue any form of business and operate anywhere in the whole world.

[18] Etzioni, A., *Modern Organizations*, Prentice-Hall Inc., Englewood Cliffs, N.J., 1964.

[19] The total percentage of 99, instead of 100, was due to rounding up errors; our findings are supported by the National Universities Commission's Publication that as of 1982, over 20% of the lecturers in Nigerian Universities were, on the average, non-Nigerians. In fact, in one of the universities, the non-Nigerian academics were more in number than the Nigerian lecturers! See Chizea, C.A., *20 Years of University Education in Nigeria*, Lagos, Nigeria, 1984.

[20] Singleton, W.T., *Management Skills*, MTP Press Limited, Lancaster, 1981, p. 68.

[21] See Chapter 5 for details. This diary finding was also supported by a survey conducted in both Britain and Nigeria and in which over one hundred academic leaders participated. See Chapter 8 for the details of the survey results.

[22] Odeleye, A.O., Professionalism in Management and Administration, *Management in Nigeria*, Jan. 1979, p. 17–21.

[23] Etzioni, A., op. cit., p. 82.

[24] Ibid.

[25] Ibid.

[26] Etzioni, A., op. cit., p. 83; "Some would refuse any administrative role, including the top one of university president or hospital chief, because of their commitment to professional values and ties to professional groups, and because they feel that they would not be capable of performing the administrative role successfully. Those who are willing to accept administrative roles are often less committed to professional values than their colleagues, or view it as a transitional status, not a career".—p. 83.

[27] Ibid., "It seems that academicians who are inclined to take administrative jobs, or who are organization-oriented, not only publish less in quantity and quality after they have entered administrative positions but also tend to publish less before they accept such jobs".—p. 83.

[28] Miner, J.B., *Motivation to Manage: A ten Year Update on the "Studies in Management Education" Research*, Organizational Measurement Systems Press, Atlanta, Georgia, 1977.

[29] Mintzberg, H., The Manager's Job: Folklore and Fact, *Harvard Business Review*, July–August 1975, p. 61.

[30] Wright, P.L. and Taylor, D.S., *Improving Leadership Performance*, Prentice-Hall International, Englewood Cliffs, N.J., 1984. One of the features of the book which is particularly useful is the provision of exercises (and answers) which readers can use in the training to develop their own skills.

[31] McCall, M.W., Morrison, M.A., and Hannan, R.L., *Studies of Managerial Work: Results and Methods, Centre for Creative Leadership*, Technical Report No. 9, North Carolina, 27402, May 1978, p. 42.

[32] Lynch, J.E., op. cit.

[33] In-tray-exercises are simulations of the different aspects of a manager's work designed to introduce participants to the practical problems and methods of handling these. The exercises are often in the form of short case studies or memos in the in-tray of the manager leaving participants to scan, rank or prioritize, and plan the handling of the different memos with the interactive implications of having to consult, inform, delegate, etc., in clearing the desk work satisfactorily and on time.

[34] Mintzberg, H., *The Nature of Managerial Work*, Harper and Row, New York, 1973, pp. 187–188. See also, Stewart R., The Nature of Management? A Problem for Management Education, *Journal of Management Studies*, Vol. 21, No. 3, July 1984, pp. 323–330.

[35] Singleton, W.T., loc. cit.

Chapter 10
Summary of the Research and its Findings

10.1 Introduction

This research has attempted to investigate the nature of academic leaders' jobs, academic leaders' perceptions about these jobs, and academic leaders' attitudes and beliefs about aspects of their jobs. It is our hope that the study has contributed to a greater awareness and a better understanding of the activities and job characteristics of academic leaders. The study was also carried out in the hope that it would lead to the ultimate objective of making universities more effective in the realization of their goals and objectives, and in the positive contributions they make to society. In essence, this research sought to identify and outline ways in which universities could achieve more effective management practices and policies through an examination of the jobs, perceptions, and attitudes of, perhaps, the most important actors and actresses on the university management scene—the academic leaders.

The research techniques employed in this investigation are a combination of the survey and the diary methodologies. To gather data about academic leaders' job characteristics, a more direct method, the diary, was used, while to elicit data on academic leaders' perceptions and attitudes, the conventional survey, a more indirect method, was used as it seems more appropriate for the purpose. Together, the methods were designed to complement and supplement each other in producing results that would be superior to either method used alone. Although our samples were drawn from only Nigerian and British Universities, it is hoped that our results would be of general applicability, especially in view of the similarity in academic culture. The remaining sections of this chapter summarize the findings of the study. In the concluding chapter, the conclusions and implications arising from these findings will be presented, and the potential applications of the work outlined.

10.2 Summary of the Findings

The detailed findings of this work were presented in Chapters Five, Six, Seven, Eight, and Nine. Chapters Five and Six presented the findings on the nature of the academic leaders' jobs, while Chapter Seven discussed a classification of academic leaders into job profiles based on how academic leaders spend their time. Chapter Eight analyzed academic leaders' perceptions of how they spend their time as well as their perceptions of particular aspects of their jobs. The latter consideration was an examination of the academic leaders' attitudes and beliefs on aspects of their jobs. Chapter Nine concluded the presentation of the findings by discussing not only the goals and objectives and the problems of university administration and management, but also by critically evaluating the selection criteria of academic leaders and by making empirically based suggestions in the areas of training and management development for academic leaders.

10.2.1 Findings on the Nature of the Academic Leaders' Jobs

The analyses of the diaries show that the average weekly total time worked by the Nigerian and British academic leaders were 41 and 43 hours, respectively. The coefficients of variation of the distribution of total working hours were similar in the Nigerian and British samples and were, in each case, less than 20 percent. These working hours represented the net figures, i.e. after deducting the time taken off for personal lunch and idle or un-accounted for periods spent between activities. All figures were rounded up to the nearest whole number. The results reveal that some academic leaders work on Saturdays and Sundays, sometimes working for as long as 8 or more hours on each of these days, a practice which is, perhaps, not widespread in the public or even the private sectors.

On the activities performed, our analyses show that the Nigerian academic leaders spent an average of about 44 percent of their total working hours on deskwork functions. The corresponding figure for the British sample was 43 percent. The variation about the mean (coefficient of variation) in both groups was similar and, in each case, higher than 30 percent. This finding reveals that paperwork is the stock-in-trade of the academic leaders, and that this function, not surprisingly, occupies most of their time.

On scheduled meetings, which in our study were mostly lectures, our British and Nigerian sampled academic leaders spent 25 and 29 percent of their respective total working hours. Although the Nigerian academic leaders spent slightly more time on this activity than the British, the differences were not statistically significant. References to previous studies on the percentage of time spent by industrial managers on scheduled meetings show that industrial managers tend to spend more time on this activity than academic leaders. Industrial managers sometimes spend as much as 50 percent of the total working hours on scheduled meetings. Mintzberg, for example, recorded a figure as high as 59 percent of the total working time spent by his sampled American managers on scheduled activities (Mintzberg 1973). Concerning unscheduled meetings, figures from past studies demonstrate clearly that industrial managers spend more time on this activity than the academic leaders. For example, for our sampled British and Nigerian academic leaders, unscheduled meetings consumed only about 7 and 11 percent of their respective total working hours, whereas corresponding figures from industry were never less than 12 percent, and were as high as 20 percent in some cases.

The time spent on the telephone was another activity that we analyzed from our diaries. Our findings reveal that in each of the Nigerian and the British samples, less than 1 percent of the academic leaders' total working time was spent on this activity. Indeed, more than half of the academic leaders in each sample did not spend any time on the telephone. Not surprisingly, therefore, the coefficients of variation were as high as 172 percent in the British sample and 152 percent in the Nigerian sample. A comparative study of the average time spent by industrial managers on the telephone shows that the time spent on this activity was never less than 5 percent of each manager's total working hours and was as much as 15 and 17 percent by some managers. Like with meetings, there is thus a wide difference concerning the time which academic leaders and industrial managers spend on the telephone.

On the subject of their activities, the diary results show that Nigerian academic leaders spent about 17 percent and the British academic leaders about 12 percent of their respective total time on teaching. The difference between these figures was not statistically significant, although it would appear that Nigerian academic leaders tended to teach more than their British counterparts. The results show that the academic leaders spent slightly more time on research than teaching, averaging 21 percent of the total time for the British, and 20 percent for the Nigerian sample. The academic leaders did not, however, spend much time on consulting, recording only 4 percent of the total time spent in the British case and only 3 percent in the Nigerian sample.

Our results show that administration and management consume the larger part of academic leaders' time. It shows that British academic leaders spent an average of 47 percent of their total time on administration and management, while the corresponding figure from the Nigerian sample was 48 percent. Thus, the time spent on administration and management was greater than the combined time spent on teaching, researching, and consulting activities. Academic leaders spend about 15 percent of their total working time on 'personal' activities such as taking a lunch break or telephoning a friend.

The diary results further show that academic leaders perform most of their jobs in their own offices. The British academic leaders spent as much as 50 percent and their Nigerian counterparts 45 percent of their respective total hours in their offices. Our figures reveal that the British academic leaders spent about 30 percent and the Nigerian academic leaders up to 36 percent of their total working hours in other university units. Examples of such units include the library, the computer room, the bursary, the registry, the health clinic, or other campuses if any. Our sampled academic leaders spent about 11 and 8 percent of their total time each working in other organizations. Each of our British and Nigerian academic leaders spent about 10 percent of their working time at home, a figure which tends to be higher than the practice in industry.

In summary, therefore, the academic leaders, on the whole, spent about 80 percent of their time on campus, resulting in an average of over 30 hours which the average academic leader spent within university premises each week. On the whole, the distribution of the average duration for all activities showed a mean of slightly more than one hour. This is true whether the distribution is with or without fleeting contacts, and it is true for both the Nigerian and the British samples. It is probably true, therefore, to say that academic leaders tend to work a bit longer on the same activity than their industrial counterparts.

The diary results on the contact with other people show that British academic leaders spent only 7 percent and the Nigerian academic leaders 16 percent of their total time with their students. While the proportions of the total time spent by the two groups are low, there is a significant difference between them, with the Nigerian figure showing a statistically significant result when compared with the British figure. Other results show that academic leaders spent more of their time with colleagues than with their students. The Nigerian academic leaders spent about 22 percent, and the British almost 26 percent, of their time with their colleagues.

In fact, the time which the academic leaders spent with the members of the administrative staff (about 15 percent in each case) was, as we can see, less than that spent with their colleagues. The proportion of time which the academic leaders spent with non-members of their universities was less than 8 percent in the Nigerian sample and about 11 percent in the British sample. Other results actually indicate how academic leaders spent most of their time—alone! The British and the Nigerian academic leaders spent about 40 percent of their time working alone (disregarding fleeting contacts or interruptions of less than 5 minutes' duration). It should be stated that the academic leader was not considered alone if he or she was on the phone with someone else. Both groups of academic leaders spent about 20 percent of their time with one person, and they spent about the same proportion of time with groups of 2–5 people. The time spent by the Nigerian academic leaders with groups of six or more people (24 percent) was significantly higher than the corresponding time spent by the British academic leaders (15 percent).

Concerning fleeting contacts and interruptions, the analyses of the diaries show that the Nigerian academic leaders experienced about 90 percent of the fleeting contacts by person as compared to 10 percent of the fleeting contacts by telephone. This result differs significantly from the situation in Britain where the academic leaders had almost as many fleeting contacts by telephone as they did by person. The academic leaders experienced more fleeting contacts from their colleagues and the administrative staff than from the students.

As with industrial managers' jobs, the academic leaders' jobs were fragmented with an average of one fleeting contact per activity. As many as 10 activities on the average occurred each day. Alone time with or without fleeting contacts were analyzed, and the results show that the academic leaders were truly alone for less than 18 percent of their total time. Analyses of the variety exhibited by the academic leaders in the performance of their jobs were made. The results show a rich pattern of variation in the daily hours worked, the interruptions experienced, the fleeting contacts made, and the activities recorded in the diaries; where activities took place, with whom, et cetera.

10.2.2 Findings on the Job Profiles of Academic Leaders

The findings on the nature of academic leaders' jobs have shown that academic leaders very widely in the proportion of time which they spend on their activities, where these took place, with whom, and so on. Chapter Seven confirms that, despite this variety in managerial job characteristics, academic leaders can be usefully grouped on the basis of how they spend their time. Because of the low samples involved and because sampled academic leaders from Nigeria and Britain exhibited similar job characteristics, the two groups of academic leaders were combined for the classification exercise.

Using 24 different criteria of their job characteristics and applying hierarchical clustering technique, using Ward's (1963) method with Euclideun distance measure, five distinct groups of academic leaders were formed. These were labelled Administrators Type 1, Administrators Type 2, Educational Leaders Type 1, Educational Leaders Type 2, and Research Leaders.

An examination of the 5 groups of academic leaders was made, and it revealed that Administrators Type 1 spent the highest percentage of time on administration and management, and with members of the administrative staff. There were 10 members of this group, and they were further distinguished by the fact that they worked the longest hours, and they spent the highest percentage of time on deskwork, and at home. This group, however, spent the least percentage of time, and remarkably so, on teaching. They also recorded the least percentage of time on scheduled meetings and with groups of 6 or more people.

Administrators Type 2 exhibited similar characteristics to the first group, differing only slightly in the percentage of their total working time spent in most of the activities that distinguished Administrators Type 1. For example, Administrators Type 2 came next to those in Type 1 in the percentage of their time spent on administration and management, on deskwork, and at home. Administrators Type 2 spent the highest percentage of their time in the office. Made up of twelve members, Administrators Type 2 spent the least percentage of time on research and consulting functions.

Administrators Type 2 distinguished themselves by spending the highest percentage of their total working time alone, and by recording the greatest number of fleeting contacts and interruptions. It was hypothesized that these characteristics are symptomatic of administrators who are strategic planners versus those who are tactical trouble shooters. It is perhaps interesting to note that teaching and research roles seem to have been interchanged by the two groups of administrators. While the Administrators Type 1 spent a relatively high proportion of their time on research but did the least teaching, the Administrators Type 2 did relatively substantial teaching, but spent the least percentage of time on research.

The Educational Leaders Type 1 were made up of only 4 members. They were a small group of academic leaders who spent the highest percentage of time on teaching and on unscheduled meetings. Two features distinguish this group not only from the next group but, in fact, from all groups. They spent the highest percentage of time on short-duration activities, recording a figure which was more than triple the corresponding figure obtained by any of the other groups. In addition, the Educational Leaders Type 1 recorded by far the highest number of activities during the week.

The Educational Leaders Type 2 worked the shortest number of hours. They attended meetings a great deal, spending the highest percentage of time on scheduled meetings which in the present context were usually lectures. There were 7 members in this group, and they stand out prominently in the percentage of time spent in other units. In this feature, they not only spent the highest percentage of time, but recorded a percentage figure which was almost double that obtained by the group that came next. Educational Leaders Type 2 also spent a higher percentage of time with students and with colleagues than any of the other groups.

The figures show that the Educational Leaders Type 2 interacted much more with large groups of people than those in Type 1. They also spent the least percentage of time on short-duration activities, and recorded the least number of activities during the week, obtaining a figure which was much lower than half of that obtained by Type 1. Both groups of academic leaders in the Educational Leaders' category worked a relatively low number of hours, each recording total average working hours well below the overall average.

The fifth and the last group of academic leaders are the Research Leaders. This group of academic leaders spent a relatively very high percentage of time on research, consulting, and on long-duration activities, recording the highest percentage of time in these activities. The Research Leaders also spent the highest percentage of time in the other organizations, and with non-members of the university who were often in small groups of 2–5 people. The Research Leaders recorded the lowest number of fleeting contacts. There were five members of this group. They also recorded the lowest percentage of time, and remarkably so, on unscheduled meetings, administration and management, and with students. However, this group came second only to the first group in the number of hours they spent working, spending more than the average time for the overall sample.

10.2.3 Findings on the Perceptions of Academic Leaders

The findings in Chapter Eight can be broadly divided into two parts. The first part discussed academic leaders' perceptions of how they spend their time. This was in an attempt to find out, among other things, the extent to which academic leaders really know their jobs. The basis for this discussion was a comparison of the academic leaders' estimates of how they apportioned their time, which was made on the questionnaire, with the empirical findings on their time allocation obtained from the diary study.

The results reveal that both the Nigerian and the British academic leaders consistently overestimated their total working hours from Monday to Friday. That is, the differences between the hours they estimated in the questionnaire were statistically significant when compared with the actual hours worked which were obtained from the diary. They also overstated the time they spent working on Saturday and Sunday, if we assume that the academic leaders who did not fill in the diaries on these days did not work during the weekend.

The analyses also reveal that the academic leaders tended to exaggerate the time they spent working at home, and that the Nigerian academic leaders estimated spending significantly more time in the office and in the other units than was recorded in the diary study. However, the British academic leaders did not reveal significant differences in their estimated and recorded time in their own office and in the other units. The estimates of both groups of academic leaders regarding the percentage of time which they spent working in other campuses and in other organizations were reasonably close to the recorded data for these locations.

On the question of with whom academic leaders spend their time, the analyses show that there were no significant differences between the estimated and the recorded time spent either with colleagues or with non-members of the university in the Nigerian and in the British samples. However, the academic leaders tended to understate the time they spent alone and definitely overstated the time spent with students. While the Nigerian sample revealed significant differences in the estimated versus the recorded time spent with members of the administrative staff, the British sample did not show corresponding significant differences with that category of staff.

As far as the subject of their activities was concerned, it was found that both British and the Nigerian academic leaders estimated almost correctly the time spent on research. However, both groups exaggerated the percentage of time spent on teaching. The Nigerian academic leaders underestimated the percentage of time spent on administration and management, and overstated the time they spent on consulting. The British academic leaders, however, did not record significant differences in their estimates and the recorded data on these activities. Finally, the academic leaders grossly underestimated their average activity duration to a figure of only about half of the recorded data.

Table 8-2 was presented to summarize the nature of the academic leaders' errors in how they spent their time. Some possible reasons for these errors were suggested. An attempt was made to examine, from the available literature, industrial managers' perceptions of how they spent their time. This examination was compared with our findings as they related to academic leaders. It showed that most managers, whether academic or industrial, are poor estimators of how they spend their time. Managers do not seem to know how they spend their time, and it may be hypothesized that they respond to conscious or sometimes unconscious rationalizations in their estimates of their time allocation.

The second part of Chapter Eight examined, in detail, academic leaders' perceptions of their primary jobs of administration and management, teaching, researching, and consulting. The examination was made from five basic consideration, which the academic leaders rated on a scale measuring from 1 (signifying low rating) to 10 (signifying high rating). These considerations were: (1) the extent to which the academic leaders considered the jobs to be their primary responsibilities, (2) the extent to which they enjoyed doing them, (3) their estimate of their competence in executing them, (4) their estimated percentage of total working time spent among them, and (5) the extent to which competence on the respective activity affected career prospects or promotional success.

To get an overall picture of the academic leaders' ratings and views on these jobs, a ranking of the jobs in order of the perceived importance, level of enjoyment, the percentage time spent, etc. was made. The rankings show that research was generally ranked first, consulting was consistently ranked last, while teaching and administration and management were mostly ranked in between. The rankings also reveal an interesting relationship between the academic leaders' jobs of research and administration and management. Whereas the academic leaders spent most of their working time on administration and management, they appeared to enjoy research more, felt that they were more competent at it, and agreed that it contributed more to their career prospects. This conclusion was supported by other more detailed analyses, including tests of significant differences between ratings and chi-square tests showing relationships between the variables considered. All the possible combinations of the four jobs and the five considerations were also made to reveal, indeed, a very comprehensive treatment of the academic leaders' perceptions of their jobs. The cultural differences evident from the ratings of the British and the Nigerian academic leaders were noted and discussed.

The logic of the consistent ratings seems to support the view that academic leaders are more committed to success at research than effectiveness in administration and management. The importance of research seems to continue to predominate academic leaders' minds, although their jobs as academic leaders are administration and management. In summary, the comparison of the academic leaders' perceptions of the main aspects of their jobs revealed that (1) the British academic leaders regarded consultancy to be of lower priority than the Nigerian, (2) the Nigerian academic leaders enjoyed teaching more and thought themselves more competent at it than the British, (3) the Nigerian academic leaders thought that competence at teaching and consultancy affected their career prospects more than the British. Comparisons were also made between the jobs rated and the dimensions enumerated. The outcome of these analyses generally substantiates earlier findings on this important and complex subject of the academic leaders' perceptions of their jobs.

10.2.4 Findings on the Selection, Training, and Management Development of Academic Leaders

Chapter Nine concentrated on the issues affecting academic leadership and management practices more directly. Continuing the focus on the academic leader, and building on the discussions in the earlier chapters, Chapter Nine emphasized on the issues of the selection, training, and management development for academic leaders. As a prelude to the consideration of these issues, the goals of universities and the peculiar management problems facing academic leaders were examined.

The bases for the discussions in Chapter Nine were the responses to a survey from over one hundred academic leaders in Nigeria and Britain. These responses were detailed in several tables presented in that chapter. However, published materials were also used to buttress the opinions held and the suggestions made. As in the preceding four chapters, the objective of Chapter Nine continued to be the identification of ways in which the academic leaders could contribute towards more effective academic management.

Chapter Nine was divided into four sections. The first section attempted to establish the goals of universities. It reviewed the models of university purpose, and identified the teaching, research, vocational, and societal models. Recognizing the complementarity of these models, a unifying model of the university purpose, the pluralistic model, was presented and discussed.

The latter part of the first section examined in general the goals of complex organizations such as the university. It distinguished between formal or legal goals, actual or real goals, and stated or perceived goals. Finally, an empirical verification of the university's stated or perceived goals was discussed, based on the academic leaders' responses to our survey. This confirmed the multiple-purpose nature of universities and established the perceived superiority of the research goal over other university goals.

The second section of Chapter Nine discussed the management problems affecting the effectiveness levels of academic leaders in the performance of their jobs. The academic leaders' responses to our survey revealed that academic shortages, dwindling resources, and excessive work constitute the major management difficulties to both the British and the Nigerian academic leaders. The latter part of the second section also identified academic leaders' important job elements on which presumably they experience their problems. Again, the academic leaders' responses to the survey identified as major academic concerns the extension of the frontiers of knowledge, staff selection and development, and policy formulation. The consistent ratings between the British and the Nigerian academic leaders on these job elements and problems give greater reliability to the findings.

The third section of Chapter Nine was on the selection of academic leaders. It explained the current selection processes in both the Nigerian and the British universities and observed that the selection criteria are based essentially on academic seniority and research publications. It noted, therefore, in consonance with our earlier findings, that the selection criteria of academic leaders are, in the main, unsupported by the nature of work which academic leaders perform. While academic leaders perform administrative and management functions, they are selected based on academic competence. It was therefore suggested that in order that academic leaders might be more effective on their jobs, the selection criteria should be reviewed to require more management and administrative skills on the part of academic leaders. Since the academic leaders do not favor making management and administrative competence a prerequisite to their appointment, it was suggested that specialized management training should be made available to academic leaders on appointment.

The latter part of section three posed and attempted to resolve the dilemma of who heads the universities. It considered the advantages and the disadvantages of a lay administrator versus a pure professional (an academic), and settled for the professional administrator who seems to combine the advantages of both a lay administrator and a pure professional. Finally, the academic leaders' own solution to the dilemma of who heads their universities was sought. The results of the survey revealed that the academic leaders would resent very much the idea of lay administrators heading them.

The last section of Chapter Nine was devoted to the issues of training and management development for academic leaders. First, the academic leaders' reaction to the idea of training was sought. Our investigations revealed that while most academic leaders seem to believe that some form of training would be beneficial to them, they would oppose making management training a prerequisite to their appointment as academic leaders. When an estimate of their motivation to manage was made, it showed that academic leaders may not be particularly motivated to effective management, and this explains in part their resentment to training. However, judging by some of the comments made in the questionnaire by the academic leaders, making management training a package to accompany their appointment would be better accepted.

It was argued that the nature of possible management training would emphasize skills development, would be specialized, and high-status to be successful. The areas of relevant skills which the academic leaders agreed would be beneficial to them include decision-making and information management, but especially interpersonal and leadership skills.

In general, the findings in Chapter 9 reveal the relative non-respect given to the role and importance of administration and management in the university setting. Academic leaders would appear doubtful of the potential and capability of this factor to make a fundamental difference in organizational success or failure. The attitude of academic leaders seems to be that management skills are trivial and unimportant.

Another general finding in Chapter 9 and related discussions on this [1] reveal the multiplicity, the dynamism, and the complexity of university goals and activities. This finding suggests the need to exercise care in testing ideas and priniciples which are hypothesized to be superior to current management and academic leaders' practices in the academia. This, in turn, calls for extensive and intensive debates on suggested changes in universities, including the training of academic leaders in skills, some of which business managers would normally possess.

For example, in recommending ideas designed to enable universities to meet some of their challenges and thus be more effective, debate and suggestions seemed to have focused on appropriate models of university governance. Instead of practising the traditional Committee Model which universities seem to favour, consultants and critics of the Committee Model recommend Collegiate or Polytechnic Model, the Industrial or Managerial Model, or the Civil Service Model of university governance [2].

Little recognized or accepted is the fact that each of the traditional and the alternative models of university administration and management has its strengths and weaknesses in a university environment. Therefore, there is the need to evaluate the Committee Model of administration and management against the alternative models proposed to bring out the advantages and disadvantages of each model in the university system, before a decision to change or retain a particular model can be justified. Even then, care must be exercised not to lay undue emphasis at organizational structures at the expense of the behaviour of operators of a system. Formal structures hardly tell the whole story.

Whilst organizational structure is undoubtedly important, for example, the idea that one can solve all organizational problems simply by designing a better structure is unduly optimistic. In the political arena, for example, Nigeria has practised both the parliamentary and the presidential systems of political administration, and both with disastrous consequences. In such a case, attention must necessarily focus on the *knowledge*, *skills*, and the *motivation* of the operations of a system rather than on the formal structure in which they operate.

Besides, the power of the external or the informal groups is a factor that militates against the significance of formal organizational structures. However good a structure may be, if the people who operate it do so badly, they can ruin it. On the other hand, if the operators of a system are aware of its strengths and limitations, with appropriate skills and motivation, almost any system can be made to function effectively. This is one of the strengths of our present research. It concentrates on the behavioural aspects of organizational members—their skills, knowledge, motivation, and attitudes, as well as on the actual jobs these members perform.

Finally, the results in Chapter Nine also reveal areas in which lack of management skills was seen by the academic leaders as being constraints on their effective performance as managers. Academics often argue correctly that universities, in comparison with private industry, have goals that are more abstract, authority that is more diffuse, interdependence that is lower, individual roles that are more in number, and performance measures that are fewer and less clear. However, the logic of such arguments calls for *more*, not *less*, preparation on the part of the academic leaders. Yet it must be admitted that academic leaders are generally not as well prepared as their industrial counterparts in the practice of administration and management, and in the handling of large and multi-million pound organizations which universities are [3].

10.3 References

[1] See also, Oshagbemi T.A., "What are universities for? An empirical verification of the perceived goals of British and Nigerian universities", Department of Management Studies, University of Jos, Seminar Series, Jan. 13, 1987.

[2] Oshagbemi, T.A., "Academic leaders and the Management of Universities", *Management in Nigeria*, Vol. 22, Nos 11 & 12, Nov./Dec., 1986.

[3] Ibid.

Chapter 11
Conclusions, Implications, and Applications of the Study

11.1 Introduction

Chapter Ten presented a summary of the research and its findings. The current chapter attempts to provide some underlying explanations to these findings. In addition, it presents the conclusions and implications of the study and outlines the potential applications of the work. This concluding chapter also summarizes the limitations of our research and highlights some suggestions for further studies.

We now summarize hereunder the conclusions and the implications of this study. As in the presentation of the previous chapter on the findings of the research, this summary is subdivided into different relevant headings.

11.1.1 Conclusions on the Nature of the Academic Leaders' Jobs

The findings in Chapter Five show, among other things, that academic leaders are, on the average, hardworking individuals. The figures of how long our sampled academic leaders work (a net of about 42 hours per week), compare favourably with the results of previous studies of the time spent by managers at work. Thus, our results suggest that, on the average, academic leaders work at least as long as industrial managers and perhaps longer than some public sector managers. In making comparisons of how long managers work, however, only studies employing the more direct diary or observation methodologies were used. This is because the literature has shown that studies based on interviews and questionnaires tend to overestimate the working hours of managers. One should nonetheless be careful of the comparability of research results, even of those using the more direct empirical methodologies. For example, while some researchers defined the total working hours to include the gross time spent, other studies, such as ours, defined the total working hours to include only the net actual working hours. In either case, it should be noted that figures for the working hours relate to the average for the sample only; there are often wide ranges of variations of managers' working hours even within the same sample.

Explanations for variations in total working hours experienced by managers were made in Chapter Five. Such explanations include the differences between organizations in which managers work, differences in the levels of the managers involved, and differences in the jobs of managers. An explanation arising from our own study, and which could also explain variations in total working time, is the concept of managers' level of motivation and their work habits. Beyond a minimum level of control arising from system imposition, for example, academic leaders determine their own jobs and their own working hours. In addition, some of them are more effective than others in the management of their time.

The findings on the activities of academic leaders indicate that the British academic leaders spent about the same percentage of their total working time on deskwork as their Nigerian counterparts—over 40 percent in each case. The variations about the mean in both samples were also not significantly different from one another. Comparison with previous studies on the time spent by industrial managers on deskwork activities show, however, that academic leaders spend more time on this activity than industrial managers. The explanation for this results is perhaps the excessive paperwork which academic leaders necessarily handle in the excecution of their primary jobs of teaching, research, and administration and management, jobs which necessitate extensive reading and writing.

The findings on the time spent by academic leaders on scheduled and unscheduled meetings and a comparison of the industrial managers' time on these activities show wide differences. They show that academic leaders tend to attend less meetings as compared with industrial managers. The conclusions from these findings would seem to suggest that industrial managers tend to be more participative than academic leaders in the management of their respective organizations. This conclusion may be difficult to accept in view of the practice of the Committee System of administration and management in the universities. This result is perhaps better understood in the context that academic leaders, unlike industrial managers, tend to spend more of their time alone.

A comparison of the time spent by our academic leaders and industrial managers on the telephone reveals that industrial managers tend to spend more time on this activity than academic leaders. A possible explanation may be that academic leaders interact more on a face-to-face basis with their students and colleagues than managers in industry. In the Nigerian case, at least, the use of the telephone has not, unfortunately, become widespread within the campuses.

The findings on teaching show that British academic leaders tend to teach a little less than their Nigerian counterparts, although the differences between the figures involved were not statistically significant. This finding may be due, in part, to relative paucity of qualified Nigerian academics vis-à-vis the British lecturers, some of whom may be senior and more experienced than the Nigerian lecturers. Invariably, therefore, the Nigerian academic leader often has to teach.

Furthermore, the findings on the subject of the academic leaders' activities show that academic leaders spend more time on research than on teaching and much less time on consulting functions. The explanation for the relative time spent on research vis-à-vis teaching may be the perceived superiority of the research function which has in fact being regarded as the "lifeblood" of the university. Consulting activities will now tend to be more popular in both countries, as the pressure to generate more cash from within the universities increases.

The analyses from the diaries also reveal where academic leaders spend their time. The findings here show that academic leaders and industrial managers both tend to spend a considerable time, about 75 percent of their total time, in organizational premises. This finding confirms the statement that managers are "homebodies". The implication is that since managers, on average, perform most organizational activities in organizational premises and do this mostly during designated office hours, in order to improve their skills and productivity, attention must be focused on what they do during the office hours.

The findings on the significantly different hours which British and Nigerian academic leaders spend with their students are interesting. One is not sure whether these findings reveal some underlying cultural differences in attitude in both countries regarding student-staff personal contacts. However, some other possible explanations for these differences were offered in Chapter Six. Contrary to academic leaders' perceptions that they spend much of their time with their students, the findings reveal that academic leaders spend more time with their own colleagues and members of the administrative staff than with students. Thus, the thinking that academic leaders spend more time with students is an illusion not borne out with reference to the facts.

In was revealed from the data that academic leaders actually spend less than 20 percent of their time truly alone, i.e. without any interruptions. This means that academic leaders who also engage in teaching should expect their research activities to suffer because of insufficient time. The implication is that promotions on the academic line will be much slower for academic leaders who are not yet professors, other things being equal. Similarly, academic leaders who are already professors would tend to publish less.

General conclusions could now be made in the observed similarities in the job characteristics of Nigerian and British academic leaders. Our findings reveal similar characteristics in the jobs performed by these two groups of managers; where these took place, their subject, and the duration of these activities. There were a couple of exceptions, these relating to the time spent with students and with groups of 6 or more people. Generally, however, the conclusion seems to be that academic jobs are roughly similar in both countries. This similarity may be due, in part, to the historical relationship between both countries. The conclusion is that cultural differences between Britain and Nigeria would not appear to affect the nature of academic jobs in both countries significantly. The exception to this statement may be the technological differences in both countries and the implications of this on the performance of the academic leaders' jobs.

If we compare the job characteristics of academic leaders on the one hand with those of industrial managers on the other, some general conclusions can also be made. There are areas of similar job characteristics between academic leaders and industrial managers. For example, the total hours worked, as well as the percentage of time spent within organizational premises were quite close as between our study of academic leaders and other studies of managers within industries. In addition, it can be observed that all managers, whether industrial or academic, exhibited rich varieties in their jobs which were, in both cases, highly fragmented.

There were a number of important exceptions, however, and these should be highlighted. Academic leaders tend to differ in the extent of the proportion of their time which is spent on some activities such as meetings and telephone. Consistently, academic leaders tend to spend a lower percentage of time than industrial managers on these activities. On the other hand, academic leaders tend to spend a higher percentage of their total time on some other type of activities. Examples of these include the percentage of time spent by academic leaders working during the weekend, working alone, or working on deskwork activities. On each of these activities, comparable figures from managers in industry would suggest that industrial managers spend a lower percentage of time than academic leaders. The activity duration of academic leaders also tends to be longer than that of industrial managers where episodes tend to be very brief.

The complexity of academic leaders' jobs should also be mentioned. Academic leaders tend to perform miscellaneous roles while, comparatively, the roles of industrial managers tend to be simpler and more clearly defined. The complexity of academic leaders' roles may be related to the multiplicity of the goals of universities. What universities have been established for continues to present a rich and interesting debate on organizational goal.

Our study therefore contributes to the notion that the concept of the universality of managerial functions would need contexual qualifications as well as qualifications based on the nature and reality of managerial work. With the bulk and with upper ranges of 75 and 89 percent of their total time spent on administration and management, academic leaders are managers by whatever definition, their technical skills and competence notwithstanding. It would be unrealistic to expect all managers to have identical job characteristics. We have seen that even within the same industry, managers exhibit a variety of job characteristics.

11.1.2 Implications of the Job Profiles of Academic Leaders

Stewart (1984) has shown that managers, in general, can be grouped together meaningfully on the basis of their job characteristics. Our classification of academic leaders into meaningful groupings has buttressed this view. Notwithstanding the earlier picture conveyed in Chapters Five and Six, that academic leaders vary widely in the practice of their jobs, Chapter Seven has shown that a meaningful classification of academic leaders is possible. It has demonstrated that academic leaders in both Britain and Nigeria can be grouped together and classified usefully on the basis of how they spend their time.

Traditionally, classification of managers tends to be based on only one criterion, functions, or levels. The cluster analysis in Chapter Seven has shown that there is an alternative and modern way of classifying managers into intelligible groups based on several criteria. Instead of using only one criterion, rank, for example, our classification was based on 24 criteria which are various measures of the job characteristics of academic leaders, especially those based on how academic leaders spend their time. This alternative method of classification offers a lot of potential, as it uses fairly comprehensive criteria of job characteristics.

For example, because the resulting classification is based on both similarities and differences in recorded job characteristics, training programmes should, perhaps, be focused on groups of managers with similar work characteristics. In essence, therefore, it is our considered view that attendance on management development programmes should not be made on one's rank alone, as this criterion may say little about each manager's work habits and skills. In our own classification, for example, the Administrators Type 2 may benefit from a course on delegation, time management, and developing human relations skills. Similarly, the Research Leaders may benefit from a training programme emphasizing the importance of effective management in the determination of an organizational success. Our classification seems to support our belief that effectiveness in managerial practices can be increased by tailor-made development programmes based on managers' work characteristics. Managers themselves can be very useful in the identification of their work habits, deficiencies in their skills, and gaps in their competences and knowledge. Unless empirical bases are undertaken to assess managerial needs, many of the general management development programmes available will not serve their purpose, as some of these are often targeted at the wrong audience. In matters of productivity and competence on the job, one's managerial level alone does not say all.

We should be careful, however, not to give the impression that our research suggests that one group of our classified academic leaders was necessarily less or more effective than the other. This is certainly not the objective in cluster analyses. In classifying managers, we merely observe and say that since each group exhibits different job characteristics, they would need different assistance programmes to increase their effectiveness levels. Beyond this observation, it is difficult to generalize. One problem of the concept of effectiveness relates to organizational goals. If university goals were only research and consulting excellence, for example, it is clear that one of our groups will tend to be more effective than the others. But in the real world of multiple goals and multiple measures, discussions on the effectiveness of groups can only be relative. It would be interesting and useful to know, however, the one of the five groups which tends to be more effective than the others in relation to the overall university goals. This may then enable us, perhaps, to identify those skills and work habits which tend to be more or less effective in general or particular managerial work situations.

It is of interest to observe that the majority (about 60 percent) of the academic leaders were classified as administrators, either strategic or tactical. This result further reinforces one of the conclusions made earlier that the jobs of academic leaders are administration and management, and that academic leaders' technical and professional competences should not becloud this fact. The result shows that, essentially, academic leaders, like industrial managers, perform managerial jobs.

It is noteworthy to further observe that in comparison to the number of academic leaders who were classified as administrators, only half were grouped as Educational Leaders. About half of the Educational Leaders were, in turn, classified as Research Leaders. It follows, therefore, that academic and research competence alone may not be the best and the sole criterion for appointing academic leaders, whose jobs are, in the main, administration and management. Notwithstanding the difficulty of assessment, perhaps some measure of competence in administration and management may also be considered useful in selecting academic leaders. Alternatively, perhaps, universities should consider assisting academic leaders in performing their management and administrative jobs effectively. This may be approached through occasional tailor-made development programmes based on the need resulting from an examination of their job characteristics. The opinion expressed here is that it would be beneficial to universities to have academic leaders, who, in addition to their technical competence, are knowledgeable and skilled in administration and management.

It should be pointed out that the naming of the groups should not be allowed to give the impression that there was complete uniformity within each category. It should be emphasized that 24 variables were used for the classification of academic leaders and that only average data for the various groups were compared. It is possible, therefore, that a given academic leader in a group may not necessarily feature prominently on the criteria from where his group name apparently emanated.

Finally, it should be restated that our grouping of academic leaders was based on a sample of 38 academic leaders from Nigeria and Britain. These people filled our diaries for one week. The small sample size and the short duration of the time during which they filled the diaries are limitations to the conclusions made on the job profiles of academic leaders. It is hoped that more senior academics could, in the future, be persuaded to take part in this type of research, filling diaries for a longer time. This would provide an opportunity to test the validity of our findings and of our classification which was not, in any case, intended to be definitive.

11.1.3 Implications of the Perceptions of Academic Leaders

There are very important implications of academic leaders' perceptions of their jobs and of academic leaders' perceptions of how they spend their time. One of these implications is related to the unreliability on managers' estimates of how they spend their time. All managers, whether industrial or academic, tend to make errors in estimates of how they spend their time. Furthermore, these errors are not consistent, either in nature or direction, and the degree of the errors involved in some instances is substantial.

This finding, in turn, has important implications on the methodology employed when designing researches to study managerial jobs. It reveals the weaknesses of the questionnaire and interview methodologies, as manager's estimates may be wrong and the researcher may not know the nature and the extent of the error involved. The diary provides a more direct approach to studying managerial jobs, and it should be much less susceptible to deliberate structuring than the questionnaire approach. Therefore, the more direct research designs, such as the diary or the observational methods, should always be employed in preference to indirect techniques when studying managerial jobs. This will enhance the reliability and validity of the findings.

However, our findings have merely demonstrated the inadequacy of the questionnaire methodology when used alone to study the job activities of managers. It has not implied that the questionnaire has no use in this or other types of research. Actually, our own research provides a strong support for the use of a multiple methodology that combines direct and indirect measures, especially when the research objectives include obtaining data on managerial perceptions and attitudes. In such a research design, the questionnaire will not only serve as a supplement but also as a complement to the diary. In our study, the questionnaire complements the diary findings, for example, on the fact that the academic leaders spent more time on administration and management than on research. It also supplements the diary findings, for example, on the academic leaders' perceptions of the relative importance of research versus administration and management to them. Together, these findings give greater depth and breadth of knowledge of the academic leaders' jobs.

Other implications arising from the findings in Chapter Eight relate to the general consistent ratings by the British and Nigerian academic leaders on their jobs and of how they spend their time. It shows that not only do British and Nigerian academic leaders have similar job characteristics, but that the academic leaders also have similar perceptions of their jobs and of their time allocation. These findings in turn strengthen the notion of the similarity of the academic culture in both countries.

The findings in Chapter Eight also have serious implications for the selection, training, and development of academic leaders, topics that were considered in greater detail in Chapter Nine. The findings in Chapter Eight suggest that, for greater effectiveness, only professors who enjoy administration and management should be selected as academic leaders, and not, as one of the respondents put it, those who "accept administration as a cost to be borne as part of holding chairs". The selection of those who would regard administration and management as their primary job should also be sought in appointing academic leaders. The latter would tend to be more committed to the job of effectively administering and managing their universities. Furthermore, only academics who demonstrate fair competence on administration and management (with successful administrative experience to back this up) should be made academic leaders. Alternatively, academics who are appointed leaders should not only accept that management skills can be learnt, but be willing to improve their management skills through training and exposure to management development programmes.

On the nature of training, our analyses show clearly that, while the demands of the academic leaders' job are in administration and management, the preferences of most of the academic leaders and or their abilities seem to be on research. The most appropriate training would therefore be one that is designed to assist academic leaders to improve their management and administrative skills. Academic leaders would also benefit from a general orientation and appreciation of the fact that effectiveness in management is crucial to the realization of organizational goals, even if that organization is the university. Irrespective of the resource-base of an organization, ineffective management practice, including faulty policy administration, will still, at the end, determine success or failure. Especially in an era when the university system is being attacked lefts, rights, and centre, competence on the part of its managers in administration and management may make a difference as to whether or not the university system will survive these attacks and criticism.

That is why it is being suggested that some measure of managerial success, however crude, should be devised to assess the promotion of academic leaders to higher managerial levels. For example, a dean who cannot manage his or her faculty well should not be a candidate for consideration as a Vice-Chancellor. A corollary of the above suggestions is that only academic leaders who are already very successful (preferably professors) should be appointed as higher level academic leaders—so that, perhaps, the distraction of the effort on research may be lessened. Implementing this suggestion may be more of a problem in Nigeria (where many academic leaders are yet to attain professorship) than in Britain. Another corollary is that "political factors" should as much as possible be replaced in favour of demonstrated merit in selecting academic leaders. Only academic leaders who are competent on administration and management and who enjoy the job should be selected to head universities. In this way, universities would tend to face squarely the challenges confronting them.

11.1.4 Implications of the Selection, Training, and Management Development of Academic Leaders

Chapter Nine has important implications on the selection, training, and management development of academic leaders. One of these implications is that since the primary goal (not the only goal) of universities seems to be research excellence, any head of the university system who himself may not be or have been a successful researcher is not likely to command respect, however good his skills in administration and management may be. However, the nature of the work which academic leaders do, and the nature of the problems and difficulties which they encounter in their jobs would suggest that academic leaders' effectiveness levels can be increased by recourse to management skills development programmes to complement their research skills.

Another implication is the identification of the academic leaders' important job elements which reveal that academic leaders tend to be more concerned with "academic matters". The implication is that overall university effectiveness can be improved if academic leaders have competent administrators and secretaries to take care of routine administrative functions, leaving strategic issues to the academic leaders.

One of the findings in Chapter Nine is that the selection process of academic leaders is not consistent with the nature of work which academic leaders perform. While academic leaders perform administrative and managerial work mostly, they are selected based on their research competence. The implication of the finding is that if academic leaders are to do their work more effectively, the selection criteria should either be modified to incorporate the requirement of more management training and experience, or some form of management training should be instituted to assist academic leaders. Perhaps, a combination of both methods should be used.

Notwithstanding the doubts sometimes expressed on the gains to be derived from management education even by some management scholars [1] one of the suggestions of Chapter Nine is that academic leaders' managerial performance can be improved by recourse to management training. The academic leaders themselves seem to confirm that management training would be generally useful to them. However, to be successful, such a training programme must have a skills orientation and be high-status. Furthermore, to be relevant the training should be specialized and related to the needs of the individual academic leaders.

In matters of training, however, one observation is that academic leaders, perhaps like some managers, seem to be conservative. Universities everywhere seem to be strong in tradition and tend to overlook or underplay important changes that have occurred in the society. Surprisingly, this attitude of proconservatism in the matters of the practice of administration is unlike the academic leaders' attitude to research activities where changes in substance and methodology are easily accepted if found to be better than earlier ideas and or practices. Academic leaders should realize that, unless they improve on the general administration and management of the universities, intervention by the governments and the society on university affairs may increase. This trend would not be beneficial either to the universities or to the larger society.

In this regard, Singleton has argued that because of the growth in size and expenditure, universities can no longer be left to themselves, and the outside world is increasingly critical of the values and achievements of universities. [2] This is so much so that the expansion of the university system in the Western world has, according to Singleton, been almost eliminated over the last few years. Unfortunately, the experience of current academic leaders seems to be limited almost entirely to the expansion era. Worse still, the new management skills which are now being required and which will increasingly be required in the future of stagnation or recession are not being now developed.

Academic leadership and management practices in the universities can be improved. It is hoped that some of the ideas expressed in this work will contribute towards this improvement.

In conclusion, perhaps, one should be very careful not to overemphasize administrative excellence over everything else in a university setting, or be seen to give the impression that good administration and management is the only thing that matters in a university. That is why Diana Warwick cautions that universities

> may have a terribly efficient management structure, have a financial control system of impeccable accuracy and be able to cost and account for every item of expenditure, but if in the process of gaining this managerial world the soul of the institution is lost, where is the profit? [3]

By my own interpretation, the "soul" of the university is research excellence. Therefore, a situation whereby some academics, after attaining professorships allegedly cease to get involved in any research, for whatever reason, should be discouraged, as this practice is not in the interest of any university. For an academic leader, obviously the priority activity should be in administration and management. However, the research function should still be encouraged to stimulate and give direction to younger academics, among other reasons. In Nigeria, for example, where textbooks and other teaching materials are in short supply, senior academics really have an obligation to show leadership in the promotion and production of these needed materials.

Actually, there is no denying the fact that, in the final analysis, research excellence is what gives respect to a university. Indeed, excellence in research activities would appear a *necessary* quality for any university worthy of its name. The message from this work is that whilst recognizing the necessary role of research to the enhancement of a university's reputation, it should now be apparent to and appreciated by academic leaders that research excellence is no longer a *sufficient* condition for university survival and success in this era of enormous challenges facing them. Stated differently, universities would increasingly find it difficult to pursue their research and other goals without also ensuring that their organizations survive and are well managed. In essence, therefore, the message from this book is that excellence in research would need to be complemented by excellence in administration and management for optimum results. Accordingly, universities should strive for excellence in their policies, structure, administrative processes, as well as in their management of human, financial, and other resources. There are beneficial relationships among research, consulting, teaching, and administration and management, and these relationships would need to be pursued by universities.

Finally, academic leaders must come out of their shells and accept that academic competence does not *ipso facto* confer leadership and management capabilities. This suggests that they should be willing to improve their management skills through appropriate skills training. This is especially necessary, as the experiences of many academic leaders seem to be limited to the expansion era which is a sharp contrast to the current situation of stagnation and recession.

11.2 Potential Applications of the Study

The practical as well as the theoretical applications of this study are wide and varied.

First and foremost, the results should be immediately usable to academic leaders and policy makers in Nigerian and in British universities. Because of the similarity in academic culture, the findings of this study may also be of practical significance to academic leaders and policy makers in other countries and in other institutions of higher learning. For example, academic leaders would be better able, and perhaps more willing, to analyze how they spend their time for better time management. They would also be able to better analyze the nature of their work and undertake self study that would generally increase their performance levels. Informal feedback from some of the subjects who completed the diary indicated that they were very surprised by what it revealed about the pattern of their work activities. Thus, filling in the diary, for say a week, whilst perhaps time-consuming and even irritating at times, could provide valuable data which would allow academic *at all levels* to organize their work activities more effectively.

For policy makers, areas of direct relevance and applications for the universities would be in the composition, selection, and training of academic leaders as well as in the structure, governance, and administration of universities generally. In particular, training courses for academic leaders can be better designed taking into consideration the nature of academic leaders' work and academic leaders' perceptions, beliefs, and attitudes. These applications will help to make the universities more efficient and more effective.

With due modifications, it is expected that this study may also be usefully applied to other organizations in the private and public sectors. This is especially, as the focus of the study is on academic leaders, whose actions and perceptions, like those of the other managers, need to be understood fully in order to help enhance their performance and the performance of their organizations. For example, this study has contributed to the concept of the universality of managerial functions that may help in the designing of both general as well as specialized management or skills development programmes for managers.

On the theoretical side, apart from shedding further light on the limitations of the concept of the universality of managerial functions, this study could be usefully applied in designing better researches to study managerial jobs. For example, the research has demonstrated the benefits to be derived from the multiple methodologies of the direct and indirect approaches in the study of managerial jobs and perceptions.

The identified job profiles of academic leaders may also be used as a basis for future researches dealing with the subject of managerial effectiveness. In doing this, the effort would be to see the extent to which some job characteristics or profiles of academic leaders correlate with some measures or indicators of managerial effectiveness.

11.3 Limitations to this Study

Only the group referred to as academic leaders has been examined in this study. Unfortunately, academic leaders are only one group of actors in a university's management scene. There are also the other university staff represented in the support offices of the bursary, registry, health, catering, library, et cetera. The heads of these units, especially those of the bursary and the registry, wield enormous power and are also important actors and actresses influencing the form and the trend of management and administrative practices. A total picture of the university administration and management scene can hardly be obtained without also examining the role of these other university staff.

However, the latter group of non-academic leaders almost always act in the advisory or supportive roles to implement policy decisions made by the academic leaders. In the culture of most universities, the academics seem to occupy a central focus, and their actions affect the structure, orientation, and performance of the administration. Besides, considering the limited time and financial resources available for this study, it was not feasible for the design of the project to be all-embracing.

Another limitation to this work is the rather small sample of British and Nigerian academic leaders who completed the diaries (38) and the duration for which this was done (one week). However, larger sample sizes of diary studies covering different organizations are not many. In addition, we complemented our study by an extensive survey which in many cases provided corroboratory evidence for the conclusions drawn from the diary study.

11.4 Suggestions for Further Study

As we suggested under the potential applications of this work, one area of useful further study is the effectiveness of academic leaders.

Whilst our study classified academic leaders into job profiles, the implications of this exercise on the effectiveness of each group was not conclusive. It would be necessary to further identify and isolate job characteristics that may correlate with less or more effective academic leaders.

Another area of further investigation would be the question of the selection processes of academic leaders. It would be helpful to know, for example, if academic leaders such as deans who are democratically elected by their colleagues tend to perform differently than academic leaders such as head of departments who are merely appointed. Similarly, it would be useful to know if government interference in the appointment of Nigerian Vice-Chancellors affect the performance of such academic leaders, and if so, in what way?

Related to this consideration is the issue of the nationality of academic leaders. In Britain, all the academic leaders who responded to our questionnaire were British. In Nigeria, 35 percent of the responding academic leaders were non-Nigerians. The question is: would academic leaders who are non-Nigerians perform better, worse, or at about the same level as Nigerians in Nigeria? Answers to these and other related questions would help in fashioning policies and recommending practices that would make universities more effective and more responsive to their societal needs.

Finally, the effectiveness of academic leaders may be influenced by the type of organizational structure within which they work. This issue was beyond the scope of the present book, but would provide a useful area for future research which would complement the findings of the present study.

11.5 References

[1] Mintzberg, H., *The Nature of Managerial Work*, Harper and Row, New York, 1973, pp. 187–188; See also, Stewart, R., The Nature of Management? A Problem for Management Education, *Journal of Management Studies*, Vol. 21, No. 3, July 1984, pp. 323–330.

[2] Singleton, W.T., *Management Skills*, MTP Press Limited, Lancaster, 1981, p. 68.

[3] Warwick, D., *The Times Higher Education Supplement*, April 12, 1985, p. 8.

Appendices

Appendix A: A Copy of the Diary Used in This Study

Dear Sir

We are studying some aspects of the job characteristics of academic leaders in Britain and Nigeria. For the purposes of our study, 'academic leaders' are defined as academic staff members occupying formal administrative positions within the university framework. Examples of this group include (but are not limited to) heads of department, deans, directors, and vice-chancellors.

Towards the objectives of our study, the attached diary has been designed. We would be grateful if you would kindly fill in the diary for a working period of one week. Academic leaders who may be deputies or who may be acting in their positions may also complete the diary. Please return the completed diary in the enclosed stamped and addressed envelope as soon as you can.

As a means to partially compensate you for your efforts, we undertake to tell you your job characteristics in relation to the average for this study. If you want this information sent to you, please identify your diary by supplying your name and address. Otherwise, you may remain anonymous. However, if you would like to know more about the project or its conclusions, please do not hesitate to write to us.

We thank you in anticipation of your cooperation.

Yours sincerely

* Please, Read These Explanatory Notes Carefully Before Filling in the Diary.

* Use a new sheet for each activity. Activities are defined as incidents of five minutes or more in duration. Tick only ONE activity in each column. If two or more activities are involved, please tick the most

important one. Incidents of less than five-minute duration are defined as fleeting contacts or interruptions. These are not to be recorded separately on a different page. There may be a number of fleeting contacts during a given activity. The appropriate column under fleeting contacts/interruptions should be ticked for as many times as they occur. If you desire, you may give details of your activities on the pages of the diary.

[a] 'Deskwork' refers to all paperwork—reading, writing, grading scripts, reports, figurework, etc. 'Travelling' refers to all your physical movements away from your campus. Lecturing or teaching is defined as a meeting; it may be scheduled (if on the timetable for example) or unscheduled. As far as possible, could you please give brief details of activities recorded as miscellaneous.

[b] The heading 'Subject Matter?' refers to the primary purpose of an activity and not necessarily the only purpose. Similarly, 'Where?' and 'With Whom?' refer respectively to the primary place where an activity featured and the major group with whom it was performed. Teaching is used to refer to the dissemination of knowledge while research refers to all activities related to the propagation of knowledge. Consulting refers to the activities pertaining to be application of knowledge especially to outside bodies and for a fee. 'Administration and management' is used here to refer to all other official activities that you perform.

[c] 'Other units' may include the lecture halls, computer rooms, library, laboratory, board rooms, common rooms, etc. located on the same campus.

[d] 'Colleagues' refer to academic staff members. Administrative staff refers to all non-teaching staff. This includes your secretary. 'External' refers to one who is not a member of the university community (i.e., not students, administrative or academic staff members).

* Please Note That This Exercise Is Designed for Seven Consecutive Days. However, Your Data Would Be Appreciated Even for a Fewer Number of Days.

Thank You.

Examples of how to Fill the Diary (Illustration 1)

Academic Leaders' Study (Diary Method)

Date (if on a new day): 6, 4, 1984.
Time at the beginning of the activity: 7.20 AM

Activity?		Subject Matter?		Where?		With Whom?	
Deskwork	☑	Teaching	☐	Own office	☑	Students	☐
Scheduled meetings	☐	Research	☐	Other Units	☐	Colleagues	☐
Unscheduled meetings	☐	Consulting	☐	Other Campuses	☐	Admin. Staff	☑
Telephoning in/out	☐	Admin. and Mgt.	☑	Home	☐	External	☐
Travelling	☐	Personal	☐	Other Organizations	☐	Alone	☐
Computing	☐						
Practicals	☐						
Coffee/Tea break	☐						
Lunch	☐						
Miscellaneous	☐						

Compiling examination results

Approx. duration (minutes)	5	10	20	30	40	50	60	Otherwise, specify time: 2 hrs 15 mins.

Activity performed with: (No o people)	0(alone)	1 ✓	2–5	6–20	21–50	51+

Fleeting Contacts and Interruptions

	Personal	Telephone
Students	✓✓✓✓	
Colleagues		✓✓
Administrative staff		✓
External person		
Self		✓

Possible Explanation of Illustration 1

On 6 April, 1984, I started some deskwork activity at 7.20 AM. in my office. The work is related to administration and management and it lasted for approximately 2 hours 15 minutes. One member of the administrative staff (my secretary) was with me in the office.

During this period, a student or some students came in briefly at 4 different intervals. 3 brief telephone calls were received, 2 of these were from colleagues and the third was from a member of the administrative staff. The other telephone conversation was a brief call made by myself.

These Notes Are for Illustration Only. You Do not Have to Write Such Detailed Notes in the Diary.

Examples of how to Fill the Diary (Illustration 2)

Academic Leaders' Study (Diary Method)

Date (if on a new day): ____, ____, 1984.
Time at the beginning of the activity: 11.00 AM

Activity?		Subject Matter?		Where?		With Whom?	
Deskwork	☐	Teaching	☑	Own office	☐	Students	☑
Scheduled meetings	☑	Research	☐	Other Units	☑	Colleagues	☐
Unscheduled meetings	☐	Consulting	☐	Other Campuses	☐	Admin. Staff	☐
Telephoning in/out	☐	Admin. and Mgt.	☐	Home	☐	External	☐
Travelling	☐	Personal	☐	Other Organizations	☐	Alone	☐
Computing	☐						
Practicals	☐						
Coffee/Tea break	☐						
Lunch	☐						
Miscellaneous	☐						

Postgraduate seminar

Approx. duration (minutes)	5	10	20	30	40	50	60 √	Otherwise, specify time:

Activity performed with: (No of people)	0(alone)	1	2–5	6–20	21–50	51+ √

Fleeting Contacts and Interruptions

	Personal	Telephone
Students		
Colleagues		
Administrative staff		
External person	√	
Self	√	

Possible Explanation of Illustration 2

On the same day (i.e. 6/4/84), I had a scheduled meeting (lecture) with students which started at 11.00 AM. It look place in one of the classrooms and lasted for an hour. The class size was larger than 50.

During the lecture, I was interrupted by a visitor who wanted to know the location of the library. I also had to go back to my office at the middle of the lecture to obtain coloured chalks for drawing diagrams on the board!

These Notes Are for Illustration Only. You Do not Have to Write Such Detailed Notes in the Diary.

Examples of how to Fill the Diary (Illustration 3)

Academic Leaders' Study (Diary Method)

Date (if on a new day): 17 , 4 , 1984.
Time at the beginning of the activity: 12.30 PM

Activity?		Subject Matter?		Where?		With Whom?	
Deskwork	☐	Teaching	☐	Own office	☐	Students	☐
Scheduled meetings	☐	Research	☐	Other Units	☐	Colleagues	☐
Unscheduled meetings	☐	Consulting	☐	Other Campuses	☐	Admin. Staff	☐
Telephoning in/out	☐	Admin. and Mgt.	☐	Home	☑	External	☐
Travelling	☐	Personal	☑	Other Organizations	☐	Alone	☑
Computing	☐						
Practicals	☐						
Coffee/Tea break	☐						
Lunch	☑						
Miscellaneous	☐						

Approx. duration (minutes)	5	10	20	30	40 ✓	50	60	Otherwise, specify time:

Activity performed with: (No of people)	0(alone) ✓	1	2–5	6–20	21–50	51+

Fleeting Contacts and Interruptions

	Personal	Telephone
Students		
Colleagues		
Administrative staff		
External person		
Self		

Possible Explanation of Illustration 3

On 17/4/84, I went home for lunch at 12.30 PM. This took approximately 40 minutes and I was alone.

There were no fleeting contacts or interruptions during this activity.

These Notes Are for Illustration Only. You Do not Have to Write Such Detailed Notes in the Diary.

Academic Leaders' Study (Diary Method)

Date (if on a new day): ____, ____, 1984.
Time at the beginning of the activity: ________

Activity?		Subject Matter?		Where?		With Whom?	
Deskwork	☐	Teaching	☐	Own office	☐	Students	☐
Scheduled meetings	☐	Research	☐	Other Units	☐	Colleagues	☐
Unscheduled meetings	☐	Consulting	☐	Other Campuses	☐	Admin. Staff	☐
Telephoning in/out	☐	Admin. and Mgt.	☐	Home	☐	External	☐
Travelling	☐	Personal	☐	Other Organizations	☐	Alone	☐
Computing	☐						
Practicals	☐						
Coffee/Tea break	☐						
Lunch	☐						
Miscellaneous							

Approx. duration (minutes)	5	10	20	30	40	50	60	Otherwise, specify time:

Activity performed with: (No of people)	0(alone)	1	2–5	6–20	21–50	51+

Fleeting Contacts and Interruptions

	Personal	Telephone
Students		
Colleagues		
Administrative staff		
External person		
Self		

The diaries contained 80 sheets

Appendix B: A Copy of the Questionnaire Used in This Study

Dear Sir

We are carrying out a study of academic leadership in British and Nigerian universities. Whilst academic researchers have studied the work of many other professions, the work of the academic leader has largely been ignored. Our research, comprising a questionnaire survey, a diary study and an observational study with different groups of senior academics, is intended to establish the nature of the academic leaders' job, their attitudes towards it, the skills required to do it effectively, and so on. Such information could have important implications for the future selection, training and development of academic leaders, issues which are particularly relevant at a time when many academic leaders are facing new and increasingly severe problems due to the decrease in financial support for universities.

As part of this study, we would be most grateful if you would complete the attached questionnaire and return it in the enclosed stamped and addressed envelope.

Yours faithfully

Academic Leaders' Study (Questionnaire Method)

Explanatory Notes

1. This questionnaire concerns only your job-related activities. The research has been centred on the job and not on the individual.

2. Academic leaders are here defined as academic staff members occupying formal administrative positions within the university framework. Examples of such academic leaders include (but are not limited to) heads of department, deans, directors and vice-chancellors. If you are in doubt as to whether or not your position falls within the definition, you should fill in the questionnaire and state your job title in question one below.

3. This instrument has been designed to facilitate quick response. This inevitably produces some element of forced choice. Please, feel free to make comments at the end of the questionnaire if you wish to clarify an answer or to criticize the ambiguity in a question.

Questions

1. Indicate your formal designation or your sphere of control. Acting heads and deputies may also complete the questionnaire.

Vice-Chancellor	☐
Director	☐
Dean	☐
Head of Department	☐
Other (please, specify)	☐

2. Indicate your national group.

Nigerian	☐
African	☐
Asian	☐
European	☐
American	☐
Other (please, specify)	☐

Questions three to seven inclusive concerns the following four activities:
Teaching,
Researching,
Consulting,
Administration and Management.

3. Please, score the activities in terms of the extent to which you consider them to be your primary responsibilities. Do this by indicating the number on each scale from 1 (low priority) to 10 (high priority) which best represents the priority of the activities in your case.

a. Teaching	1	2	3	4	5	6	7	8	9	10
b. Researching	1	2	3	4	5	6	7	8	9	10
c. Consulting	1	2	3	4	5	6	7	8	9	10
d. Administration and Management	1	2	3	4	5	6	7	8	9	10

4. Score the activities in terms of the extent to which you enjoy doing them. Do this by indicating the number on each scale from 1 (do not enjoy at all) to 10 (enjoy doing a lot) which best represents the rating of the activities in your case.

a. Teaching	1	2	3	4	5	6	7	8	9	10
b. Researching	1	2	3	4	5	6	7	8	9	10
c. Consulting	1	2	3	4	5	6	7	8	9	10
d. Administration and Management	1	2	3	4	5	6	7	8	9	10

5. Score the activities in terms of your competence in executing them. Do this by indicating the number on each scale from 1 (low competence) to 10 (high competence) which best represents the situation in your own case.

a. Teaching	1	2	3	4	5	6	7	8	9	10
b. Researching	1	2	3	4	5	6	7	8	9	10
c. Consulting	1	2	3	4	5	6	7	8	9	10
d. Administration and Management	1	2	3	4	5	6	7	8	9	10

6. Estimate the percentage of your working time spent among the activities.

a. Teaching, including preparation time	%
b. Researching	%
c. Consulting	%
d. Administration and Management	100%

7. Score the activities in terms of the degree to which competence in executing them affects (or affected) your career prospects or promotional success in the university. Do this by indicating the number on each scale from 1 (competence in activity affects success a little) to 10 (absolutely essential for success) which best represents the practice in your university.

a. Teaching	1	2	3	4	5	6	7	8	9	10
b. Researching	1	2	3	4	5	6	7	8	9	10
c. Consulting	1	2	3	4	5	6	7	8	9	10
d. Administration and Management	1	2	3	4	5	6	7	8	9	10

8. What is your estimate of the extent to which academics are motivated towards or interested in being effective managers? Please, indicate your estimate on a scale which is from 1 (little interested) to 10 (very interested).

1 2 3 4 5 6 7 8 9 10

9. To what extent do you believe that some form of training will assist academic leaders in being more effective managers? Rate this on a scale which is from 1 (very little) to 10 (a large extent).

1 2 3 4 5 6 7 8 9 10

10. To what extent are you willing to approve of a management training programme as a prerequisite to or accompanying the appointment of academic leaders? Rate this on a scale ranging from 1 (totally unwilling) to 10 (extremely willing).

1 2 3 4 5 6 7 8 9 10

11. To what extent do you think the following skills are helpful in the performance of your present job? Indicate the point on each scale from 1 (not helpful) to 10 (extremely helpful).

a. Decision making	1	2	3	4	5	6	7	8	9	10
b. Interpersonal	1	2	3	4	5	6	7	8	9	10
c. Information management	1	2	3	4	5	6	7	8	9	10
d. Leadership	1	2	3	4	5	6	7	8	9	10
e. General management	1	2	3	4	5	6	7	8	9	10

12. Estimate the importance of the following elements in or aspects of your job. The scale is from 1 (low importance) to 10 (high importance).

a. Conflict resolution	1	2	3	4	5	6	7	8	9	10
b. External representation	1	2	3	4	5	6	7	8	9	10
c. Internal resource allocation	1	2	3	4	5	6	7	8	9	10
d. Extension of the frontiers of knowledge	1	2	3	4	5	6	7	8	9	10
e. Staff selection and development	1	2	3	4	5	6	7	8	9	10
f. Policy formulation	1	2	3	4	5	6	7	8	9	10
g. Admitting good students	1	2	3	4	5	6	7	8	9	10
h. Other (please, specify)	1	2	3	4	5	6	7	8	9	10

13. Score the following selected goals in order of how important you believe they are to the university. One (1) on the scale represents low importance and 10, high importance.

a. Research excellence	1	2	3	4	5	6	7	8	9	10
b. Teaching excellence	1	2	3	4	5	6	7	8	9	10
c. Services to the community	1	2	3	4	5	6	7	8	9	10
d. Competence and skill in a particular field	1	2	3	4	5	6	7	8	9	10
e. Attracting good students	1	2	3	4	5	6	7	8	9	10
f. Other (please, specify)	1	2	3	4	5	6	7	8	9	10

14. How often, on the average does your job require you to switch your attention from one subject, person or problem to another?

Every 5 minutes	☐
Every 10 minutes	☐
Every 15 minutes	☐
Every 20 minutes	☐
Every 30 minutes	☐
Every one hour	☐
Every two or more hours	☐

15. What is the nature of your most serious management problem? Score the gravity of a particular problem on a scale measuring from 1 (little problem) to 10 (very severe problem).

a. Communication problems	1	2	3	4	5	6	7	8	9	10
b. Excessive work, i.e. lack of time	1	2	3	4	5	6	7	8	9	10
c. Colleagues do not cooperate	1	2	3	4	5	6	7	8	9	10
d. Subordinates are not effective	1	2	3	4	5	6	7	8	9	10
e. Students are troublesome	1	2	3	4	5	6	7	8	9	10
f. Dwindling resources	1	2	3	4	5	6	7	8	9	10
g. Academic staff shortages	1	2	3	4	5	6	7	8	9	10
h. Other (please, specify)	1	2	3	4	5	6	7	8	9	10

16. On the average, how many hours a day do you spend working from Mondays to Fridays?

04–06 hours	☐
07–09 hours	☐
10–12 hours	☐
13–15 hours	☐

17. What is your estimate of the total number of hours spent working on Saturdays and Sundays (both days combined)?

None	☐
00–02 hours	☐
03–05 hours	☐
06–08 hours	☐
09–11 hours	☐
12–14 hours	☐
15–17 hours	☐

18. Estimate the percentage of your working time spent with the following groups of people.

a. Students	□%
b. Colleagues	□%
c. Administrative staff	□%
d. Non-members of your university community	□%
e. Alone	□%
	100%

19. Estimate the percentage of your working time spent in the following places.

a. Own office	□%
b. Other units of the university in your campus	□%
c. Other campus(es) of the same university	□%
d. Home	□%
e. Other organizations	□%
	100%

20. To what extent do you believe that administration and management in universities should be handled by professional managers and not by the academics? Score your belief on a scale from 1 (weak belief) to 10 (belief strongly).

1 2 3 4 5 6 7 8 9 10

21. In the following classification, indicate the nearest to which your unit can be grouped.

a. Sciences	□
b. Arts	□
c. Management	□
d. Not applicable for vice-chancellors	□

Comments by the Respondent

Appendix C: A Copy of the Individual Analyses Sent to the Academic Leaders who completed the Diaries

Dear

Thank you for your completed diary which we received recently. We observed that you identified your diary by writing your name and address on it. According to our earlier directions we interpret this to mean that you are interested in a report of the summary of your job characteristics. This is now ready and it is provided in the attached sheets.

Unfortunately, as at the time of writing this report, the total diary entries for this study are not yet available. Regrettably therefore, we are unable to supply you with the average figures for the whole study as well. However, an evaluation of the duration of your average daily working hours in relation to a previous pilot study is made.

Once more, we thank you very much for cooperating with us to fill in the diary. We hope that the frequency of your activities and especially how you spend your time as are detailed in the attached sheets will be of some use to you.

Yours sincerely

Frequency Analyses

Your Activities

1. ______ The percentage of the frequency of your activities which were desk work.
2. ______ The percentage of the frequency of your activities which were unscheduled meetings.
3. ______ The percentage of the frequency of your activities which were scheduled meetings.
4. ______ The percentage of the frequency of your activities which were telephoning.
5. ______ The percentage of the frequency of your activities which were travelling.
6. ______ The percentage of the frequency of your activities which were computing.
7. ______ The percentage of the frequency of your activities which were practicals.

8. ______ The percentage of the frequency of your activities which were Lunch.
9. ______ The percentage of the frequency of your activities which were tea/coffee breaks.
10. ______ The percentage of the frequency of your activities which were miscellaneous.

The Subject Matter of Your Activities

1. ______ The percentage of the frequency of the subject matter of your activities which were teaching.
2. ______ The percentage of the frequency of the subject matter of your activities which were researching.
3. ______ The percentage of the frequency of the subject matter of your activities which were consulting.
4. ______ The percentage of the frequency of the subject matter of your activities which were administration and management.
5. ______ The percentage of the frequency of the subject matter of your activities which were 'personal'.

The Location of Your Activities

1. ______ The percentage of the frequency of the location of your activities occurring in your office.
2. ______ The percentage of the frequency of the location of your activities occurring in other units.
3. ______ The percentage of the frequency of the location of your activities occurring in other campuses.
4. ______ The percentage of the frequency of the location of your activities occurring at home.
5. ______ The percentage of the frequency of the location of your activities occurring in other organisations.

Contacts With People

1. ______ The percentage of the frequency of your total contacts spent with students.
2. ______ The percentage of the frequency of your total contacts spent with colleagues.
3. ______ The percentage of the frequency of your total contacts spent with administrative staff.

4. ______ The percentage of the frequency of your total contacts spent externally.
5. ______ The percentage of the frequency of your total contacts spent alone (i.e. without any contact).

The Duration of Your Activities

1. ______ The percentage of the frequency of the duration of your total activities accounting for less than 10 minutes.
2. ______ The percentage of the frequency of the duration of your total activities accounting for less than 30 minutes.
3. ______ The percentage of the frequency of the duration of your total activities accounting for less than 60 minutes.
4. ______ The percentage of the frequency of the duration of your total activities accounting for more than 60 minutes.

Contacts With Groups of People

1. ______ The percentage of the frequency of your total contacts spent with 1 person.
2. ______ The percentage of the frequency of your total contacts spent with 2–5 people.
3. ______ The percentage of the frequency of your total contacts spent with 6–50 people.
4. ______ The percentage of the frequency of your total contacts spent with 50+ people.

Time Analyses

The Time Spent on Your Activities

1. ______ The percentage of your total time spent on deskwork.
2. ______ The percentage of your total time spent on scheduled meetings.
3. ______ The percentage of your total time spent on unscheduled meetings.
4. ______ The percentage of your total time spent on telephoning.
5. ______ The percentage of your total time spent on travelling.
6. ______ The percentage of your total time spent on computing.
7. ______ The percentage of your total time spent on practicals.
8. ______ The percentage of your total time spent on Lunch.
9. ______ The percentage of your total time spent on coffee/tea breaks.
10. ______ The percentage of your total time spent on miscellaneous.

The Time Spent on the Subject Matter of Your Activities

1. ______ The percentage of your total time spent on teaching.
2. ______ The percentage of your total time spent on researching.
3. ______ The percentage of your total time spent on consulting.
4. ______ The percentage of your total time spent on administration & management.
5. ______ The percentage of your total time spent on personal.

Where You Spent Your Time

1. ______ The percentage of your total time spent in own office.
2. ______ The percentage of your total time spent in other units.
3. ______ The percentage of your total time spent in other campuses.
4. ______ The percentage of your total time spent at home.
5. ______ The percentage of your total time spent in other organisations.

With Whom You Spent Your Time

1. ______ The percentage of your total time spent with students.
2. ______ The percentage of your total time spent with colleagues.
3. ______ The percentage of your total time spent with administrative staff.
4. ______ The percentage of your total time spent with external.
5. ______ The percentage of your total time spent alone.

The Duration of Your Activities

1. ______ The percentage of your total time spent in activities with 10 minutes or less in duration.
2. ______ The percentage of your total time spent in activities with 30 minutes or less in duration.
3. ______ The percentage of your total time spent in activities with 60 minutes or less in duration.
4. ______ The percentage of your total time spent in activities with 60 minutes or more in duration.

How You Spent Your Time With Different Groups Of People

1. ______ The percentage of your total time spent with 1 person.
2. ______ The percentage of your total time spent with 2–5 people.
3. ______ The percentage of your total time spent with 6–50 people.
4. ______ The percentage of your total time spent with 50+ people.

General

Please note that unless otherwise stated, "the week" refers to the period from Monday to Friday.

1. ______ Total hours worked for the week. Data supplied for ______ days.
2. ______ Average (Arithmetic Mean) of the daily hours worked during the week.
3. ______ Total number of diary entries ("activities") for the week.
4. ______ Average number of daily diary entries ("activities") for the week.
5. ______ Total number of fleeting contacts or interruptions for the week.
6. ______ Average number of daily fleeting contacts or interruptions during the week.
7. ______ Total hours worked on Saturday and Sunday.
8. ______ Total number of fleeting contacts or interruptions on Saturday and Sunday.

Conclusion

From the results of a previous pilot study, the duration of the average daily working hours which you recorded was *above*, *below*, *about* the average for the other respondents.

Appendix D: A Copy of the Follow-up Letters Sent to the Academic Leaders who Failed to Respond to our Diary or the Questionnaire

Dear

Our records indicate that we sent a diary to you about a month ago. So far, we do not appear to have heard from you. We wonder whether you have not received the diary and the covering letter. In this event, we shall be happy to send another diary to you if you so indicate.

We appreciate the demands on your time especially for having to complete the diary over a period of one week. As noted on the diary, however, data from a fewer number of days would still be very useful and much appreciated, as this would allow us to assess the generality of the more detailed data we have obtained from other respondents.

As stated in the covering letter we will be happy to send you a summary of the data you supply, giving a detailed breakdown of time spent on different activities, who was involved, and so on. Apart from this, the data will be kept entirely confidential; it will only be used in an aggregated form and individual respondents will not be identified.

We do hope you will find time to complete the diary and send it to us soon.

Yours sincerely

Dear Sir,

Our records indicate that we mailed a questionnaire to you sometime last month. So far, we do not appear to have received a reply from you. This may be due to the fact that the postal services between England and Nigeria can sometimes be very slow. Perhaps, you have posted the completed questionnaire back to us and it is still in the mail. If so, please ignore this letter. On the other hand, we are not sure that the questionnaire got to you. We are therefore enclosing another copy for your kind attention.

As was stated on the cover letter to the questionnaire, we are employing a multiple research methodology designed to establish the nature of the academic leaders' job, their attitudes towards it, the skills required to do it effectively, and so on. The aim of the research is to identify ways in which academic leaders in general could perform their roles more effectively e.g. through improved selection or training methods.

All data collected in the course of the survey will be treated as strictly confidential; it will only be used in an aggregated form and individual respondents will not be identified. If, however, you are interested in results and conclusions, please do not hesitate to write to us.

We thank you, in advance, for your cooperation.

Yours sincerely,

Appendix E: The Classification of the Responses From the Diary and the Questionnaire on the Basis of the Position of the Academic Leaders

Responses from the Diary

Position	Vice-Chancellor	Director	Dean	Head of Dept.	Total
Britain	1	3	3	5	12
Nigeria	0	6	5	15	26
Total	1	9	8	20	38

Responses from the Questionnaire

Position	Vice-Chancellor	Director	Dean	Head of Dept.	Total
Britain	3	7	7	17	34
Nigeria	5	16	21	33	75
Total	8	23	28	50	109

Appendix F: The List of the 24 Variables that was Used to Classify Academic Leaders into Job Types

1. Total number of hours worked from Monday to Friday.
2. Total number of activities (entries) recorded.
3. Total number of fleeting contacts and interruptions.
4. Percentage of total time spent on desk work.
5. Percentage of total time spent on scheduled meetings.
6. Percentage of total time spent on unscheduled meetings.
7. Percentage of total time spent teaching.
8. Percentage of total time spent researching.
9. Percentage of total time spent consulting.
10. Percentage of total time spent on administration and management.
11. Percentage of total time spent on own office.
12. Percentage of total time spent in other university units.
13. Percentage of total time spent at home.
14. Percentage of total time spent in other organizations.

15. Percentage of total time spent with student.
16. Percentage of total time spent with colleagues.
17. Percentage of total time spent with the administrative staff.
18. Percentage of total time spent with non-members of the university.
19. Percentage of total time spent alone.
20. Percentage of total time spent with one other person.
21. Percentage of total time spent with 2–5 other people.
22. Percentage of total time spent with 6 or more other people.
23. Percentage of total time spent on short-duration activities i.e., less than or equal to 10 minutes.
24. Percentage of total time spent on long-duration activities i.e., greater than or equal to two hours.

The variables were given equal weight

Appendix G: Hierarchical Clustering Dendrogram

	Items Grouped		
Cycle	I	J	Coeff
1	23	26	.236
2	2	3	.239
3	17	18	.306
4	22	24	.388
5	19	25	.413
6	6	10	.512
7	1	2	.539
8	21	29	.547
9	14	19	.576
10	17	21	.673
11	22	23	.689
12	14	20	.708
13	1	4	.722
14	9	31	.722
15	7	35	.727
16	1	5	.807
17	36	38	.865
18	6	33	.883
19	8	11	1.113
20	27	34	1.416
21	14	22	1.624
22	8	16	1.665
23	7	9	1.732
24	13	32	1.909
25	27	37	2.041
26	8	12	2.102
27	13	14	2.342
28	15	30	2.621
29	13	36	2.662
30	17	28	2.948
31	1	17	3.182
32	15	27	3.491
33	6	8	4.295
34	1	13	4.320
35	1	7	6.050
36	1	15	7.040
37	1	6	10.894

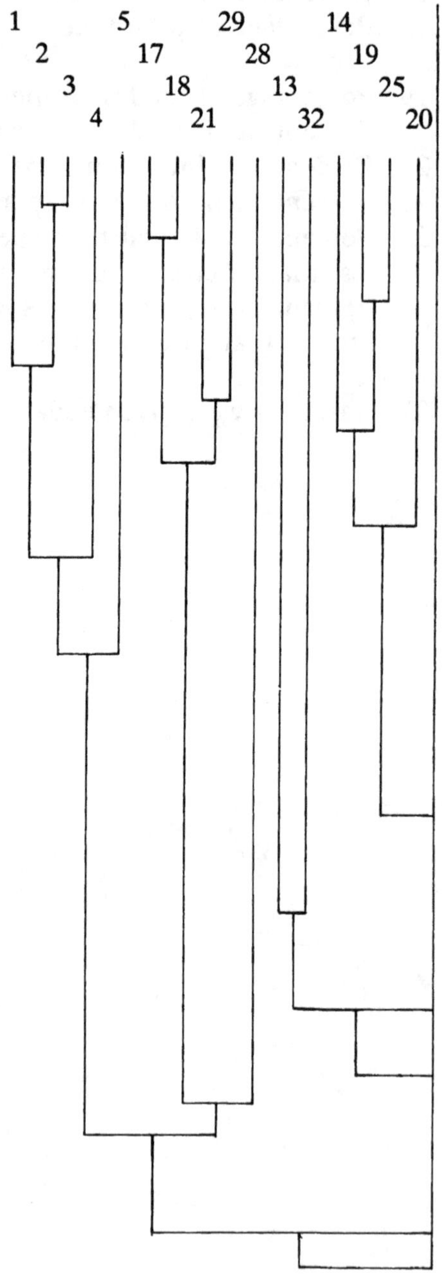

Basis: 24 Variables of Academic Leaders' Job characteristics
Procedure: Ward's Method Using Euclidean Distances

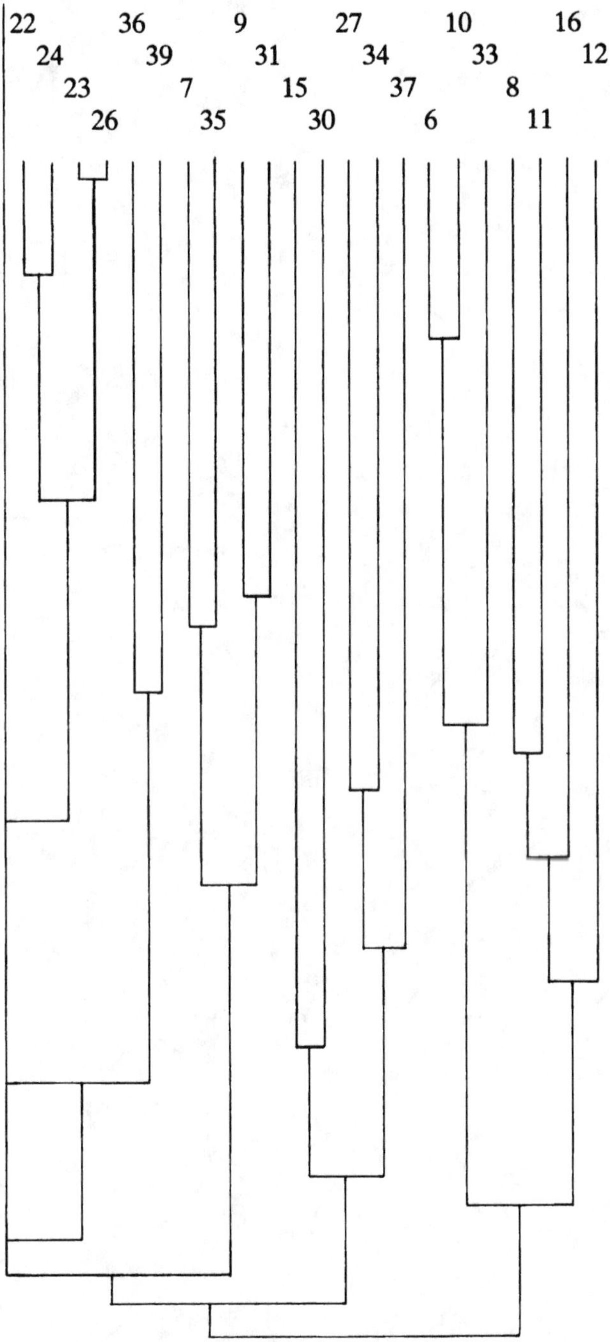

Bibliography

Adamolekun, N.K. and Gboyega, A. (eds.) (1979): *Leading Issues in Nigerian Public Service*, Proceedings of a National Symposium, April 1975; Ile-Ife, Nigeria: University of Ife Press.

Adaralegbe, A. (ed.) (1972): *A Philosophy for Nigerian Education*, Report of the National Curricula Conference, 8–12 Sept., 1969, Ibadan, Nigeria: Heinemann Educational Books.

The Association of Commonwealth Universities (1982a): *Commonwealth Universities Yearbook*, Vol. I: 206–833.

The Association of Commonwealth Universities (1982b): *Commonwealth Universities Yearbook*, Vol. III: 2021–2111.

Ball, G.H. (1971): *Classification Analysis*, Stanford, CA: Stanford Research Institute.

Berdie, D.R. and Anderson, J.F. (1974): *Questionnaires: Design and Use*, Metuchen, N.J.: The Scarecrow Press Inc.

Birley, D. (1970): *The Educational Officer and His World*, London: Routledge and Kegan Paul.

Blau, P.M. (1954): Patterns of interaction among a group of officials in a government agency, *Human Relations*, Vol. 7: 337–338.

Brewer, E. and Tomlinson, J.W.C. (1964): The Manager's Working Day, *The Journal of Industrial Economics*, Vol. 12: 191–197.

Burns, T. (1954): The Directions of Activity and Communication in a Departmental Executive Group, *Human Relations*, Vol. 7(1): 73–97.

Burns, T. (1957): Management in Action, *Operational Research Quarterly*, Vol. 8(2), June: 45–60.

Carlson, S. (1951): *Executive Behaviour: A Study of the Work Load and the Working Methods of Managing Directors*, Stockholm: Strombergs.

Chizea, C.A. (ed.) (Various Dates): *Bulletin of the National Universities Commission*, Lagos, Nigeria: National Universities Commissions' Publication.

Chizea, C.A. (ed.) (1984): *20 Years of University Education in Nigeria*, Lagos, Nigeria: National Universities Commission's Publication.

Cohen, M.D. and March, J.G. (1974): *Leadership and Ambiguity: The American College President*, New York: McGraw-Hill.

Committee of Vice-Chancellors and Principals (1985): Press Briefings on Jarrat Committee Reports on Efficiency in Universities, London: Committee of Vice-Chancellors and Principals, April 1985.

Copeman, G., Luijk, H., and Hanika, F. deP. (1963): *How The Executive Spends His Time*, London: Business Publications Limited.

Cyert, R.M. and March, J.G. (1963): *A Behavioural Theory of The Firm*, Englewood Cliffs, N.J.: Prentice-Hall.

Dahl, T. and Lewis, D.R. (1975): Random Sampling Device Used in Time Management Study, *Evaluation*, Vol. 2(2): 20–22.

Dale, E. and Urwick, L.F. (1960): *Staff in Organization*, New York: McGraw-Hill.

Drucker, P.F. (1967): *The Effective Executive*, London: Heinemann.

Dublin, R. and Spray, S.L. (1964): Executive Behaviour and Interaction, *Industrial Relations*, Vol. 3: 99–108.

Etzioni, A. (1964): *Modern Organizations*, Englewood Cliffs, N.J.: Prentice-Hall Inc.

Everitt, B. (1974): *Cluster Analysis*, London: Heinemann Educational Books.

Fafunwa, B. (1983): Nigerian Varsities: Problems and Challenges, *National Concord*, 12 January.

Fayol, H. (1949): *General and Industrial Management*, trans. Constance Storrs, London: Pitman.

Fielden, J. and Lockwood, G. (1973): *Planning and Management in Universities*, London: Chatto and Windus.

Fleischman, E.A. (1953): The Description of Supervisory Behaviour, *Journal of Applied Psychology*, Vol. 37: 1–6.

Flexner, A. (1930): *Universities: American, English, German*, London: Oxford University Press.

Friedman, H.P. and Rubin, J. (1967): On some invariant criteria for grouping data, *Journal of American Statistical Association,* Vol. 62: 1159–1178.

Gibbs, S. (1982): The Role of the Manager, M.B.A. Dissertation, University of Bradford.

Goode, W. and Hatt, P. (1962): *Methods in Social Research*, New York: McGraw-Hill.

Government of Nigeria (1974): Views on the Report of the Public Service Review Commission, Lagos: Federal Government of Nigeria.

Guest, R.H. (1956): of Time and the Foreman, *Personnel*, Vol. 32: 478–486.

Gulick, L.H. and Urwick, L.F. (eds.) (1937): *Papers on the Science of Administration*, New York: Columbia University Press.

Harbison, F.H. (1973): *Human Resources as the Wealth of Nations*, New York: Oxford University Press.

Hemphill, J.K. (1959): Job Description For Executives, *Harvard Business Review*, Vol. 37(5), Sept.–Oct.: 55–67.

Hemphill, J.K. (1960): *Dimensions of Executive Positions*, Columbus, OH: Ohio State University, Bureau of Business Research.

Henkel, R.E. (1984): *Tests of Significance*, Beverly Hills, Cal.: Sage Publications.

Hill, L. (1938): *The Local Government Officer*, London: George Allen and Unwin.

Hinrichs, J.R. (1964): Communications Activity of Industrial Research Personnel, *Personnel Psychology*, Vol. 17: 193–204.

Hinrichs, J.R. (1976): Where has all the time gone: *Personnel*, Vol. 54(4): 44–49.

Hodgkinson, H.L. and Edelstein, S. (1972): Questionnaires: In fact, there is error, *Educational Researcher*, Vol. 1(8), August: 9–10.

Homans, G.C. (1950): *The Human Group*, New York: Harcourt Brace Jovanovich.

Hornby, A.S. (1982): *Oxford Advanced Learner's Dictionary of Current English*, London: Oxford University Press.

Horne, J.H. and Lupton, T. (1975): The Work Activities of 'Middle' Managers—An Exploratory Study, *The Journal of Management Studies*, Vol. 2(1): 14–33.

Ike, M.C. (1977): Manpower or Manhood? *Management in Nigeria*, Jan.: 6–17.

Jasinki, F.J. (1956): Foreman Relationships Outside the Work Group, *Personnel*, Vol. 33: 130–136.

Jacques, D. and Richardson, J.T.E. (1985): *The future for higher education*, Guildford, Surrey: The Society for Research into Higher Education and NFER-Nelson.

Jedamus, P., Peterson, M.W., and Associates (1980): *Improving Academic Management: A Handbook of Planning and Institutional Research*, San Francisco: Jossey-Bass Publishers.

Kelly, J. (1964): The Study of Executive Behaviour By Activity Sampling, *Human Relations*, Vol. 17: 277–287.

Kelly, J. (1969): *Organizational Behaviour*, Homewood, Ill.: Irwin Dorsey.

Kerr, C. (1963): *The Uses of the University*, Cambridge, Mass.: Harvard University Press.

Kogan, M. and Van der Eyken, W. (1973): *County Hall: The Role of the Chief Education Officer*, Harmondsworth, Middlesex: Penguin.

Koontz, H.J. (1961): The Management Theory Jungle, *Journal of the Academy of Management*, Vol. 4, No. 3, December: 174–188.

Koontz, H. and O'Donnel, C. (1972): *Principles of Management: An Analysis of Managerial Functions*, New York: McGraw-Hill, 5th ed.

Kurke, L.B. and Aldrich, H.E. (1983): Mintzberg was right! A replication and extension of the nature of managerial work, *Management Science*, Vol. 29, No. 8, August: 975–984.

Landsberger, H.A. (1961): The Horizontal Dimension in Bureaucracy, *Administrative Science Quarterly*, Vol. 6: 299–332.

Lawler, E.E., Porter, L.W., and Tennenbaum, A. (1968): Manager's attitudes toward interaction episodes, *Journal of Applied Psychology*, Vol. 52: 432–439.

Lawrence, P. (1984): *Management in Action*, London: Routledge and Kegan Paul.

Lorr, M. (1983): *Cluster Analysis For Social Scientists*, San Francisco: Jossey-Bass Publishers.

Lupton, T. (1983): *Management and the Social Sciences*, Harmondsworth, Middlesex: Penguin Education.

Lynch, J.E. (1981): Strategic Marketing Planning in U.K. Universities: An examination of the relevance to university managements of externally-orientated planning concepts and systems supported by a series of illustrative applications, Ph.D. Thesis, University of Bradford.

Mahoney, T.A., Jerdee, T.H., and Carroll, S.J. (1965): The Job(s) of Management, *Industrial Relations*, Vol. 4; 97–110.

Mansfield, R. et al. (1981): *The British Manager in Profile*, London: British Institute of Management Foundation.

Marples, D.L. (1967): Studies of Managers—A Fresh Start?, *The Journal of Management Studies*, Vol. 4: 282–299.

Marples, D.L. (1968): Roles in a Manufacturing Organization, *The Journal of Management Studies*, Vol. II: 183–204.

Marshall, J. and Stewart, R. (1981a): Managers' Job Perceptions, *Journal of Management Studies*, Vol. 18, Part I: 177–190.

Marshall, J. and Stewart, R. (1981b) Managers' Job Perceptions, *Journal of Management Studies*, Vol. 18, Part II: 263–275.

McCall, M.W. and Lombardo, M.M. (1979): Looking Glass Inc.: The First Three Years, *Centre for Creative Leadership*, Technical Report No. 13, North Carolina, 27402, Columbus, OH: Ohio State University.

McCall, M.W. and Segrist, C.A. (1980): In Pursuit of the Manager's Job: Building on Mintzberg, *Centre for Creative Leadership*, Technical Report No. 14, North Carolina, 27402, Columbus, OH: Ohio State University.

McCall, M.W., Morrison, M.A., and Hannan, R.L. (1978): Studies of Managerial Work: Results and Methods, *Centre for Creative Leadership* Technical Report No. 9, North Carolina, 27402, May, Columbus: Ohio State University.

McCorkle, C.O. and Archibald, S.O. (1982). *Management and Leadership in Higher Education*, San Francisco: Jossey-Bass Publishers.

Miner, J.B. (1977): *Motivation to Manage: A ten Year Update on the "Studies in Management Education" Research*, Atlanta, Georgia: Organizational Measurement Systems Press.

Mintzberg, H. (1973): *The Nature of Managerial Work*, New York: Harper and Row Publishers.

Mintzberg, H. (1975): The Manager's Job: Folklore and Fact, *Harvard Business Review*, July–August: 49–61.

Morrison, D.G. (1967): Measurement Problems in Cluster Analysis, *Management Science*, Vol. 13: 775–780.

Morse, J.J. and Wagner, F.R. (1978): Measuring the Process of Managerial Effectiveness, *Academy of Management Journal*, Vol. 21, No. 1: 23–35.

Neustadt, R.E. (1960): *Presidential Power: The Politics of Leadership*, New York: Wiley.

Newman, C.J.H. (1959): *The Idea of a University*, Garden City, New York: Image Books, A Division of Doubleday and Company, Inc.

Newman, W.H. (1951) *Administrative Action: The Technique of Organization and Management*, Englewood Cliffs, N.J.: Prentice-Hall.

Odeleye, A.O. (1979): Professionalism in Management and Administration, *Management in Nigeria*, Jan.: 19–21.

Opoola, M. (1983): Ageing U.I.: Coping with the problems of university education, *New Nigerian*, May 24.

Oshagbemi, T.A. (1982): The Cultural Factor in Nigeria's Development Equation, *Journal of Social and Economic Studies*, Vol. X, Parts 1 and 2: 243–257.

Oshagbemi, T.A. (1984) The Job Characteristics of Academic Leaders: A Pilot Study, *Management Research News*, Vol. 7, No. 2: 20–23.

Oshagbemi, T.A. (1985): Leadership and Management in Universities: An Exploratory Study of the Job Characteristics and Perceptions of Nigerian and British Academic Leaders, Ph.D. Thesis, University of Bradford.

Oshagbemi, T.A. (1986): Academic Leaders and the Management of Universities, *Management in Nigeria*, Vol. 22, Nos. 11 & 12, Nov/Dec.

Oshagbemi, T.A. (1987): What Are Universities for? An Empirical Verification of the Perceived Goals of British and Nigerian Universities, Department of Management Studies, University of Jos, Nigeria, Seminar Series, January 13, 1987.

Oshagbemi, T.A. (in press): *Nigerian Business Policy and Strategy*, London: Hutchinson.

Payne, S.L. (1951): *The Art of Asking Questions*, Princeton, N.J.: Princeton University Press.

Prince, G.M. (1970): *The Practice of Creativity*, New York: Harper and Row.

Ponder, Q.D. (1957): The Effective Manufacturing Foremen, in: E. Young (ed.), *Industrial Relations Research Association Proceedings of the Tenth Annual Meeting*, Madison, Wisconsin.

Public Service Review Commission (1974): *Main Report*, Lagos, Nigeria: Federal Ministry of Information.

Report of the Presidential Commission on Salary and Conditions of Service of University Staff, Nigeria (1981), Lagos, Nigeria: Federal Government of Nigeria.

Richman, B.M. and Farmer, R.N. (1974): *Leadership, Goals And Power In Higher Education*, San Francisco: Jossey-Bass Publishers.

Robbins, L. (1963): *Report of the Committee on Higher Education*, Cmnd. 2154. London: Her Majesty's Stationery Office.

Robert, D. (1983): Culture and the Management of Time: A Comparison of Japanese and American Top Management Practice, *Asia Pacific Journal of Management*, Vol. 1, No. 1, Sept.: 65–71.

Salami, A. (1982): Universities: Alternative Sources of Finance to Government Funding, *Sunday Standard*, October 31.

Sayles, L. (1964): *Managerial Behaviour*, New York: McGraw-Hill.

Searle, J. (1972): *The Campus War*, London: Pelican.

Shapira, Z. and Dunbar, R.L.M. (1980): Testing Mintzberg's Managerial Roles: Classification Using In-basket Simulation, *Journal of Applied Psychology*, Vol. 65: 87–95.

Shartle, C.L. (1949): Leadership and Executive Performance, *Personnel*, Vol. 25: 370–380.

Singleton, W.T. (1981): *Management Skills*, Lancaster: MTP Press Limited.

Sokal, R.R. and Sneath, P.H.A. (1963): *Principles of Numerical Taxonomy*, London: Freeman.

Stewart, R. (1965): The Use of Diaries to Study Manager's Jobs, *The Journal of Management Studies*, Vol. 2: 228–235.

Stewart, R. (1967): *Managers and their jobs: A study of the similarities and differences in the ways managers spend their time*, London: Macmillan.

Stewart, R. (1976): *Contrasts in management: A Study of Different Types of Managers' Jobs, Their Demand and Choices*, London: McGraw-Hill.

Stewart, R. (1984): The Nature of Management? A Problem for Management Education, *The Journal of Management Studies*, Vol. 21, No. 3, July: 323–330.

Stieglitz, H. (1969): The Chief Executive—And His Job, *National Industrial Conference Board*, New York: Personnel Policy Study.

Stogdill, R.M., Shartle, C.L., Scott, E.L., Coons, A.E., and Jaynes, W.E. (1956): *A Predictive Study of Administrative Work Patterns*, Columbus, OH: Ohio State University, Bureau of Business Research.

Taylor, F.W. (1947): *Scientific Management*, New York: Harper and Row.

Terry, G.R. (1953): *Principles of Management*, Homewood, Ill.: Irwin.

Thomason, G.F. (1966): Managerial Work Roles and Relationships (part I), *The Journal of Management Studies*, Vol. 3: 270–284.

Thomason, G.F. (1967): Managerial Work Roles and Relationships (part II), *The Journal of Management Studies*, Vol. 4: 17–30.

Thorndike, R.L. (1953): Who belongs in a family? *Psychometrika*, Vol. 18: 267–276.

Torrington, D. and Weightman, J. (1985): *The Business of Management*, Englewood Cliffs, N.J.: Prentice-Hall International.

Truscot, B. (1943): *Redbrick University*, London: Faber.

Walker, C.R., Gust, R.H., and Turner, A.N. (1956): *The Foreman on the Assembly Line*, Cambridge, Mass.: Harvard University Press.

Ward, J.H. (1963): Hierarchical grouping to optimise an objective function, *Journal of the American Statistical Association*, Vol. 58: 236–244.

Warwick, D. (1985): *The Times Higher Education Supplement*, April 12, p. 8.

Wikstrom, W.S. (1967): Managing at the Foreman's Level, *National Industrial Conference Board*, New York: Personnel Policy Study, No. 205.

Wishart, D. (1978): *Clustan User Manual*, Inter-University Research Council Series, Report No. 47, (3rd ed.), Jan. (And the Supplement to this edition by the same author, April, 1982.) Bradford: University of Bradford.

Wren, D.A. (1979): *The Evolution of Management Thought*, New York: Wiley.

Wright, P.L. and Taylor, D.S. (1984): *Improving Leadership Performance*, Englewood Cliffs, N.J.: Prentice-Hall International.

Name Index

Subject Index

www.ingramcontent.com/pod-product-compliance
Lightning Source LLC
LaVergne TN
LVHW010549300926
849162LV00002B/282